Cutting Rhythms

Cutting Rhythms
Shaping the Film Edit

Karen Pearlman

AMSTERDAM • BOSTON • HEIDELBERG • LONDON
NEW YORK • OXFORD • PARIS • SAN DIEGO
SAN FRANCISCO • SINGAPORE • SYDNEY • TOKYO
Focal Press is an imprint of Elsevier

Focal Press is an imprint of Elsevier
30 Corporate Drive, Suite 400, Burlington, MA 01803, USA
Linacre House, Jordan Hill, Oxford OX2 8DP, UK

Library of Congress Cataloging-in-Publication Data
Pearlman, Karen.
   Cutting rhythms : shaping the film edit / Karen Pearlman.
      p. cm.
   Includes bibliographical references and index.
   ISBN 978-0-240-81014-0 (pbk. : alk. paper) 1. Motion pictures—Editing. 2. Motion
pictures—Philosophy. 3. Motion picture plays—Editing. 4. Rhythm. I. Title.
   TR899.P42 2009
   778.5′35—dc22

                                                                     2008044538

British Library Cataloguing-in-Publication Data
A catalogue record for this book is available from the British Library.

ISBN: 978-0-240-81014-0

For information on all Focal Press publications
visit our website at www.books.elsevier.com

09 10 11   5 4 3 2 1

Printed in the United States of America

Table of Contents

Preface

My interest in writing this book began when I was finishing the practical course work for my M.A. in Editing at the Australian Film Television and Radio School (AFTRS). I was approached by the head of the editing department, Bill Russo, ASE, about the possibility of researching editing history and theory for the purposes of teaching incoming students there. From that discussion, the idea was to base my research on words that are frequently used, but infrequently defined in the regular course of editing a film,[1] such as "structure," "montage," and "rhythm." Bill's expertise in editing, as with most senior editors now working, came about through many years of practical experience. The AFTRS, in trying to train an editor in a few short years, was already very focused on providing a variety of practical editing experiences. Bill responded enthusiastically to my ideas for research because he wanted to know: What could film school offer that was different from working in the field? And, more importantly: Could principles be articulated and communicated that might otherwise be understood only through years of practice or experience?

In the course of my research I found that it was a relatively straightforward matter to draw together and teach many specific principles about Soviet montage theory, techniques of continuity cutting, structure, devices, and common scenes by studying films and books and talking to writers, directors, and editors. However, rhythm, as a topic, was elusive. A literature search yielded contradictory, limited, or inconclusive definitions. Experienced editors, although in agreement that rhythm (along with structure) is what an editor devises or realizes in a filmmaking process, were reluctant to try to articulate a definition of the word "rhythm" or talk about how it is made, beyond saying "it's intuitive." Finally, David Bordwell and Kristen Thompson's *Film Art* threw down the gauntlet with the comment "the issue of rhythm in cinema is enormously complex and still not well understood."[2] Perhaps perversely drawn to the most ineffable, or at least the trickiest, topic of study I had yet found, I set out on my quest to understand rhythm in film editing.

Scholarly discussion of rhythm in film editing is rare, so I have had the opportunity to draw on a range of disciplines, including film studies, dance, and neurology, to formulate some principles about my topic. In this book I develop ideas about intuition in the cutting of rhythms, editing as a choreographic process, and the tools and purposes of rhythm in film editing, before going on to look at the different kinds of rhythms with which editors work and some of the different kinds of scenes and scenarios that vary the editor's approach to the film's rhythm.

Cutting Rhythms is a book about editing theory and practice and the creative processes, tools, and functions of rhythm in film editing. It is designed to enhance readers' creativity in film editing by providing them with methods for developing their rhythmic intuition, a functional vocabulary for collaborative discussion of rhythm in film, and an analysis of kinds of rhythm in film and how they work. There are many books available on the technology of editing, some books on the history and craft, but few that offer editors and filmmakers specific ways of making their edits work better. *Cutting Rhythms* looks at something central to the art of filmmaking: rhythm, a word often used and rarely defined. Its ideas about what rhythm is, how it is shaped, and what it is for are intended to be useful to scholars of film studies who want to know how film is made and how it has its effect on spectators and, especially, for students and professional filmmakers who are interested in making great films.

ENDNOTES

1. In this book, I use the word "film" to refer to any screen work of a fixed duration, designed to be viewed from beginning to end. This includes video, animations, and, in some instances, digital media. It does not include any work with an unfixed duration or intended for nonlinear interaction, such as CD-ROMs, computer games, video or film installations, or web-based screen work. The rhythm of these is a fascinating matter for another inquiry and will not be addressed herein.

2. Bordwell, D., and Thompson, K., *Film Art: An Introduction,* pp. 196–197.

Acknowledgments

This book is based on the doctoral thesis *Cutting Rhythms: Ideas about the Shaping of Rhythm in Film Editing*, by Dr Karen Pearlman, University of Technology, Sydney, 2006.

An earlier version of Chapter 1 of this book was published as "The Rhythm of Thinking—speculations on how an editor shapes the rhythm of a film," in a special feature section on editing in *Metro Magazine*, a publication of the Australian Teachers of Media, No. 141, pp. 112–116, 2004.

Sections of the thesis and *Thursday's Fictions* were presented at Dance, Corporeality, the Body and Performance Practices, a conference for researchers at the University of New South Wales, in Sydney, on November 14, 2003, and at Cinemoves—a Forum for Dance on Film at the Sydney Dance Company, September 25, 2004.

Excerpts from Chapters 4, 5, and 6 have been published in a series of three articles in the journal of the Dance Films Association, New York, 2005–2006 (*Dance on Camera Journal*, July–August 2005, Vol. 8, No. 4; *Dance on Camera Journal*, September–October 2005, Vol. 8, No. 5; and *Dance on Camera Ezine*, February 9, 2006).

I'd like to acknowledge the wonderfully unflagging energy, commitment, and excellent advice of my primary doctoral supervisor, Sarah Gibson, and my co-supervisor, Professor Ross Gibson, whose own writings have been so significant in shaping my ideas. I'd like also to acknowledge the tremendous influence and inspiration of my original supervisor, Dr. Patrick Crogan, in getting this project started and the exceptional job he did in clearing a pathway for my thinking and research.

Acknowledgment and thanks are due to Bill Russo, ASE, Head of Editing at the Australian Film Television and Radio School (AFTRS), for his curiosity, challenges, and discussions and his own exemplary editing. I would also like to acknowledge Paul Thompson, former Head of Screenwriting at the AFTRS, for his articulation of ideas about "hope and fear," and to thank Philippa Harvey and all of my colleagues at the AFTRS for their insights and interest, as well as my former and current students at the AFTRS and at the University of Technology, Sydney (UTS), whose energy and passion for their work have been so inspiring.

The lecturers at UTS in the Department of Media Arts and Production, especially Associate Professors Gillian Leahy, Norie Neumark, and Martin Harrison, and Megan Heyward, Ann-Marie Chandler, Andrew Taylor, and Chris Caines, have all been great to work with and have often, perhaps without knowing it, dropped in a remark or an idea that has set me thinking. And special thanks to the Dean of the Faculty of Arts and Sciences at UTS, Professor Theo van Leeuwen, for his work on rhythm in film and for bringing key texts to my attention. My esteemed colleagues on the Australian Screen Editors Guild Committee have been a great inspiration for me, and I'd particularly like to acknowledge the input, advice, and encouragement of Henry Dangar, ASE; Emma Hay, ASE; Peter Whitmore, ASE; and Mary Jane St. Vincent Welch, ASE. I also acknowledge the advice and assistance of Dr. Stephen Malloch, Dr. Greg Hooper, and Dr. Mark Seton in discussion of particular problems and in locating particular texts. Dr. Christopher Allen, Michelle Hiscock, Dierdre Towers, Darmyn Calderon, J. Gluckstern, and Ross Murray have all been kind enough to read some parts of the manuscript, and I thank them for their comments and suggestions.

Finally, for having gotten this far I owe a debt to my family: my father, Dr. Alan Pearlman, whom I "mirror" in all of my thinking, and his wife, Gail Bass, whose knowledge of music has provided stimulating debates about rhythm; my mother, Joan Pearlman, an endless source of enthusiasm and loving support, and her husband, Professor Peter Kivy, who gave me my first books on film theory and continues to send me all the best books I have. To the memory of my father-in-law, Robert Allen, and special thanks to my mother-in-law, Jocelyn Allen, who lifted the burdens of all my daily cares and held them aloft so graciously while I sheltered with her and wrote. Then there are the gorgeous ones, my children Sam and Jaz, my *raisons d'être*, who inspire me to get up in the morning and in absolutely everything else, and my darling partner, Richard, the astounding river of energy, vision, and love running through it all. With love and thanks to you all, here it is!

Introduction

Cutting Rhythms is about rhythm in film editing. It begins with the question: What can be said about the shaping of a film's rhythm in editing beyond saying "it's intuitive"? This question leads to an in-depth study of editors' rhythmic creativity and intuition, the processes and tools editors work through to shape rhythms, and the functions of rhythm in film. Through this research *Cutting Rhythms* has carved out a number of theories about rhythm in film editing—what it is, how it is shaped, and what it is for. Case studies about creating rhythm in films edited by the author and examples of rhythm in a range of other films describe and illustrate practical applications of these theories.

Cutting Rhythms begins in Chapter 1 with an inquiry into intuition. What kinds of thinking and practice are editors referring to when they say the processes of creating rhythm are "intuitive"? *Cutting Rhythms* hypothesizes that the editor's intuition is an acquired body of knowledge with two sources—the rhythms of the world that the editor experiences and the rhythms of the editor's body that experiences them. These are the sources of the editor's somatic intelligence about rhythm, and they are also the triggers that activate the editor's creativity in cutting rhythms. This chapter describes the neurological and experiential connections between these two sources of rhythmic knowledge. It stresses the importance of physiology in the accrual of rhythmic knowledge and introduces ideas about thinking physically and using kinesthetic empathy creatively.

Chapter 2 of *Cutting Rhythms* argues that editing is a form of choreography in that editors manipulate the composition of moving images and sounds to shape a film's rhythms. It builds on the ideas in Chapter 1 that we perceive rhythm physically and develops the idea that the way we perceive rhythm is through perception of movement. The premise is that movement is what editors experience as a source of rhythmic knowledge, and it is also the material that editors work with in shaping a film's raw imagery and sounds into rhythms. This chapter looks at some of the ways in which choreographers work with movement and proposes that dance and dance-making processes might provide productive crafting information for the rhythm-making process in film editing.

The tools of this choreographic process of cutting rhythms are discussed in Chapter 3, which breaks down and describes the various editing operations being referred to with the terms "timing" and "pacing." This chapter also introduces "trajectory phrasing," a term devised to describe some of the key operations an editor performs that are not precisely covered by timing or pacing. The notion of trajectory phrasing draws on work done in dance theory to present ideas about the shaping of the direction and energy of movement phrases in film editing.

Chapter 4 looks at the purposes for which movement in film is shaped into rhythms. It describes the psychosomatic effect of rhythmic cycles of tension and release and the effect of synchronization that a film's rhythm can have on the rhythms of a spectator.

These four chapters cumulatively propose that: *Rhythm in film editing is time, movement, and energy shaped by timing, pacing, and trajectory phrasing for the purpose of creating cycles of tension and release.*

Cutting Rhythms then applies its hypotheses about intuition, choreographic approaches, and the tools and purposes of rhythm to different types of rhythm that editors encounter. The terms "physical rhythm," "emotional rhythm," and "event rhythm" are offered as ways of describing kinds of rhythm and the variations of choreographic and intuitive approaches that editors might take to work with them.

Finally, *Cutting Rhythms* offers a series of chapters that address particular editing figures or problems. It starts with a chapter on style, looking at the rhythmic issues involved in cutting montage versus decoupage, and the kinds of decisions an editor makes about timing, pacing, and trajectory phrasing when establishing and sustaining a style. Chapter 10 looks at devices such as parallel action, slow motion, and fast motion—things an editor can use to vary the rhythmic texture of a film—how they work best and when they descend into cliché. Finally, a chapter on common scenes looks at shaping two-handers and chases, with examples and case studies that provide instances of the principles in practice.

Cutting Rhythms is written to address editors and filmmakers who are learning their craft and more experienced practitioners who find their work benefits from discussion of their craft. Knowledge about rhythm helps students and editors to shape rhythms contrapuntally and maximize their material's rhythmic potential. It is also relevant to the screen studies scholar who is interested in the connection of theoretical ideas to practical methods and outcomes. Its purpose is to stimulate ways of thinking and talking about rhythm in film and to understand and deepen rhythmic creativity.

METHODOLOGY: THEORY

A survey of recent literature about editing[1] shows that the question of rhythm in film editing is rarely addressed as a topic in and of itself. One notable exception is the work by Theo van Leeuwen, who notes in the introduction to *Rhythmic Structure of the Film Text* that:

> There was a time when few works of film theory failed to address the role of rhythm in film. . . . More recently the study of rhythm in film has been all but abandoned. Since the publication of Mitry's *Esthetique et Psychologie du Cinema* (1963) little if any original thought has been contributed to the subject.[2]

Handbooks on editing craft sometimes supply rules about the rhythm-making tools of timing and pacing. These books and interviews with editors may also provide examples of rhythms from specific films, but say that there are no rules for editing rhythms and do not offer any substantial definitions of rhythmic creativity in film editing.

In his book *The Technique of Film and Video Editing: Theory and Practice*, Ken Dancyger describes rhythm as part of pace, and says, "The rhythm of a film seems to be an individual and intuitive matter."[3] *The Technique of Film Editing*, by Karel Reisz and Gavin Millar, positions rhythm as an attribute of timing.[4] In *Film Art*, Bordwell and Thompson describe a number of attributes of rhythm in their discussion of the "Rhythmic Relations between shot A and shot B,"[5] but most of them are subsumed under the operations I will call pacing as in frequency of cuts. Bordwell and Thompson preface their remarks by saying that "cinematic rhythm as a whole derives not only from editing but from other film techniques as well." Unlike their discussion, mine is an effort to consider cinematic rhythm as a whole inasmuch as the editor devises its final shape and form. In other words, although I am focused exclusively on editing operations, my question concerns their impact on the larger aspects of cinematic rhythm that they shape. I will define, therefore, a number of considerations the editor has in the affective shaping of cinematic rhythm, and frequency of cuts is only one of those operations.

Don Fairservice, author of *Film Editing: History, Theory and Practice*, gives a summary view of the literature available on rhythm in film editing when he says:

> Any discussion about film editing will inevitably sooner or later raise the matter of rhythm. It tends to be used rather as a compendium word, a sort of catch-all which tends to obscure as much as it reveals about something that is difficult to define.[6]

Cutting Rhythms avoids putting forward any rules about rhythm or creativity in rhythm. Instead, it articulates some principles of rhythm in film editing as questions that editors, filmmakers, or film studies scholars can ask themselves and of their material in order to expand the scope and sensitivity of their rhythmic intuition. This approach, to articulate questions that editors can ask themselves or ask about their material, is a way of tying the theory proposed herein to the more pragmatic and pressured moments of practice. When one is working on a film, and someone in the edit suite says "it isn't right," "it doesn't feel right," or "the rhythm is off," the ideas articulated herein about rhythm may present possibilities an editor can consider for herself to make it "right."

Given this practical, craft-based purpose and my interest in connecting theory to practice, I have chosen, primarily, a cognitive approach to my discussion of the properties and processes involved in working with rhythm in film editing.

Cognitivism, as described by David Bordwell and Noël Carroll, "seeks to understand human thought, emotion and action by appeal to processes of mental representation, naturalistic processes, and (some sense of) rational agency."[7]

Cognitivists consider the physiological makeup of humans when they are studying how we understand and are affected by something like film. The underlying principle is that there are certain things hardwired into all human beings, things that are part of our makeup before we are shaped by our particular moment in time or upbringing, such as "the assumption of a three dimensional environment, the assumption that natural light falls from above, and so forth. These contingent universals make possible artistic conventions which seem natural because they accord with norms of human perception."[8]

These assumptions are present in most editing practice—we do not spend our time in the editing suite wondering about the nature of being or the universe; rather, we are trying to shape an experience that resonates with the knowledge and beliefs many people hold. The ability to tap into those aspects of human experience that are physiological or deeply ingrained in perception and knowledge is an asset in trying to create resonant stories or experiences. So the discussions between working collaborators about a film project are generally grounded in this cognitive approach, and the cognitive approach will be used as a practical theorizing basis from which to work with the vocabulary in the filmmaking process in order to expand and refine it.

In particular, this book seeks to understand rhythm in film editing and the process of creating rhythm "through the physiological and cognitive systems 'hard-wired' into all human beings."[9] *Cutting Rhythms* makes numerous references to "physical thinking" when describing the cooperative functioning of known neurological processes with the rhythmic activity of the living breathing bodies of editors and spectators. By taking this approach, I follow, to some extent, the great Soviet director and montage theorist Sergei Eisenstein, who believed that "in its fullest manifestation, cognition becomes kinesthetic."[10] In other words, deep knowledge is not just something you know, but something you are and you feel. My argument that the *body* thinks about and creates a film's rhythms is made in practical terms that are intended to enhance access to this embodied knowledge.

In saying that the mind is physical and the body thinks, I am not making any comment about what else the mind may be, if anything. There is no revelation about consciousness or Consciousness, and no material versus extramaterial value judgment implied. I don't know what else the mind may be, or how else it may function, and I do not intend to address that question. My ideas rely on the evidence that the mind is a physiological entity as well as, despite, without regard for, and without implication of, anything else it may or may not be. And given that the mind is physical and the body thinks, I am developing an idea about cutting rhythms that looks at the way an editor shapes the flow of a film as a unified action of mind, emotion, and body.

The cognitive approach is effective in making my arguments accessible to practitioners; however, there is an anomaly in this approach for my particular topic. The study of rhythm is a study of something that is not, or is not primarily, apprehended cognitively. Dictionary definitions of the word "rhythm" frequently emphasize that "rhythm is a *felt* phenomenon."[11] This quality of being felt and created through feeling is a substantial thread in my overall inquiry. It is this quality that causes rhythmic creativity to be characterized as subjective and ineffable in writings on the craft of editing. It is also this quality that finds expansive, sympathetic discussion in the phenomenological and Deleuzian approaches to the study of cinema. For more information on this approach to understanding film, readers may find it interesting to go directly to the source and read Deleuze, *Cinema 2: The Time Image*, in which they will find a discussion of "the sensory (visual and sound), kinetic, intensive, affective, rhythmic"[12] from another perspective.

However, through an analysis of the shaping of the "the sensory (visual and sound), kinetic, intensive, affective"[13] into rhythms through various procedures and for particular purposes, *Cutting Rhythms* makes the case that, although rhythm is a felt phenomenon, it is not *just* felt. Creativity in rhythm and spectators' expectations about rhythm are also learned, and the process of creating and learning rhythms can be described.

Cutting Rhythms appeals to knowledge in the discipline of neurology to explain the actual physical processes of experiencing and creating rhythm. In particular, it draws on recent theorizing by neurologists about the functioning of mirror neurons in the recognition of intentional movement. By describing the processes through which the brain apprehends rhythm (in part through recognition of intentional movement) and phenomenological theories of the ways that living bodies have kinesthetic empathy with movement they perceive, *Cutting Rhythms* develops a model of a thinking body, a body that gathers, stores, and retrieves information about rhythm and uses it strategically—in other words, a body that thinks, but does so primarily through a directly physical, experiential process.

I make use of work by the philosophers Deleuze and Henri Bergson and various scholars, drawing on the phenomenological study of film and dance within my thinking body model because their studies of perception of cinema, time, space, energy, and movement provide insights into the ways in which rhythm is perceived and the meanings of those perceptions. However, my objective is not to "create new concepts" or to "alter our modes of thinking about time and movement,"[14] as Thomas E. Wartenburg and Angela Curran describe the work of Deleuze in their textbook *The Philosophy of Film*, but to engage in what Bordwell and Carroll describe as "problem driven research."[15] The problem is to find a way to describe the materials, processes, and purposes of rhythm and modes of physically thinking about rhythm so that rhythmic creativity in film editing can be understood and extended.

METHODOLOGY: PRACTICE

A substantial portion of my research into rhythm is necessarily practical. I have edited a number of short dramas, short and longer form documentaries, and the occasional educational or promotional video. Each of these has provided insights into the editing process. I have made observations and notes about each project I've worked on, so all of them have had an impact, in some way, on my research processes. By integrating theory with practice, testing my own and other's ideas against the practical experience of cutting to discover and articulate knowledge about rhythm, my intention has been to produce a set of ideas that are useful to practitioners and that may also provide useful data or ideas for other theoretical inquiries.

SOUND

Sound is an inestimably large force in the creation and perception of rhythms in film; therefore, the picture editor's work with sound must be accounted for in a discussion of rhythm. The standard process for editing, and the pathway that I learned, follows a timeline in which the raw footage is handed over to the editor (meaning the picture editor) for composition of final form, structure, and rhythm. Then she hands it over to the sound editor for sound design. This process may change, but for the time being, the implications of this process are that the editor *does* handle sound, inasmuch as she handles synchronized sound, and whatever sound effects and sound atmospheres are necessary to create a finished picture edit of the film, but the sound designer is the expert in sound.

As an editor, I almost always work with sound, but I only sometimes find or create sounds to make the pictures work. I usually use what is readily on hand that satisfies the criteria of timing and energy that I think are needed. I play around a bit with levels, a bit with various kinds of sound effects, and a lot with timing. But I leave the specifics of quality, source, direction, nuance, and layers to the sound team that will follow on from my work. Sound is a factor in the rhythms I create, but the art of sound design is a separate decision-making process that follows from and responds to the rhythms created in the picture edit.

In my discussion of rhythm, I include sound in my general statements about editing, and when I do, I mean sound as a picture editor works with it, not as a sound designer works with it. I distinguish sound as a specific element only when particularly noted. Otherwise, when I say, for example, "movement," I mean movement in image and in sound; when I talk about energy, I mean energy in picture and sound, but *only* inasmuch as a picture editor would be expected to be manipulating sound.

MUSIC

Similarly, with regard to the use of music, the work discussed herein is that of a picture editor and not a composer. Picture editors don't create the music that is so substantially a part of the viewer's perception of rhythm in a finished film. However, unless a particular piece of music is written into the script, the composition of music generally follows the completion of a locked-off picture edit. Musical rhythms are, like sound rhythms, composed to underline, counterpoint, enhance, contradict, shade, and so forth, the story, structure, and rhythms created in picture editing. Music is, in fact, one of the things that make the topic of rhythm in picture editing so hard to pin down. When a film is finished, the music applies a seamless composition to images that are in actuality riddled with seams. Music, which is perceived as a flow rather than a series of individual notes, enhances the flow of images and ameliorates much of the disruptive potential of cutting, thereby making the cuts and the compositions of the cuts' rhythms much harder to see.

Many editors use temporary, or "temp," music while they are cutting. There are a few ways to do this, and some of these are more useful than others. One method of using temp music is to find pieces of music that match the mood the editor is trying to create and then lay them down and cut pictures to them. I do not usually do this for a number of reasons. The first of these is that it muddies my direct experience of the rhythms inherent in the images and performances. Furthermore, temp music applies a rhythm of something else that was already shaped to something I am trying to shape, thus blocking the potential for the rhythm I am creating to be its own unique solution to the problem at hand[16].

Perhaps in an ideal world, a composer, sound designer, and editor would work side by side on constructing the final flow of the rhythm, the movement of sound and image, and the experience of the screen story. The impediments to this ideal are the usual: time and money. The process of cutting image first and then handing over to sound and music saves both time and money in that the composer and sound designer don't spend any time working on images or timings that may change or even be dropped. Less time wasted is certainly less money wasted. But the artistic possibilities of changing the workflow pathway to one that, though possibly more expensive, leads to a more balanced positioning of sound, music, and image in the production of film have yet to be fully explored.

Therefore, an editor has to look at yet another consideration when deciding whether to use temp music, which is that music is stronger than picture in its affect. To paraphrase Phillip Glass from a public forum on his work in Sydney in 2005, putting different pieces of music to images will change the images, but putting different images to a piece of music won't change the music.[17] I avoid temp music whenever possible for all of the above reasons, and especially this one: a piece of temp music will make the flow of images seem to be working, which is a deception I cannot afford when trying to make the best possible edit.

There are two other ways of using temp music that should also be mentioned. One is to cut first and then lay in a particular piece of temp music. This is a form of communication between editor and composer, who may never meet on a tightly budgeted project. Editors can use temp music in this way to "show" composers what they mean or intend. To some extent this practice limits the composer's creativity and artistry. However, there are many edited projects in which deadlines and budgets supersede these concerns, so composers are happy to get this "help" and editors are glad to have an effective tool for communication. The other significant use of temp music is to sell the cut to the producers. If an editor lays in a compelling temp music track, it helps to inspire the producer's faith in the eventual results of the editing process by giving the roughly edited footage a feeling of having a polished rhythm. If temp music is being used in this way, then the best scenario is to have the composer come in and advise the editor on what music to use. This involves the composer in the creative editing process and gives him a chance at least to shape the impression a producer gets of the film toward the direction it will eventually take it when he composes the music.

Although both of these last two methods of applying temp music to a cut are useful for particular reasons, neither one really supports the editor's quest to find the best visual and kinesthetic flow of images and sounds in the editing process. Therefore, unless music is specifically mentioned, I do not include it herein as part of the discussion of the process of shaping rhythms in moving images.

MAKING DECISIONS

Cutting Rhythms breaks with the usual practice of referring to the director as the decision maker in the editing process, a practice found even in books about how to edit. These books consider the director the creative decision maker because the director is ultimately responsible for the decisions that are made. The director may give instruction as to what decisions should be made in the edit suite, but there is a great deal of variation among directors in the style and precision of these instructions. Furthermore, in the editing process, unless the director actually has his hands on the editing gear and is cutting the film himself, thousands of decisions are made by the editor *before* an edit of a whole film, a sequence or scene, or even an individual shot-to-shot relationship is presented to the director. The editor presents successive cuts, but not every possible choice that could be made, to the director for ratification. The director makes choice from among the variations offered to him by the editor. The editor makes choices from among millions of possible combinations of the material of what to present to the director.

Editor–director relations are a fascinating area of study, as they are delicate, complex, inspiring, frustrating, and very often nonverbal. It is not possible to overestimate their importance in the shaping of both the process and, of course, the eventual product of the edit. However, as they are not the central area of inquiry for this book, I have just added particularly relevant notes on the subject of working with directors on shaping rhythm in sidebars and reserved the larger topic of director–editor collaborations for another book!

ENDNOTES

1. In *Editing: The Art of the Expressive,* Valerie Orpen discusses various kinds of books available on editing, saying, "The existing literature on editing can be divided into three categories: textbooks or general studies on film, either solely on editing or with a section on editing; editor's handbooks; and interviews with editors, which include autobiographies, transcripts of lectures, essays, anthologies of interviews and individual interviews in periodicals." See Orpen, V., *Film Editing: The Art of the Expressive,* p. 10. My literature survey includes texts in all three categories.

2. Van Leeuwen, T., "Rhythmic structure of the film text," in *Discourse and Communication: New Approaches to Analysis of Mass Media Discourse and Communication,* p. 216.

3. Dancyger, K., *The Technique of Film and Video Editing: Theory and Practice,* pp. 307–315.

4. Reisz, K., and Millar, G., *The Technique of Film Editing,* pp. 246–247.

5. Bordwell, D., and Thompson, K., *Film Art: An Introduction,* pp. 278–280.

6. Fairservice, D., *Film Editing: History, Theory and Practice,* p. 273.

7. Bordwell, D., and Carroll, N., *Post-Theory: Reconstructing Film Studies,* p. xvi.

8. Stam, R., *Film Theory: An Introduction,* p. 236.

9. Ibid.

10. Bordwell, D., *The Cinema of Eisenstein,* p. 125.

11. Brogan, T. V. F., "Rhythm," in *The Princeton Encyclopedia of Poetry and Poetics,* p. 1068.

12. Deleuze, G., *Cinema 2: The Time Image,* p. 29.

13. Ibid.

14. Wartenburg, T. E., and Curran, A., *The Philosophy of Film: Introductory Text and Readings,* p. 7.

15. Bordwell, D., and Carroll, N., *Post-Theory: Reconstructing Film Studies,* p. xvii.

16. I am indebted to Robin de Crespigny, former lecturer in directing at the Australian Film Television and Radio School (AFTRS), and Edward Primrose, former Head of Screen Composition at AFTRS, for their discussions of temp music.

17. Phillip Glass spoke at Popcorn Taxi at the Valhalla Cinema in Glebe, Sydney, on January 9, 2005. A documentary record of the proceedings is available for the purposes of study or research through Popcorn Taxi at http://www.popcorntaxi.com.au.

CHAPTER 1

Rhythmic Intuition

How does an editor make decisions about where and when to cut in order to make the rhythm of a film?

When asked, most editors will say something along the lines of "by intuition" or "you just know when it's right." For example, in *First Cut, Conversations with Film Editors* by Gabriella Oldham, editors are quoted talking about rhythm and editing as "magic" (Sheldon Kahn), "feels right" (Carl Kress), "it's intuitive" (Bill Pankow), "it's intuition" (Paul Hirsch), "having a sense" (Donn Cambern), "you just know" (Sidney Levin), "exclusively in the realm of intuition" (Merle Worth), "an internal sense" (Richard Marks), and "we go by intuition" (Alan Heim).[1] These are extremely estimable editors, and there is no question of the validity of their answers. They are, in my experience, absolutely right, and if there is one thing this book aims to respect and support, it is the power of intuition.

But these editors' comments leave one wanting to know more. What kinds of thinking and practice are editors referring to when they say that shaping rhythm is intuitive? Intuition is not the same as instinct. People are born with instincts, but intuition is something we develop over time, through experience; in other words, it is learned. So, if we can pinpoint what kind of intuition is at work in shaping a film edit, then we can ask, "How is this intuition developed or acquired and how is it actually working in the process of editing rhythms?"

1

To say that something is intuitive is often used to draw a protective veil around the knowledge. As Donald Schon wrote in the preface to *The Reflective Practitioner*, "When people use terms such as 'art' and 'intuition,' they usually intend to terminate discussion rather than to open up inquiry."[2] The implication is that intuition can't be further examined without disrupting the ecology of mind that permits it to flourish.

The explanation for most editors' lack of discussion of rhythmic intuition may be the fear that analyzing or theorizing—in other words, "thinking too much"—will interfere with intuition. It is true that analyzing creativity and doing something creative are incompatible activities to perform simultaneously. Analysis is an activity that engages neural pathways that are distinct from the pathways engaged by moving or responding directly to a stimulus. So, trying to break down and observe an action at the same moment as doing it causes the brain's attention to be split and diffused, disrupting the efficacy of either the analysis, or the action, or both. Neurologist Richard Restak explains:

> In terms of brain performance, "just doing it" involves the smooth non-self-conscious transfer of learned actions from working memory, stored in frontal lobes, to the pre-motor and motor areas that transform the working memory into those effective, winning plays that result from thousands of hours of practice....[3]

In other words, disrupting impulses by thinking too much is a specific neurological response to the effort of activating two distinct neurological pathways simultaneously. However, this disruption does not occur as a result of the accrual of explicit knowledge about a craft or skill. In fact, explicit knowledge is an essential support to intuition. It is the learned knowledge that gets transferred from working memory. The more that is explicitly known, the more readily accessible intuitive responses will be. "Geniuses ... share a similar talent for storing vast amounts of information in long-term memory and then retrieving the information as circumstances demand."[4]

This discussion of intuition therefore proceeds from the premise that articulation of ideas about what kinds of learned knowledge inform an editor's intuition need not disturb the balance of thinking and doing that allows editors to use intuition in the creation of the rhythms in films.

Not everyone will agree with this premise, and furthermore, some editors who disagree are, in fact, extremely credible given their experience, knowledge, and swags of awards. To quote Martin Walsh, Academy Award-winning editor of *Chicago* (Rob Marshall, 2002), "Don't read any books about film editing, especially those that theorize about mathematical possibilities and how many feet of film they had to deal with back in the 20th century. And blinking. I read one once … I'm still in therapy."[5]

I can only hope that the readers of my ruminations (particularly those from the Final Cut Pro generation who have easier access to gear and technical manuals than to ideas about editing) will, instead of requiring therapy, find some useful thoughts.

In any case, the discussion of intuition that follows is consciously designed to avoid disrupting intuition and to respect and even enhance the immediacy of rhythmic knowledge and its "smooth non-self-conscious transfer of learned actions from working memory."[6]

INTUITIVE THINKING

Guy Claxton, educator and co-editor of *The Intuitive Practitioner*, summarizes what particular types of thinking are at work, or what people mean when they say "intuition," as the following six things: expertise, implicit learning, judgment, sensitivity, creativity, and rumination. Each of these things could be at work at any moment that intuition is activated and often in complex combinations. But to pull them apart for a moment and see how they work in the process of editing, I have listed them below, first with Claxton's definition,[7] followed by my thoughts about some of the ways they apply specifically to an editor's intuitive processes.

1. *Expertise*—the unreflective execution of intricate skilled performance

   An example of expertise is the way a professional editor with years of experience uses her gear. It's like touch-typing or riding a bicycle; she doesn't have to think about what button to push in order to do an operation, and this frees her concentration to focus on the material she's working with. I call it "breathing with the Avid," but it's not restricted to Avid. ... It's a matter of knowing your gear of choice so expertly that its operation doesn't require conscious thought.

   Another important instance of expertise is that which arises from years of experience with the editing process. Editors often say that each new project is like learning to edit all over again, and in my experience this is an accurate description of what it feels like. However, after accruing a degree of experience in structuring documentary footage or shaping a story or scene, an editor becomes expert, in the sense that she can see a possible organization or flow very quickly and without conscious thought. Note, however, that there is practice and learning at work in acquiring this expertise that, just like learning the gear, can be made explicit.

2. *Implicit learning*—the acquisition of such expertise by non-conscious or non-conceptual means

   A lot of implicit learning about editing is acquired by watching films. There are conventions of filmmaking that show up in most TV programs, ads, movies, and digital games. An editor may not know the names of these conventions or techniques but has seen them enough to know what they are without ever having consciously learned them.

3. *Judgment*—making accurate decisions and categorizations without, at the time, being able to justify them

   Judgment can be seen at work whenever an editor makes an adjustment to a cut and it works better. Once the "working better" is visible, an editor is rarely called upon to explain why or how. In fact, there are reasons that can be elucidated and described, but the use of judgment implies making good decisions without going through the process of justifying them. Judgment is, however, acquired by having a thorough understanding of the material, the story, the conditions, and the traditions within which you are working, and the capacity to make judgments can be enhanced and developed through explicit teaching and learning.

4. *Sensitivity*—a heightened attentiveness, both conscious and nonconscious, to details of a situation

   An editor has sensitivity or heightened attentiveness to movement and emotion in the material. Developing sensitivity is a matter of learning to see the potential of movements and moments before they are shaped—a subject that will be taken up at length in this book!

5. *Creativity*—the use of incubation and reverie to enhance problem solving

   Creativity is a complex and much-discussed notion, sometimes understood to mean generating new ideas or concepts, but just as often considered to be the process of making new associations or links, which, of course, is exactly what an editor does. Editing creativity is the lateral association of images or sounds to solve the problem at hand, which is the shaping of the film and its rhythms. The editor's reveries yield connections between images, sounds, and movements in the raw material, which will create new and coherent meanings. Practice, and trial and error, informs these reveries, of course, but also the editor's acquired knowledge of the world, herself, and her sensitivity to movement and emotion give her the basis from which to make creative connections and associations.

6. *Rumination*—the process of "chewing the cud" of experience in order to extract its meanings and its implications

   Rumination is what is at work when you are washing the dishes and suddenly the solution to an intractable sequence is clear to you. It is the kind of thinking that happens when you're thinking about something else, and you have immersed yourself so deeply in your material that it inhabits a part of your brain even when you're not actually looking at it or working on it. Rumination is what happens on the weekend or while you're making a cup of tea and can yield some of your best solutions and ideas, which is why healthy work/rest cycles are so important to editing: they enhance your intuition!

Looking at intuition as these six types of thinking clearly demonstrates that intuitive thinking need not draw a protective veil around itself. The ecology of mind that allows these kinds of thinking to flourish is nourished by acquisition of explicit skills and knowledge. Claxton, in fact, is quite clear on this point when he quotes Nobel Laureate Konrad Lorenz: "This apparatus which intuits has to have an enormous basis of known facts at its disposal with which to play."[8] In short, intuition isn't something you just have. It is something that can be developed, enhanced, and even acquired through practical and theoretical experience and education. The question implied by Claxton's list is this: Where, specifically, does the experience and education of rhythm, which editors use as fodder for their intuition, come from?

The philosopher Henri Bergson describes intuition in physical, spatial terms that are useful starting points for describing the editor's means of acquiring rhythmic knowledge:

We call intuition here the *sympathy* by which one is transported into the interior of an object in order to coincide with what there is unique and consequently inexpressible in it.[9]

It is a feeling *for* something that moves one's understanding not just from outside to inside an object, but into a relationship of feeling *with* the object, a position at which one can *coincide* with some aspect of the object. This feeling *with*, in the case of rhythm, is what I will call kinesthetic empathy.

Even more directly, this quote from Australian editor Dany Cooper, ASE, sums up rhythmic intuitions and points distinctly and succinctly to what I will argue is the editor's method of accrual and storage of rhythmic information: "It's a body thing."[10]

Picking up on Bergson's spatial metaphor and applying it quite practically to the body of the editor, I propose that an editor learns where and when to cut to make rhythm from two sources: one is the rhythms of the world that are experienced by an editor, and the other is the rhythms of the body that experiences them.

In the next three sections of this chapter, I describe first the rhythms of the world as a source of knowledge in rhythmic intuition. Then I look at kinesthetic empathy and mirror neurons as two phenomena that pertain particularly to the editor's accrual of knowledge about rhythm. Finally, I look at the ways in which an editor's own body is also a source of rhythmic information in the edit suite.

PERCEIVING RHYTHM

The universe is rhythmic at a physical, material level. Seasons, tides, days, months, years, and the movement of the stars are all examples of universal rhythms, and our survival depends on us oscillating with these rhythms and functioning as part of a rhythmic environment.

Waking/sleeping, eating/digesting, working/resting, and inhaling/exhaling are just some of living beings' ways of following the rhythms of the world, of surviving by oscillating or moving with the rhythms of their physical world.

Going beyond rhythmic survival and into rhythmic creativity is partly a matter of *perceiving* rhythm. To enhance their rhythmic intuition, editors actively perceive the rhythmic movement of life and of the world around them. The world's external rhythms are a primary source of knowledge about rhythm in film, because they are the rhythms that frame our existence, expectations, and knowledge of the movement of time and energy in life.

If we actively see and hear and feel the world's rhythms, what we are actually seeing, hearing, and feeling is *movement*. Editors need actively to perceive and shape the flow of time and energy through movement to shape a film's rhythms. Russian filmmaker Andrey Tarkovsky uses the metaphor of a reed quivering to describe the way that movement shows us time and energy in life and in film:

> "Cinema ... is able to record time in outward and visible signs, recognizable to the feelings. ... Rhythm in cinema is conveyed by the life of the object visibly recorded in the frame. Just as from the quivering of a reed you can tell what sort of current, what pressure there is in a river, in the same way we know the movement of time from the flow of the life-process reproduced in the shot."[11]

When Tarkovsky writes, "... we know the movement of time from the flow of the life-process,"[12] he describes movement as the means by which we perceive time and energy.

ACTIVELY PERCEIVING RHYTHMS

As living beings, editors inherently have some knowledge of rhythms of the world, but it is also possible for them to develop and enhance their rhythmic intuition by engaging an *active* awareness of rhythms of the world through the perception of movement of energy and time. For example, almost every one of the twenty-three distinguished editors interviewed in *First Cut, Conversations with Film Editors*[13] mentions music, their love of music, or their musical training. One interpretation of these editors' engagement with music is that through their experience of music, their awareness of rhythm in the movement of sound has been specifically and consciously activated. This activation educates their intuition about rhythms more generally—in life and in film. It may even cause them to perceive rhythms in the world around them quite actively, to become consciously aware of the rhythms with which people walk and talk, with which nature ebbs and flows. Music is an intentionally formed instance of rhythm, but knowledge of music has developed these editors' capacity to perceive any rhythm.

I have also heard editors speak about surfing, rowing, dancing, painting, and cooking as experiences of rhythm that help them to develop their rhythmic intuition. These editors draw on their direct experiences of the movement of these rhythms to accrue a cache of rhythmic knowledge.

PRACTICAL EXERCISE

Becoming Aware of Rhythms of the World

Becoming aware of the rhythms of the world is a way of adding to your rhythmic knowledge. We all behave rhythmically all of the time—how else would we avoid being hit by cars, for example, if we didn't judge their speed and our trajectory in relation to their speed? By recognizing our everyday lives as rhythmic entities, we can refine our sense of the rhythms of the world from rhythmic survival into rhythmic creativity.

Choose something that you do often, something physical that you do without thinking about it, something that is not dangerous; for example, brushing your teeth or locking and leaving the car once you've parked it. As you go through the motions of this activity, notice the speed of movements relative to each other, the efforts, the sounds, the emphasis points or punctuation points in gestures and actions, and particularly their relationship to one another. You could map this flow with a line drawing of accents, or hum it to yourself, or just see it in your mind's eye as a flow of energy, directions, and actions.

When I pull into the garage at night I do a very polished rhythmic routine, and I do it without conscious thought—but it is not instinctive; I have trained myself to do it. It goes: ignition off, parking brake on, seatbelt unclick, door open, keys into bag, relock door, and slam. Each of these actions has duration, a sound, an amount of effort required (mostly very small!), and together, they make a rhythm, a flow, a pattern with lulls and accents. This is a rhythm of the world, one of thousands, that informs my sense of what feels right as far as duration, emphasis, and rate of movement are concerned.

Do this exercise only outside of the cutting room, where analysis won't disrupt action. The objective is to develop a heightened sense of rhythms of the world, happening and intersecting all around you, all of the time. Later, in the cutting room, this sense will support and inform intuition or the "unreflective execution of intricate skilled performance."[14]

PERCEIVING RHYTHM IN THE RUSHES OR DAILIES

In the process of shooting a film, a small, specific "world" is created. The rushes, or raw material of a given film project, are the immediate source of information that feeds the editor's rhythmic intuition about a particular project and its rhythmical world. The same active awareness that editors use to accumulate rhythmic information about the larger world is employed, but now in a very specifically directed way, to accumulate information about rhythms in the rushes or dailies.

The editor finds specific cues to rhythmic possibilities in the uncut material, as Tarkovsky suggests, in the *movement* inherent in the recorded images and sounds. This may be movement of the frame, movement within the frame, or movement of the eye around the frame. And, as will be discussed in greater detail later, it may also be movement of events or emotions. The editor who tunes her awareness to movement in the rushes—its pulse, effort, speed, shape, size, causes, purposes, and so forth—gathers information about the rhythmic potential of the film. An editor who is shaping a rhythm in the editing process directs her attention to the shaping of movement in the images and sound, because movement is the visible and audible manifestation of energy and time.

The processes by which specific sensitivities to the movement of the world and the movement of the more limited world of the raw material become sources of the editor's rhythmic intuition are the subject of the next section, which looks at kinesthetic empathy and mirror neurons, two physiological motion detectors built into humans.

MIRRORING RHYTHM

There are at least two physiological activities that an editor engages in when intuitively perceiving and shaping movement in the rushes into an edited rhythm. The first is *kinesthetic empathy*. Kinesthetic empathy is feeling *with* movement, a sensitivity we have developed by perceiving and being movement and a sensitivity that, I propose, is particularly relevant to editors of moving pictures. Neuropsychologist Arnold Modell describes the activation of kinesthetic empathy by saying, "The perception of feelings relies on the corporeal imagination, which in turn is determined by the history of the self."[15] I am drawn to his phrase "corporeal imagination," which suggests that the body not only thinks, it imagines, in this case imagining how another body feels. And it imagines in relation to its own experience, drawing on remembered sensations to recognize feeling in movement.

Our physical response to movement is based on direct or indirect experience of movement, the history of our individual bodies in movement, and physically innate reflexes connected to protection from movement or pleasure in movement. In other words, even if we ourselves have not moved in a particular way, for example, if we have not fallen in a fast, straight, hurtling trajectory, our bodies know to duck if something comes hurtling at them, just as they know to brace for impact if they themselves are falling. We know the laws of physics in our bodies because we live them. So, movement speeds, directions, and energies have meaning when we see them, even if we have not experienced them. Through our kinesthetic memory of life lived in time, space, energy, and movement, we can account for responsive attention to movement in filmed rushes.

When movement is intentional, our responsive attention to its rhythms is augmented by a special feature of our advanced brains: mirror neurons. Mirror neurons are explained in layperson's terms by neurologist Richard Restak:

> Neuroscientists have recently discovered the existence of "mirror neurons" in the brains of monkeys that discharge both when the monkey performs certain movements and when the animal merely observes another monkey performing the movement. Strong evidence

suggests a similar mirroring process in humans—certain nerve cells are activated both during an activity and while observing another person performing the activity ... the brain is a powerful simulating machine designed to detect and respond to a wide range of intentions on the part of other people. Neuroscientists are further exploring how our observations of another person's behavior allow us to infer his or her conscious or even unconscious intentions.[16]

This breakthrough discovery of mirror neurons by neuroscientists gives us a physiological accounting for empathetic engagement with intentional movement. Neurologically speaking, we physically participate in the movement of people we see, even if we are sitting still. Moving with intention lights up certain neurons in our brains, and watching someone do the same movement lights up the same neurons.[17] So, watching movement really is a physical thing; it is a special brain process that interacts differently with differently intended movements. Scientist V. S. Ramachandran writes:

With knowledge of these neurons, you have the basis for understanding a host of very enigmatic aspects of the human mind: "mind-reading" empathy, imitation, learning and even the evolution of language. Anytime you watch someone else doing something (or even starting to do something) the corresponding mirror neurons might fire in your brain, thereby allowing you to "read" and understand another's intentions, and thus to develop a sophisticated "theory of other minds."[18]

One of the ways the editor knows how to cut rhythm is through her mirror neurons. Mirror neurons allow us to participate in another person's intentional movements. Our neurons do the movement with them, whether they are live or on the movie screen.

So, what an editor may be doing in making rhythm in moving pictures is engaging her corporeal memory and/or mirroring, neurologically, parts of what she sees and hears. Some part of what she sees or hears in the movement of the rushes will light up the editor's mirror neurons or her kinesthetic memory, and that part will be selected and juxtaposed with another part that also "lights up her lights".

Putting two shots together, each of which inherently has rhythm, makes a third rhythm, which is not the same, or even just the sum of the first two. So the edit begins to have a rhythm of its own. At this point the editor cannot simply recognize a "right" rhythm in, for example, a performance, which is a process of comparatively drawing on knowledge of the rhythms of the world. The editor's own internal rhythms must come into play to shape rhythm through an editing process. As editors begin to do more than neurologically imitate existing rhythms, they draw on rhythms inside themselves, *as well as* those things captured in the rushes, to create the film's rhythm.

PRACTICAL EXERCISE

Mirroring Intentions

The purpose of this exercise is to recognize how much you already know about movement, emphasis, energy, and intention.

Sit in a café and observe a conversation between two people—observe, but don't listen in. You don't want to know what the conversation is actually about, you just want to become aware of how much you know by seeing movement dynamics rather than hearing dialog. Watch the movements of your subjects' heads, eyes, posture, and hands, and notice how much you know about their intentions just by their body language. You know, for example, when one person leans forward whether they are leaning forward conspiratorially or aggressively. And you know, just by watching the energy and quality of movement, whether the other person is delighted (leaning in to catch the gossip) or ambivalent (shifting to one side, looking away) or scared (leaning back warily).

The people you are watching may not lean forward and back but they will, without fail, use their hands, eyes, posture, speed, and attack on movement to express things—things they themselves may not even be aware of. Furthermore, they will also read each other's intentions and respond through movement. If one leans forward aggressively and the other leans back warily, the first person will, consciously or unconsciously, make a decision to pursue (lean farther forward) or retreat (relax, back off, withdraw …). The decisions made and expressed in movement are arrived at through interpretation of the information being provided by mirror neurons, by the neurological readings of each other's intentions as expressed in movement.

Observing the conversation from the outside, you are not called upon to make decisions about how to respond, but your mirror neurons are activated just by watching the two people move. You know what they mean because you yourself have done similar movements, and your neurons recognize the intentions that drive those movements. If you were constructing the same conversation from a number of available takes in the editing suite, you would be making decisions about which nuances of the movement to emphasize and which to elide to create a rhythm that feels right. The intuition about what feels right, and what doesn't, comes, in part, from mirror neurons doing their work of interpreting intentions in movement. The shaping of the flow of these movements is the editor's work of creating the appropriate interchange for a given moment in a film.

FIGURE 1.1

In this scene from Quentin Tarantino's film Pulp Fiction *(1994), Tim Roth's character Ringo is trying to convince Yolanda (Amanda Plummer) to do something. In the first image (a) he is leaning forward, arms open to her in a gesture that reads as sincere, serious, and intent. She is focused on him, but her arms are clenched close to her body, shoulders slightly hunched, and face turned very slightly to the side so that she would have to look at him out of the corner of her eye. Her posture in relation to his is protective, maybe unwilling or skeptical. In the next image (b) Ringo looks as though he is about to jump out of his seat with vehemence. Yolanda has opened her arms and is leaning farther forward, looking straight at him; in other words, she has physically and psychologically opened up to his plan and is moving toward it. Even without hearing the dialog, we know what these characters mean because we recognize the intention in their movement. [Photo credit: Miramax/Buena Vista; The Kobal Collection; Linda R. Chen]*

BEING RHYTHM

The editor is a material, physical, rhythmical entity that accrues rhythmic knowledge of the world. However, her body has another function in the creation of rhythm. It doesn't just recognize and store information about rhythm, it also *provides* rhythms. The editor's living, breathing body is the other source of rhythm available in the edit suite. Rhythm is in her own physical presence.

Roland Barthes' discussion of the difference between playing music and hearing music in his essay "Musica Practica" could also be a description of the way in which the editor's body participates in the creation of rhythms:

> … the body controls, conducts, coordinates, having itself to transcribe what it reads, making sound and meaning, the body as inscriber and not just transmitter, simple receiver.[19]

The musician's, or in this case the editor's, physical presence and physical engagement with the material becomes part of the creative process. The rhythms of an editor's body act on the material of the film's rushes in a very direct, physical way. Her own rhythm of blinking, breathing, heartbeat, synapses firing, as well as the rhythm of her cycles of sleeping, eating, thinking, and feeling, choreograph the film's rhythm. The next section will articulate some theories about how this works, how the rhythm of the material passes through the rhythms of the editor on its way to being formed.

THINKING RHYTHMICALLY

Thinking rhythmically is what I will call the intersection of the rhythms of the world and the rhythms of the editor's body with the editor's learned craft skills, including her ability to operate the editing gear. The three knowledges—knowledge of the world, of the body, and of the craft—are deeply entwined. The entwining occurs during the learning of craft skills and gear operation. During this process the body develops a new rhythm, a rhythm of editing as physical movement and work.

Also during this process some of the editor's significant neural mirroring patterns are formed. To quote Walter Murch on learning rhythms from working closely with other editors:

> You pick up the good things that other editors are doing and you metabolize those approaches into what you're doing, and vice versa. It's kind of like women who live together eventually having their periods at the same time.[20]

Murch's metaphor alludes to a process that is very much embodied. The picking up of good things is a process of metabolizing; i.e., taking the crafting knowledge into your body. Sharing a common rhythm of menstrual cycles is an example of oscillating with the rhythms of the world and an example of a body becoming a source of rhythmic knowledge about the world. In Murch's description of learning from other editors, the rhythms of the world and the rhythms of the body become entwined with the skills of editing.

Murch also talks about blinking and tuning oneself to the rhythm of the filmed material:

> One of your tasks as an editor is sensitizing yourself to the rhythms that the (good) actor gives you, and then finding ways to extend these rhythms into territory not covered by the actor, so that the pacing of the film as a whole is an elaboration of those patterns of thinking and feeling. And one of the many ways you assume those rhythms is by noticing—consciously or unconsciously—where the actor blinks.[21]

I propose that an editor doesn't just notice where the actor blinks, she imitates it. This might mean that the editor literally imitates it, or at least tries to, by syncing up her own blinking rhythm with that of the actor and making a cut. Then, in playing back that cut, if the rhythm of her own blinks and the rhythm of the actor's blinks don't sync up, perhaps the rhythm of the film doesn't "feel right." So, the editor will have a look, adjust the cut, and then try re-syncing her rhythm to the rhythm in the material she has just cut into place. The editor needn't literally blink with the actors (although some do), her mirror neurons imitate the blinks. They mirror the movement of the actor, and perhaps, on the first rough assembly, the blinks fail to light up all the mirror neurons that could be lit up in association with that moment of the film, in which case, the cut gets adjusted.

What editors are doing to tune themselves to the rhythm of the material is drawing on their own experiences of the rhythms of, for example, blinking. This knowledge of blinking rhythms they have perceived is implicitly compared to the rhythms they see in the rushes and cuts they are working on. As they continue to refine the cuts, they use their mirror neurons and kinesthetic empathy to relay the external rhythms, which they perceive in the developing edits, *through* their internal rhythms, to create the rhythm of the film.

Ross Gibson, in his essay "Acting and Breathing," picks up on Murch's ideas about blinking and extends them into a discussion of breath rhythm as an affective rhythm that actors use:

> When we watch a body in performance, we watch its breathing, and most crucially we also imbibe its breathing. Performers with strong presence can get us breathing (and blinking also) in synch with them. As we experience the patterns of their corporeal existence, we also get gleamings (*sic*) of their thoughts and feelings—we get these gleamings in our bodies, nervously, optically, and cardio-vascularly ... we feel ourselves occupied and altered by the bodily rhythms of another.[22]

Gibson is writing about live performance at this point in the essay, but the same "imbibing" of breath can take place in the cinema. The difference is that, in cinema, the actor's breath rhythms have passed through the hands, or perhaps the lungs, of the editor.[23] Gibson goes on to discuss the activity the viewers are engaged in, what their bodies are doing, when they are being moved by a performance:

> By blinking and breathing in synch with the performer, you can feel the actor representing you in the world of the drama. And through the proxy of the actor ... you can feel the imaginary world course through you. Your representative breathes you and blinks you and thereby helps you imagine experiences other than your own.[24]

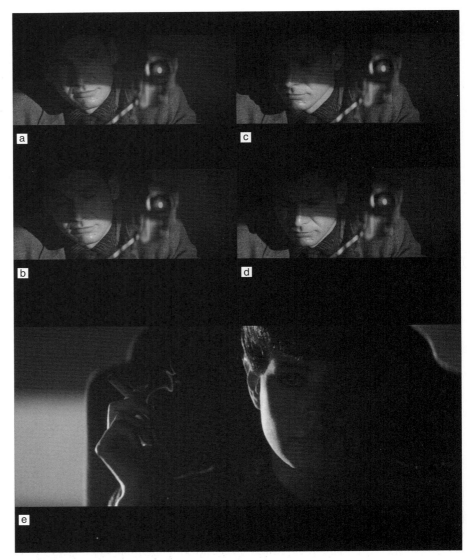

FIGURE 1.2

In this scene from Blade Runner *(Ridley Scott, 1988) Deckard (Harrison Ford) puts Rachael (Sean Young) through a test to determine whether she is a human or a "replicant." The test measures her eye movement as a way of determining her thoughts. So the scene, in a sense, illustrates Murch's premise about blinking revealing thinking. Interestingly, Harrison Ford blinks fairly often in this scene, shifting his thoughts and focus from himself to his job, to his subject, to his concerns about the whole operation, and so on. Sean Young blinks not at all, an impenetrable presence, until, toward the end, when she becomes confused and flustered by the test results, she uncharacteristically blinks three or four times in one shot.*

Before the spectator can have this wonderful experience of blinking and breathing with the performer in the cinema, the editor has to do it. She has to use her own physical presence as a stand-in for the spectator's and measure the rhythms of the film's breath by comparing it with the feeling of her own breathing. To do so, the editor has to imbibe the breath first. Then the editor can deploy her two caches of rhythmic knowledge on it: the rhythms she has seen, in the world or in the rushes (or both); and the rhythms she has "been," in the sense of her own experiences of breathing and blinking.

FIGURE 1.3

In this scene from American Beauty *(Sam Mendes, 1999) there is a quartet of breath rhythms carried on the voices of the four actors, each of whom has a different pattern and different state of mind and different objective. But the scene is unmistakably driven by the breathing of Lester (Kevin Spacey), who is overwhelmed by desire for his daughter's friend, Angela (Mena Suvari). Each of his utterances is borne on a particular breath expressing his desire, and each of his exhalations and inhalations adds to the sense of his purpose and intent. The other three characters each respond: Lester's wife (Annette Bening), with a chirpy, high-pitched insistence that glosses over everything; Janie (Thora Birch), with a strangled breath and sound that barely escapes through gritted teeth; and Angela, with an easy poise, a breath rhythm that promises much but gives little away. [Photo credit: DreamWorks/Jinks/Cohen; The Kobal Collection]*

I propose that Murch's ideas about blinking and Gibson's about breathing can be extended to take the actor's whole body and the whole of the mise-en-scene into account as a source of kinetic communication. As an editor, my body tenses and relaxes responsively to what I see because my kinesthetic empathy and mirror neurons are activated by all of the sources of movement on the screen. If I can be at some level tuned to these physical responses to what I see and hear, then I can use them to make the rhythm feel right.

In this case, the method editors use for constructing a rhythm is this: they breathe and blink with the actors, feeling their way through a shot, a performance, a scene, and the whole film. They tune their awareness of the movements in the film to the rhythms of their own bodies. Some even hear the film's movement as a song in their heads. Others sway, shrug, nod, or squint with the energies made visible by movement passing before their eyes. Maybe something is off. The sigh of the actor doesn't feel long enough—literally. I know because I can feel his sigh in my body.

Because the editor is conducting rhythms of the whole world of the rushes, as we have seen, Murch suggests "sensitizing yourself to the rhythms that the (good) actor gives you, and then finding ways to extend these rhythms into territory not covered by the actor."[25] The actor's intentional movements provoke empathetic engagement in the editor's body and implicit comparison, by the editor, of the rhythms of the performance to her own rhythms and the rhythms of the world. The editor uses this form of intuition (the Bergsonian sense of being in "coincidence"[26] with the actor's rhythms) to make decisions about when and where to cut the performance to shape its rhythms. During this process a rhythm of the film begins to take shape in the rushes, and in the editor there awakens a physical experience of this nascent rhythm. This physical experience is used to map the rhythms in the film where the actor is not present, to give the story, emotions, and visuals rhythm.

USEFUL QUESTIONS

If an editor is stuck, and she knows that some of her intuition about rhythm comes from her knowledge of the rhythms she has seen or heard in the world or rhythms of her own being, she may ask herself what rhythmical experience she can use for comparison to the rhythm she is trying to construct.

This question is generally deployed unconsciously when confronted with an editing project. It is part of the comparison that is implied by the statement, "It doesn't feel right"; i.e., it doesn't feel right compared to some internal or external experience of rhythm. So, an editor could employ this question consciously as a strategy for giving rhythmic intuition a structure to work within. She could ask herself: To what rhythm am I comparing the rhythm of this edit? This question pushes the editor to broaden the range of rhythms she refers to during the process of editing and brings the editor's body of knowledge about perceiving rhythms and being rhythms into active engagement with the rhythms she is shaping from the uncut, raw, filmed material.

SUMMARY

Intuition in editing is a mode of thinking that includes creativity, expert judgment, sensitivity, and "unreflective execution of intricate skilled performance."[27] It also includes activation of implicit learning, which is learning acquired through nonconscious means. This chapter has proposed that the specific learning that supports intuition about the creation of rhythms in film editing is acquired through living in a rhythmic body and in a rhythmic universe. However, although this learning *is* implicit in being alive, it is not necessarily *only* implicit. Just as Murch suggests that we can sensitize ourselves to the rhythms a good actor provides, we can also sensitize ourselves to the rhythms of the world and of the body to expand and enhance our intuitions about cutting rhythms.

ENDNOTES

1. Oldham, G., *First Cut: Conversations with Film Editors,* p. 27 ("magic," Sheldon Kahn), p. 91 ("feels right," Carl Kress), p. 177 ("it's intuitive," Bill Pankow), p. 194 ("it's intuition," Paul Hirsch), p. 209 ("having a sense," Donn Cambern), p. 301 ("you just know," Sidney Levin), p. 320 ("exclusively in the realm of intuition," Merle Worth), p. 372 ("an internal sense," Richard Marks), p. 381 ("we go by intuition," Alan Heim).

2. Schon, D., *The Reflective Practitioner: How Professionals Think in Action,* p. vii.

3. Restak, R., *The New Brain,* p. 22.

4. Ibid.

5. Online at www.moviemaker.com/hop/vol3/02/editing2.html; accessed March 2007.

6. Restak, R., *The New Brain,* p. 22.

7. Claxton, G., "The anatomy of intuition," in *The Intuitive Practitioner,* p. 40.

8. Lorenz, Konrad, as quoted in Claxton, G., ibid., p. 44.

9. Bergson, H., *Introduction to Metaphysics,* pp. 81–82, as quoted in Fraleigh, S. H., *Dance and the Lived Body: a Descriptive Aesthetics,* p. 167.

10. Rowe, C., "Dany Cooper interview," *Inside Film Magazine,* p. 43.

11. Tarkovsky, A., *Sculpting in Time,* pp. 119–120.

12. Ibid.

13. Oldham, G., *First Cut, Conversations with Film Editors.*

14. Claxton, G., "The anatomy of intuition," in *The Intuitive Practitioner,* p. 40.

15. Modell, A. H., *Imagination and the Meaningful Brain,* p. 145.

16. Restak, R., *The New Brain,* pp. 35–37.

17. The meaning of "intentional" has significant potential for variation when moving between scientific studies and philosophical studies. As Robert Sokolowski says in *Introduction to Phenomenology,* "The core doctrine of phenomenology is the teaching that every act of consciousness we perform, every experience that we have is intentional: it is essentially 'consciousness of' or an 'experience of' something or other ... We should note that this sense of 'intend' or 'intention' should not be confused with 'intention' as in purpose we have in mind when we act" (p. 8). In the phenomenological sense, all human movements are intentional. In the "practical" (p. 34) sense of having purpose in mind, not all human movements have intention. The discussions of mirror neurons that I have researched do not specifically address this question of the philosophical versus the practical sense of intention. However, my readings do seem to suggest that any human movement can and will be mirrored by another human. When introducing the topic of mirror neurons, Restak begins by discussing how the brain can distinguish "biologically based movements, such as walking, from random other movements" (Restak, R., *The New Brain,* p. 34). Walking is an example of a movement that is potentially intentional in either sense. It may be that one walks with a specific intention or desire, or it may be that walking is intentional in the sense that the biological being, who is walking, has consciousness. What is important is that in *either* case, walking is mirrored by the mirror neurons. This book takes the point of view that other human movements, such as breathing and blinking, which may not be intentional in the sense of having a purpose in mind, are still intentional movements that trigger responses from mirror neurons.

18. Ramachandran, V. S., "Mirror neurons and imitation learning as the driving force behind "the great leap forward" in human evolution," online at www.edge.org/3rd_culture/ramachandran/ramachandran_p2.html; accessed 11 September 2004.

19. Barthes, R., "Musica Practica," in *Image–Music–Text,* p. 149.

20. Ondaatje, M., *The Conversations: Walter Murch and the Art of Editing Film,* p. 62.

21. Murch, W., *In the Blink of an Eye,* 1992, pp. 62–63.

22. Gibson, R., "Acting and breathing," in *Falling for You: Essays on Cinema and Performance,* p. 39.

23. These breath rhythms have also, of course, been considered, shaped, and captured through the rhythms of directing and shooting, passing through the lungs, as it were, of the director, the cinematographer, and the rest of the crew.

24. Gibson, R., "Acting and Breathing," in *Falling for You: Essays on Cinema and Performance,* p. 41–42.

25. Murch, W., *In the Blink of an Eye,* 1992, p. 62.

26. Bergson, H., *Introduction to Metaphysics,* p. 167.

27. Claxton, G., "The anatomy of intuition," in *The Intuitive Practitioner,* p. 40.

CHAPTER 2

Editing as Choreography

Chapter 1 established that movement is what editors use to shape rhythms; it is what they mirror neurologically, what activates their kinesthetic empathy, and what they work with intuitively. Building on that premise, this chapter compares cutting rhythms to another art of shaping movement: dance.

Choreography is the art of manipulating movement: phrasing its time, space, and energy into affective forms and structures. In their work with rhythm, editors do similar things. This chapter compares editing to choreography for the pupose of uncovering some principles that choreographers use that may be applicable to the editor's work with the shaping of the film edit. It begins by examining the uses of the more common metaphor for editing: music. It then puts forward that, although the word "rhythm" is commonly linked to ideas about music, the actual materials that editors shape in time are movement and energy. The pulse, which is the smallest expressive unit of the movement of time and energy, is discussed before looking at the choreographic processes of shaping pulses into phrases. The ways that choreographers construct dance movement phrases are compared to the ways in which an editor assembles movement into phrases and sequences when creating rhythms. Finally, the questions choreographers might ask themselves when shaping movement are recast as questions editors might ask themselves when shaping rhythm in film.

SHIFTING THE DISCUSSION FROM MUSIC TO MOVEMENT

Editing is often compared with music making. Many people understand the use of the word "rhythm" in film to be a musical metaphor. The discussion of rhythm in, for example, the 2004 book about the editing craft, *The Eye Is Quicker*, opens with the following quote: "'All art constantly aspires towards the condition of music.' —Walter Pater."[1] Another example is filmmaker Martin Scorsese's quote: "For me the editor is like a musician, and often a composer."[2] And "Eisenstein ... often makes implicit appeal to musical analogies, whence the frequent recourse to musical concepts such as meter, overtones, dominant, rhythm, polyphony, and counterpoint."[3] Music is a very rich source of language and ideas for the consideration of rhythm; however, sometimes the terms it supplies are used quite vaguely or generally. This section will look closely at some of the specific words used when comparing editing to music to discover the ways in which they are or are not useful.

When using the musical metaphor, the processes of composing, orchestrating, and conducting are often made analogous to the process of editing, particularly the creative editing process of shaping the film's rhythm. Each of these activities is analogous in some ways to editing a film, but, for different reasons, none of them are particularly precise comparisons.

Composing, in general, is more like writing than it is like editing. A composer delineates the form and structure on which the musicians base the performance of their craft. A screenwriter does the same for the cast and crew of a film. The composer makes up the music and its rhythms, whereas an editor doesn't exactly make anything up. Editors compose rhythms in the sense that someone might compose a flower arrangement: not by making the flowers, or in this case the shots, but by choosing the selections, order, and duration of shots.

The use of the word "orchestrate" comes from the idea that there are many different elements within shots, and between them, that an editor coordinates. These might include performance, composition, texture, color, shape, shot size, movement energy and direction, and many more. Eisenstein called these "attractions," as in the different elements within shots and films that might attract the spectator's attention.[4] Orchestration, in this case, is a metaphor for giving each set of attractions due consideration in relation to the others. However, orchestration is *actually* a distribution of parts to various instruments rather than a joining together of shots, in which the "instruments," or constituent parts of a shot, such as the frame, the design, the performance, and the lighting, have already been orchestrated in relation to each other. The description of what Theo Van Leeuwen calls "initiating rhythms" in his essay "Rhythmic Structure of the Film Text" is perhaps more useful for describing what an editor does than "orchestrate." Van Leeuwen suggests that there may be and usually are a few things attracting the attention, creating emphasis, or shaping time in the raw material, so that "editors are faced with the problem of synchronizing" the various elements into a coherent rhythmic experience. To do so, the editor chooses one of the lines of movement, energy, or emphasis "as an initiating rhythm and subordinates to this rhythm the other profilmic rhythms."[5] Shaping "initiating rhythms" is a more precise description of the editor's decision-making process than orchestration.

Conducting is perhaps a more apt musical metaphor because, like the conductor, the editor decides on the pacing, timing, and emphasis presented in the final composition. However, in music, conducting also suggests that a finished composition has already been submitted to the conductor and he *interprets* it, which is not really what happens in editing.

There is a nonmusical meaning to the word "conducting" that might be more useful for describing what an editor does. This is conducting in the sense of facilitating the flowthrough of rhythm like wires facilitate the flowthrough of electricity or, as filmmaker Andrei Tarkovsky suggests, pipes facilitate the flowthrough of water:

> Time, imprinted in the frame, dictates the particular editing principle;
> and the pieces that "won't edit"—that can't be properly joined—are

those which record a radically different kind of time. One cannot, for instance, put actual time together with conceptual time, any more than one can join water pipes of different diameter. The consistency of the time that runs through the shot, its intensity or "sloppiness," could be called time pressure: then editing can be seen as the assembly of the pieces on the basis of time pressure within them.[6]

Tarkovsky's implicit comparison of shots to water pipes shifts the discourse about rhythm away from music and toward the more visible *movement* of time "imprinted in the shots." Although Eisenstein and Tarkovsky generally present aesthetically and procedurally oppositional ideas about the nature and purpose of the editing process, this shift from music to movement also has precedent in Eisenstein's writing. When Eisenstein writes "in rhythmic montage it is movement within the frame that impels the montage movement from frame to frame,"[7] he succinctly summarizes the core principle of what he calls "rhythmic montage," one of his Five Methods of Montage, described in full in *Film Form*. Rhythm is not categorically or completely defined by Eisenstein's discussion of "rhythmic montage." However, it does, for our purposes, firmly shift the focus of the discussion of rhythm from music to movement.

The next question, then, is: What can be said about the art of shaping movement that can inform our intuition for shaping rhythm in film editing? For insight into this, I turn to studies of the art of choreography, which, of course, is the art of shaping movement.

A team of Australian researchers, including psychologists, scientists, and choreographers, provides a useful starting point for looking at editing as a form of choreography. Their study, *Choreographic Cognitions*, talks about how dance is made and how it is perceived and understood by audiences. This cognition of dance is, I argue, similar to the cognition of rhythm in film.

The *Choreographic Cognitions* team explains that time is the artistic and expressive medium of contemporary dance. So, when we watch

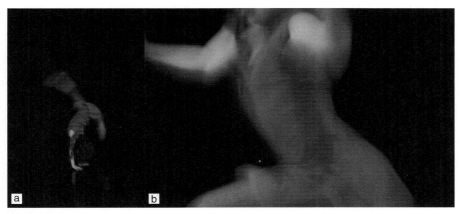

FIGURE 2.1

Jaz Allen performing a phrase of movement from Doesn't Fit in a Box *(Karen Pearlman, 2008). [Photo credit: The Physical TV Company; Christophorus Verheyden]*

dance, we see movement, but we understand what movement *means* by how it expresses the invisible elements of time and energy. In the *Choreographic Cognitions* team's words, "the artistry of movement is in trajectories, transitions, and in the temporal and spatial configurations in which moves, limbs, bodies, relate to one another ... change to a single component can affect the entire interacting network of elements. In a dynamical system, time is not simply a dimension in which cognition and behavior occur but time, or more correctly dynamical changes in time, are the very basis of cognition."[8]

If we apply this to editing, we could say that, like choreographers, editors shape the trajectories of movement across shots, scenes, and sequences, the transitions of movement between the shots. Like choreographers, editors work with the temporal and spatial dynamics of movement to create a flow of moving images that carries meaning. And, just like choreographers, editors will often describe the way a "change to a single component can affect the entire interacting network of elements."[9] Editors less often describe rhythm and time as a basis of cognition. But I argue that, in a sense, they are. As we shall see in the upcoming discussions of pulse and phrasing, and later in the chapters on emotion and events, rhythm is how we understand the meaning of information, interchanges, and images in relation to one another. Rhythm is part of the sensual experience of the film and a core means by which we interpret and understand what we see and hear. So, the "dynamical changes in time"[10] that are the core of the choreographer's art are also the core of the editor's rhythm shaping art.

The next section will look at the pulse, the smallest unit of movement shaped by choreographers and editors into rhythm, and the role of pulse in defining dynamical changes in time.

PULSE

Pulse is the smallest, the most constant, and perhaps the most ineffable unit of rhythm in film. It is ever present, just as it is in your body, and unnoticed, just as in your body. Pulse in film has a few other characteristics in common with a living body—it tends to stay within a certain range of speeds, it organizes the perception of fast and slow, and it keeps the film alive. Just as in a living body, if a film's pulse stops, slows, or speeds too much, the results can be dire for the rhythm, the story, or the experience of the film.

Pulse defines and demarcates what Tarkovsky calls "the consistency of time" or the "time pressure"[11] within shots. A single pulsation is the extra effort placed on one part of a movement compared to the less intensively energetic other parts of the movement. So, just as in the beating of a heart, there is a continuous on/off of emphasis points, accents on words, gestures, camera moves, colors, or any other pro-filmic event. Actors may develop characters in part by developing a distinguishing pulse; that is, the energy and speed with which they put emphasis on words, gestures, etc. Pulses are shaped by the energy or intention behind movement or speech and make that energy or intention perceptible to the spectator.

Feeling Pulse

Try speaking without placing an accent on any syllable.

Without training or practice this is very difficult to do because we learn language with emphasis points built into it. That is, we learn language in order to say what we mean, and without emphasis points, meaning is indistinguishable. If you can master the speaking of a couple of sentences with equal emphasis on each syllable and equal time between each syllable, try speaking these sentences to someone and see how well they understand you. Chances are they will focus a great deal more on how strangely you are speaking than on the meaning of the words you are uttering. This is because you have created a monodynamic utterance, and the meaning of every interchange resides to some extent in the dynamic—your listener will focus more on the dynamic than the words.

An editor works with and shapes the dynamics of interchanges when shaping rhythm. She chooses takes or shots with different emphases, she places these shots in relation to one another to create a pattern of emphasis, and she curtails the duration of shots to shape the rate of the accents. Underlying all of these decisions, whether they result in maintaining or varying the film's pulse in a given moment, will be a feeling for the overall strength, speed, and consistency of the pulse being shaped in the film.

Professor Theo Van Leeuwen writes, "'pulsing' plays a key role in articulating the meaning because it foregrounds the sounds or movements that carry the key information."[12] The film editor does not necessarily set the pulse of a shot—the director and actors do that mostly—but the editor has choices to make about the sustaining, changing, and coordinating of pulses into phrases. These choices are made through the selection of takes (the pulse in any two takes of the same action may be different) and the choice of cutting points. Pulse accents can also be emphasized or de-emphasized and even shifted by cuts.

Pulses in movement are shaped by choreographers and editors into phrases. The next section of this chapter describes two choreographic methods for shaping phrases and compares them to two of the various kinds of editing challenges. It then looks at how a choreographic approach could apply to the shaping of nondance movement in the context of a narrative drama.

MOVEMENT PHRASES

Movement phrases in dance, and in film editing, are compositions of movement into perceptible and intentionally formed rhythmically expressive sequences. A phrase in the choreographic sense is distinct from a linguistic phrase in that it may be of any length and may contain more than a single choreographic "thought." A choreographic phrase is a series of related movements and grouped emphasis points.

There is a broad spectrum of approaches a choreographer might take to shaping movement phrases in dance. What follows is a description of two points along that spectrum, provided to illustrate the commonalities of the choreographic and editing approaches to the shaping of movement phrases.

One choreographic approach is for the choreographer to create a movement sequence with inherent timing, spatial organization, and emphasis, and then teach that phrase to the dancers. This approach to choreography has an affinity with Tarkovsky's water pipes. If a film director works in this way, he provides the editor with rushes that

FIGURE 2.2
The Mirror *(Andrei Tarkovsky, 1974). In all Tarkovsky films, the phrasing is not created in editing; rather, it resides in the shot. The movement of the camera, the actor, the dialog, and the sound are all coordinated in the rehearsal and shooting process to create the flow of time and energy, which expresses the meaning. [Photo credit: Mosfilm; The Kobal Collection]*

have immutable, self-contained phrases of movement. So, the editor's job is not to create the phrase's rhythm, but to respect and realize the phrase's rhythm. In this approach the editor's choreographic input comes in extending these rhythms to the construction of the larger sequences. She does this by shaping the *joins* of phrases. So, she is still grappling with the shaping of movement "trajectories, transitions … and temporal and spatial configurations," but the smallest unit for transitioning or configuring is not the pulse or the single gesture or movement fragment, but the phrase.

A different approach a choreographer might take is to give her dancers "movement problems" to solve, such as, "Find five gestures of frustration and helpless anger." These five gestures are fragments, like a series of short shots. The choreographer connects the fragments into phrases and in doing so designs their temporal flow, spatial organization, and emphasis. In film, the connecting and shaping of fragments into rhythms is done by the editor. This approach has more affinity with Eisenstein's sense of montage than Tarkovsky's. Tarkovsky's approach to rhythm considers time to be present in the shot, and the editor's job to be to construct the film so that time flows effectively almost in

FIGURE 2.3
In Battleship Potemkin *(Sergei Eisenstein, 1925) shots are cut together to form phrases. Eisenstein's films make use of cutting as a form of movement, not just camera movement and actor movement. So each cut is a move to a different shot, a move of the spectator's mind and eye, and a move that contributes to the phrasing. [Photo credit: Goskino; The Kobal Collection]*

spite of cuts. In Eisenstein's view the course of time is *created* in the cutting. The editing process actively choreographs rhythms; i.e., editing connects bits of movement on film to *create* the passage of time. In this approach, the editor takes fragments of movement and designs them into phrases. Rises and falls of emphasis, direction and speed changes, size, shape, and performance are all shaped into the dynamic flow that is the "cine-phrase's" meaning.

Choreographers often work with abstract or nonnaturalistic movement, and editors often work with naturalistic movement of actors or subjects, but the choreographic principles can still be applied. A movement phrase is not just a unit of rhythm in abstract movement. A naturalistic character's movement in narrative drama is also shaped choreographically into phrases. For example, the action in a given script calls for a character to enter a room, drop the keys on the table, and open the fridge. This is a series of movements that may be handed to the editor with its phrasing intact in one shot, or it may be a series of gestures covered in a variety of shots from which the editor must select and shape fragments into a phrase. In either case, the phrasing of the movement's rhythm will carry and impart a significant portion of the movement's meaning.

A choreographer trying to elicit affective phrasing from a *live* performer would just say, for example, "Come in quickly, hesitate, then walk very deliberately." An editor may have one take in which the performer does all of this—walks in the door quickly, hesitates before dropping his keys, and then walks deliberately to the fridge. Within this single take, each of these movements contains one or more pulses, and together they constitute a phrase.

Or the editor may need to *construct* this quick–hesitant–deliberate relational nuance of the movements out of three or even more takes if that is the rhythmic phrasing she wants. If she has coverage in a selection of wide, medium, and closer shots, the editor would phrase this series of movements by choosing the performer's quickest entrance, cutting

FIGURE 2.4

Russell Crowe and Jennifer Connelly in A Beautiful Mind *(Ron Howard, 2001).* A Beautiful Mind *is just one example of hundreds that follow a middle way between Tarkovsky's and Eisenstein's views, creating some of the phrasing in the shots and some through the cuts. Ron Howard's films have a very silky smooth (some would say slick) feel to them, with every aspect of movement, including camera movements, performers' movements, and movements between shots expertly gauged to propel the narrative and not to draw the eye away from story. Cuts are tucked almost imperceptibly between similarly composed shots, with the performance movement motivating the cut or used as punctuation at the beginning or end of phrases. [Photo credit: DreamWorks/Universal; The Kobal Collection; Eli Reed]*

to his hesitation before dropping his keys, and then inserting a shot or two of his deliberate walk to the fridge.

Once it is phrased, the movement becomes the emotional content in the context of the story. If the character comes home very late in a domestic drama and rushes in the door, the hesitation before dropping the keys might be a questioning, "Is everyone asleep?" Or more melodramatically, "The house feels deserted, has my wife left me?" The deliberate walk to the fridge then becomes thoughtful, maybe even anxious, depending on the story context. The story context tells us the focus of the emotional content—what the questioning and the anxiety are directed *toward*—but it is the hesitation and the deliberate walk that gives us the *feeling* of questioning and anxiety. This is important because we don't go through a conscious process in our thoughts to understand the feeling we are seeing. We feel *with* it, we use our mirror neurons and our capacity for kinesthetic empathy to grasp the pulsation of the movement directly. When a movement phrase is satisfactorily choreographed by an editor, it gives us the kinesthetic information the story requires. It does so without confusing us or making us stop feeling and start asking questions about what we're supposed to be feeling, and it does so immediately—it lets us feel and move on to what happens next.

PHRASING CONSIDERATIONS

One reason to compare editing to choreography is to create the possibility of using knowledge about the craft of choreography to extend ideas about the crafting of rhythm in editing. If the construction of rhythm in film editing is understood to be a choreographic process, then some of the questions with which choreographers grapple may become useful questions an editor can ask herself in the process of shaping a film's rhythm.

The following ideas about methods of crafting dance are presented as questions editors can ask themselves. This is for two reasons. First, because they are not rules. These concepts are simply questions with which choreographers grapple to shape the affective qualities of movement. Second, these questions are not meant to be prescriptive. They are lateral ways of looking at the flow of movement through material, and their use value is most likely to arise when the more standard questions of story construction are failing the editor in her effort to make a film feel right.

American dancer and choreographer Doris Humphrey wrote about the craft of choreography in her book *The Art of Making Dances.* Her book is divided into chapters on some of the various considerations at work in shaping movement into dances. Taking the table of contents of *The Art of Making Dances* and reframing its topics into considerations for shaping any movement, not just dance movement, provides a series of questions editors can ask themselves. The following topics are Humphrey's chapter subheadings; the questions they raise are mine and represent just a sampling of the line of questioning raised by taking a choreographic approach to rhythm in film editing.[13]

Symmetry and Asymmetry

Just as the tension between symmetry and asymmetry can be used expressively by a choreographer, it can be manipulated by an editor who is thinking about the film's style of cutting and the rhythms created by that style. A smooth, classical style will tend to emphasize symmetry in both the composition of frames and the evenness of pulse. Disruption of symmetry then becomes an important dramatic break. For the editor, the questions of the overall film may be: Should the rhythm, and its movement phrasing, emphasize balance or imbalance? Even or uneven patterns? Measured or manic paces? These questions can also be applied to a specific break in a rhythmic pattern, as in the question of when to switch from even to uneven or from measured to manic.

One and More Bodies

For an editor, the question of one and more bodies is concerned with the choice of shots and the concentration of movement they contain. In the shaping of an expressive moment an editor may, for example, have choices between tightly framed individuals or looser frames of groups. Or she may have choices about the concentration of movement within different takes. Her questions about a given moment or an overall film might be: Is the concentration of movement high or low, scattered or unified, moving toward chaos or order? To shape these variations into an affective flow, the editor may consider the distribution of movement at a given moment and whether to amplify movement or personalize it by emphasizing a group or an individual.

FIGURE 2.5
Thandie Newton symmetrically framed in a moment of quiet reflection in Crash *(Paul Haggis, 2005).*
[Photo credit: Lions Gate; The Kobal Collection]

FIGURE 2.6
Thandie Newton and Matt Dillon falling asymmetrically from one side of the frame to the other in a
*moment of crisis (*Crash, *Paul Haggis, 2005). [Photo credit: Lions Gate; The Kobal Collection]*

FIGURE 2.7

Movement is scattered and diffuse in this image of a community mourning the deaths they feel sure are coming in Whale Rider *(Niki Caro, 2002). [Photo credit: New Zealand Film Comm.; The Kobal Collection]*

FIGURE 2.8

But the individual movements of Keisha Castle-Hughes in Whale Rider *(Niki Caro, 2002) are, in contrast, focused and directed as she saves the whales and reunites the community. [Photo credit: New Zealand Film Comm.; The Kobal Collection]*

The Phrase

As discussed above, the phrase is a composition of movement into a perceptible and intentionally formed rhythmically expressive sequence. The questions at work in shaping phrases of rhythm in editing include: What is the cadence of this rhythm? What is the rate and strength of its pulse? Where are its rests and high points? Where are its breaths and shifts of emphasis? Does it have even or dynamic variation of accent by stress? What about accent by duration?

The Stage Space

In this section of *The Art of Making Dances*, Humphrey asks choreographers to consider the use of space as an affective tool. The same questions apply for an editor faced with the frame and working to determine rhythm through the use of various shots. Of course the director and cinematographer have already given in-depth consideration to the frame and movement in the frame by the time the material reaches the editor. So, the editor's concern is with the choreographic composition of the joins of frames and the impact the material has when seen in a flow rather than as individual shots. The questions are: Are shots put together to progress smoothly from wide to close, jump from close to wide, or jump around in size? Does movement

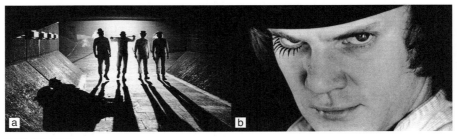

FIGURE 2.9

Bill Butler, the editor of Stanley Kubrick's A Clockwork Orange *(1972), cuts extremes of shot sizes hard together at certain moments, creating a jarring, destabilizing rhythm. [Photo credit: Warner Bros., The Kobal Collection]*

flow in a consistent direction, in alternate directions, collide from all screen directions, or are there different patterns at different times? What about angles? What kind of effect are they having and is it to be used sparingly or relentlessly?

Humphrey's ideas about the art of making dances are helpful to me in demonstrating the principles at work in rhythm, and they may be helpful to an editor if she is stuck. But, as we have seen in Chapter 1, these questions don't necessarily have to be verbally articulated by an editor to be the ones with which she is grappling, and there are other ways to solve problems than to articulate them. If an editor is working with the movement of time and energy in a film, she is working with these principles of movement distribution, concentration, phrasing, and spatial organization whether she knows it or not. Where these questions may be useful is if the editor *knows* she is working with movement to create rhythm and wants to know how to engage with choreographic principles of composition.

A choreographer will build up phrases of dance movements, vary them, juxtapose them, interpolate them, and otherwise manipulate them, shaping them within themselves and in relation to one another to make an overall experience of time, energy, and movement called a dance. In film editing, an editor is rarely simply making an experience of time, energy, and movement; she is also shaping story, character relationships, and other kinds of information. Furthermore, film editors rarely work exclusively with human movement. However, in shaping the rhythm of the film, time, energy, and movement are the salient factors; they shape the qualitative experience of the story and information. The movement through time and energy of all of the filmed images in a given project is shaped choreographically into phrases of related movements and grouped emphasis points. These phrases are then varied, juxtaposed, interpolated, and shaped within themselves and in relation to each other to make the overall experience of time, energy, and movement in a film that is known as rhythm.

PRACTICAL EXERCISE

Time, Space, and Energy: Part 1

This exercise requires at least five people. It demonstrates the affective power of time, space, and energy and shows how much impact an editor's manipulation of just these three things can have on the emotion and the story.

To set up the exercise, ask two people within the group to enact the following scene:

A: sits at a table, reading.

B: walks in and stops, looking at A.

A: looks up.

B: shakes head "no."

A: looks away.

B: sits down.

A: looks back at B; they lock eyes.

A: stands up and starts to walk out, pauses near B, and then leaves.

Once they have the script staged, three other people each get a chance to direct the scene, but each person gets to direct only *one* quality.

The first director can give directions only to do with time. He may say anything to do with speed—faster or slower; and anything to do with duration—for a longer time or a shorter time. Give the director and performers a few minutes to work and then watch the results. Notice how the whole feeling and meaning of the scene changes when things are given different emphasis by being done more quickly, or slowly, or for a longer or shorter time. This is what an editor does when she decides which take to use, the quicker or the slower one, and where to cut into the action, after a short time or a long time.

Now the second director gets a chance, and this one gets to direct only space. He can change stage directions, proximity, or direction of gestures or movements and nothing else. Again, after this director and the performers work for a few minutes, there is a marked difference in the meaning and emotion of the scene. This is the element the editor is manipulating when choosing whether to use the close, medium, or long shot of a given moment. Proximity and distance can create intimacy, discomfort, isolation, and a range of other feelings. Stage direction moves the eye around the space and can create smooth or abrupt flows of the action and a range of dynamics in between.

Time, space, and energy are all considerations in phrasing. The tools an editor has for manipulating them will be discussed in greater detail in the next chapter. The completion of this practical exercise, the directing of energy, can be found in the next chapter after the discussion of energy and trajectory phrasing.

SUMMARY

In this chapter the discourse about editing rhythms has been shifted from music to movement, thus creating the possibility of looking at editing as a choreographic process. The core unit of movement, time, and energy that editors and choreographers manipulate has been described as a pulse. Choreographic methods of shaping movement phrases have been mined for information about how making dances is and is not like making rhythms in films. In particular, the movement phrase has been looked at as a choreographic construction that is found either within a shot, through the juxtaposition of shots, or both. Whether the movement phrase is within the shot or between the shots, it is expressing time and change over time. The movement of a steady, inexorable press of a stranger through a bedroom door expresses one kind of time. Sharp flashes of steel, blood, water, and shower curtain create another. Movement is the action or the image of time and energy; it is the material the editor works with to make rhythm. Editing involves the *phrasing* of movement, or the aesthetic shaping of movement into that aspect of empathetic engagement with film that we call rhythm.

The next chapter will examine the specific tools an editor has for the shaping of rhythm in film.

ENDNOTES

1. Pepperman, R. D., *The Eye is Quicker, Film Editing: Making a Good Film Better*, p. 207.
2. Scorsese, M., as quoted in *Motion Picture Editors Guild Newsletter*, www.editorsguild.com/newsletter/specialjun97/directors.html.
3. Stam, R., *Film Theory: an Introduction*, p. 43.
4. Eisenstein also uses "orchestration" in a discussion of the relationships of sound and images. This is a more accurate use of orchestration in the sense of distribution of parts—the sound plays one part in creating affect, the images another, and Eisenstein et al. exhort us to use the parts contrapuntally, not redundantly. See "A statement on the sound-film by Eisenstein, Pudovkin and Alexandrov," in Eisenstein, S., *Film Form: Essays in Film Theory*, pp. 257–260.
5. Van Leeuwen, T., "Rhythmic structure of the film text," in *Discourse and Communication*, p. 218.
6. Tarkovsky, A., *Sculpting in Time*, p. 117.
7. Eisenstein, S., *Film Form: Essays in Film Theory*, p. 75.
8. Stevens, K., et al., "Choreographic cognition: composing time and space," in *Proceedings of the 6th International Conference on Music Perception & Cognition*, p. 4.
9. Ibid.
10. Ibid.
11. Tarkovsky, A., *Sculpting in Time*, p. 117.
12. Van Leeuwen, T., *Introducing Social Semiotics*, p. 183.
13. See Humphrey, D., *The Art of Making Dances*, p. 11.

CHAPTER 3

Timing, Pacing, and Trajectory Phrasing

What are the tools editors use to create rhythm? This chapter introduces timing, pacing, and trajectory phrasing as the three key tools utilized by editors to shape rhythmic sequences.

Timing and pacing, as discussed in the introduction, are often confused or substituted for rhythm as a whole. Timing and pacing are also used to describe a variety of aspects of rhythm or the rhythm-making process. The words "timing" and "pacing" are sometimes used when discussing *attributes* of rhythm (things that films have when they have rhythm). They are also used as words to describe *faculties* inherent in the editor. One hears "she has good timing" or "she has a strong sense of pacing" as descriptions of intuition about rhythm. Finally, they are *tools* that can be used to create rhythms in the editing process. Their function as tools is the primary concern of this chapter. However, given that timing and pacing are also attributes of rhythm and faculties of editors shaping the rhythm, the functioning of timing and pacing as attributes and faculties will also be touched upon herein.

My own contribution to the discussion of the tools for shaping rhythms is the concept of *trajectory phrasing*. Trajectory phrasing shapes the energy and spatial organization of movements in shots and across edits into rhythms. Although trajectory phrasing is not in the everyday lexicon of most film editors, I suggest that it is necessarily deployed as a tool in the creation of rhythms, and it therefore is also an attribute of rhythm and a faculty that editors with skills at creating rhythm have.

TIMING

Timing is the attribute of rhythm that arises as an editor determines *when* cuts and shots occur. There are three aspects of timing to be considered when discussing rhythm in film editing: choosing a frame, choosing duration, and choosing the placement of the shot.

Choosing a Frame

Choosing which frame to cut on is one sense of timing. It creates the specific frame-to-frame relationship of two shots and their contents. "Etymologically the word [rhythm] probably implies 'not flow, but the arresting and firm limitation of movement' (Jaeger, 1959)."[1] Timing is the tool at work in firmly limiting the movement of one shot by

FIGURE 3.1

In the days when "cutting film" meant actually cutting pieces of film, you could hold up a film strip to the light and choose the precise frame on which to cut. The process of editing was altogether more physical, and, when holding those strips of film, you actually had the sensation of holding time in your hands. [Photo credit: The Kobal Collection].

choosing the precise frame on which to begin and end it. If, for example, the editor is constructing a conversation in a shot–reverse shot configuration, and there is a shot in which a man looks up and then smiles, followed by a shot in which a woman looks away, the editor might choose to cut on the frame before the smile starts. In that case the scene would play as "the man looks up, then the woman looks away." As little as one frame later, the smiling becomes perceptible, so cutting exactly one frame later would make the scene play as "the man looks up and starts to smile, but the woman looks away." A world of different meanings can unfold if the woman seems to look away because the man is smiling or because the man looked up.

Choosing Duration

"Timing" frequently refers to duration or the length of time a shot is held. It is the aspect of rhythm being referred to when one says something feels long or short. Holding a shot for a long time or for what *feels* like a long time are both functions of timing. Choosing duration is distinct from choosing the precise frame on which to cut because, although a shot may change meaning quite dramatically by holding or dropping one frame, the feeling of its *duration* is not really affected by one frame (which is only 1/24 of a second). A 10-second shot will feel long if it is juxtaposed with a series of 1-second shots. The same 10-second shot, used in the same context, will still *feel* just as long if it is actually only 9 seconds and 20 frames. And the same 10 (or so)-second shot will *feel* quite short if juxtaposed with a series of 60-second shots. The feeling of a shot's duration is created by the relative durations of the shots near to it and the concentration of information, movement, and change within it.

Choosing the Placement of a Shot

The decision about *where* to use a shot is also called timing. This sense of timing refers to "where" as in *when* to reveal the punch line or the surprise. It is related not so much to duration or precise frames; rather, it shapes rhythm in broader strokes by determining trajectories and emphasis. If, for

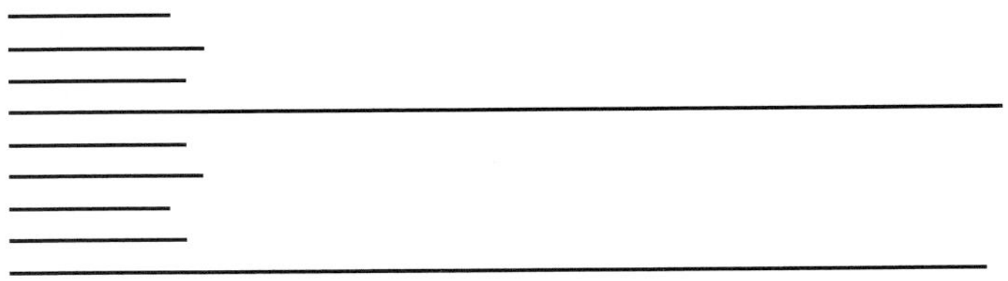

FIGURE 3.2

Even though the long lines are not exactly the same length, they both feel long compared to the short lines. Similarly, the short lines all feel short; although their shortness varies in relation to one another, they are roughly the same in relation to the long lines.

example, the plot is moving toward the discovery of a clue, does the detective stumble over traces of gunpowder in the foyer or discover a smoking gun first? The movement of the plot—direct or indirect—is determined by the timing of *where* the shots are placed. The detective's sequence of movements reveals something of his character, such as how astute or dimwitted he seems to be, by placing shots in an order that makes him move directly to the clues or meander, bumbling, toward them.

When as in where is also a way of placing emphasis by repetition. If an editor has standard coverage for a scene (a single on each character and a two-shot of both characters), she will be able to use patterns of repetition of shot setups expressively. A common pattern, for example, is to alternate between the singles of the two characters as they discuss something and then to cut to the two-shot, introducing change, at the moment at which their discussion is resolved. This sense of *when as in where* uses shot setups in a choreographic pattern to express the underlying emotional trajectory of the scene. This aspect of shaping rhythm will be discussed more thoroughly in the chapter on common scenes.[2]

Movement qualities within shots can also work with patterns of repetition for emphasis. An editor does not have to repeat three gestures of hesitation *exactly* to emphasize hesitancy; she can cut together a hesitant glance, a hesitant reach, and a hesitant step to place a big emphasis on hesitancy, or she could drop all three of those shots and go straight to the smoking gun to remove any hesitancy from the detective's timing.

All of the uses of timing—the precise frame on which cuts are made, the duration of shots, and the sense of timing as in *where* a shot is placed—intersect with one another and the other tools of rhythm: pacing and trajectory phrasing. Separating and identifying these things may have some value for understanding the processes of cutting rhythms. At the very least, all of these uses of the word "timing" can be turned into specific questions an editor can ask: Which shot where? For how long? On which frame do I cut? All are, in part at least, timing questions.

PACING

Pacing is a felt experience of movement created by the rates and amounts of movement in a single shot and by the rates and amounts of movement across a series of edited shots. Pacing as a tool for shaping rhythm defines the resulting pace of a film.

When Bordwell and Thompson describe "pace" in *Film Art,* they define it as "what musicians call tempo."[3] *The Grove Dictionary of Music and Musicians* tells us that:

> The system of musical tempo clearly has its origins in the functions of the human body and mind. It is related in particular to the speed of a normal heartbeat, between 60 and 80 beats per minute; on either side of this lie the sensations of "fast" and "slow" …[4]

Pacing is the manipulation of pace for the purpose of shaping the spectator's sensations of fast and slow. The word "pacing," like the word "timing," is used to refer to three distinct operations: the rate of cutting, the rate or concentration of movement or change in shots and sequences, and the rate of movement or events over the course of the whole film.

Rate of Cutting

Pacing refers to the rate at which cuts occur, as in how often per second or minute or hour. This is not just another way of saying "duration of shots," although the two ideas do overlap. Pacing in this sense can most easily be seen when the rate of cutting occurs in patterns; e.g., accelerating the number of cuts per minute as a chase gets closer to its climax. (In this case the durations of the shots get shorter, and the two meanings overlap.) However, pacing, as in "rate at which cuts occur," is also a factor in the rhythm of film even when it is not patterned by design. For example, cutting frequently around a conversation may make the performances seem edgier or sharper. Here we are not looking at durations of shots directly, but at the content curve of movement within the shots and either cutting it very sharply, which creates a sense of the pace being quicker, or leaving it loose, with full arcs of movement intact, which makes the pace seem slower. Thus, the pacing, in the sense of the rate at which the cuts occur, manipulates the sensation of the movement of the conversation. Further, the rate at which cuts occur defines the rate at which new visual sensations are introduced—every cut is in itself a change, so lots of cuts make a faster rate of change.

Rate of Change or Movement Within a Shot

Pacing is not just a matter of the rate at which cuts occur; it also refers to the juxtapositions of rates of movement or change within shots. If the rate of change within a shot is fast paced—for example, in one 5-second shot *the door opens—the vase falls over—the cook screams—and the burglar slips out,* and that shot is juxtaposed with another 5-second shot in which *the thief is cornered—he kicks the cop—he gets bitten by the dog and jumps over the wall*—the pacing of the sequence may be seen as very fast, even though the cuts are relatively infrequent. (Making one cut in 10 seconds is not a "fast" rate of cutting in contemporary cinema.[5]) If the editor chooses to present each of these events in its own shot, thereby making a cut every 3 seconds rather than one cut in 10 seconds, she would make the rate of change slow down—these events each shown in a single 3-second shot would take 24 seconds, not 10. The editor would have sped up the rate of cutting, but the overall effect would be of slowing the pacing.

FIGURE 3.3

The rate of change within a single shot in any Marx Brothers movie, including this one, A Night at the Opera *(Sam Wood, 1935), is extraordinary. Even in this still image it is possible to see that at least four separate transactions are taking place at one time. Breaking these down into individual shots to "cut faster" would not only slow the pace but also lose the humor created by overlapping all of these unlikely events in one continuous time and space. [Photo credit: MGM; The Kobal Collection]*

However, it would not necessarily be correct to assume that the sensation of slowing the pace arises solely from a sequence taking more time. The actual reason the pacing could feel slower may arise if the full action of each movement is being revealed by putting in a 3-second shot of each "gesture." When it is possible to see the whole of an action—its beginning, middle, and end—and not just the height of its activity, a certainty about source and direction of movement replaces the uncertainty that makes one feel as though things are moving fast.

Rate of Overall Change

Pacing also refers to movement of the overall film. A film's pacing may be the rate at which events move in the film or the rate at which movement of images or emotions occurs in the film. Each of the following three examples creates a fast pace through a different aspect of high concentration of movement overall.

1. A film with a series of moving camera shots traveling around a breathtaking array of characters, alluding to complex and fraught interpersonal relationships, has a high concentration of quick movement in visuals and emotions, which creates a sensation of fast pacing. At the same time, it has only one plot event, such as "the house guests settle in." But this will feel like a fast-paced film even though there are few events, because the rate of physical and emotional movement is high (Fig. 3.4).

2. A film with rapid dialog, relatively infrequent cuts, not much camera movement, but a rapid series of events or changes in the character's fortunes can still be considered to have rapid pacing (Fig. 3.5).

3. A film with lots of cuts, timed to maximize the energy of the movement trajectory and the collision of the movements between shots, but with basically no movement of events or no emotional change, as in a music video, may also be considered fast paced (Fig 3.6).

In each of these three films the high rate of overall movement or change and the consequent sense of fast pace are achieved through manipulation of a different aspect of pacing. The same three aspects of pacing could each be employed in the opposite manner to make a film's overall pace slower.

In general, all three of these uses of the word "pacing" interact with one another to determine a film's pace. Pacing is very important, especially for the creation of sensations of time, but rhythm also has other methods with which to shape time, energy, and movement.

FIGURE 3.4

Robert Altman's 2001 film Gosford Park *feels fast paced because characters, camera, and emotions all move quickly, but the plot doesn't move quickly, and it is not cut especially fast. The furious rainfall, the pressing forward against the rain of the figures under the umbrella, and the alert focus of the two attendants on either side of the car all make this frame feel fast paced, but all that is happening is people getting into the car. [Photo credit: USA Films; The Kobal Collection]*

FIGURE 3.5

Cary Grant and Rosalind Russell in His Gal Friday *(Howard Hawks, 1940). With its rapid-fire dialog and quickly changing plot events,* His Gal Friday *is well known as a fast-paced film, even though there are almost no camera moves and, by today's standards, cuts are infrequent. [Photo credit: Columbia; The Kobal Collection]*

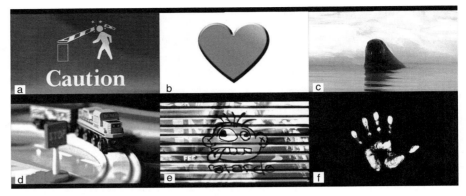

FIGURE 3.6
Music videos do not need to have plot changes or character changes to feel fast paced; instead, they can have lots of cuts and/or lots of camera moves. In "Come Together" played by The Tinku Band (Luke Eve/More Sauce Productions, 2007), these six stills, and ten others, all flash by in the first second of the music video at a rate of one or two frames each. The editor, Katie Flaxman, weaves together diverse ideas (expressed in simple graphics) into a sequence of lateral associations with the song's lyrics that is almost subliminal on first viewing because of its extremely fast pace.

TRAJECTORY PHRASING

"Trajectory phrasing" is a term I have devised to cover an area of editing rhythms that is not precisely addressed by the terms "timing" and "pacing." Trajectory phrasing describes the manipulation of *energy* in the creation of rhythm. The word "trajectory" means "the path described by a body moving under the action of given forces."[6] So "trajectory" describes a combination of the direction of a movement and the energy that propels it. My term "trajectory phrasing" describes joining together the movement trajectories found in different shots with particular attention to the shaping of the flow of energy between them. The three operations that trajectory phrasing describes are making smooth links or abrupt collisions of energy and direction, choosing from among different energetic variations done by performers in different takes, and creating emphasis points, or accents, by manipulation of the trajectory of movement. These three operations will be broken down in greater detail in a moment. But first, before looking at the tools for shaping the flow of energy, the word "energy" itself requires some definition.

My use of the word "energy" draws, in part, on movement analysts Rudolf Laban and Irmgard Bartenieff's ideas about Effort. Effort, as described in their in-depth study of movement, roughly translates as the *attitude and intention* behind movement that informs the way it is done.[7]

The kind of Effort with which a person moves is what he or she means or intends with his or her movement. A punch means aggression, violence, forceful intentions, *if* its Effort is aggressive, violent, and forceful. A punch can be playful; in other words, it may originate from a playful state of mind, and the Effort that propels it will be entirely different. It may move along the same spatial pathway as an aggressive punch, be a similar speed and have the same shape, but its Effort, or energy, will tell us that it means something different. It can even be abstracted completely by changing its energy. A closed fist moving limply is not seen as a punch. It is an abstract movement, unless the narrative context explains the energy in some way. For example, a dying man may move his closed fist in a straight line quickly but limply to give his grandson a magic bean that he has hidden in his hand. We wouldn't see that as a punch. The energy has changed it completely, and the narrative context has explained the change.

Energy is inseparable from movement and made visible through it.[8] However, although the energy cannot be separated, as in extracted, from the movement, energy can be *described* separately (as above) from movement's temporal and spatial properties. The three examples of punches—the aggressive, the playful, and the limp movement in the shape of a punch—each describe a different trajectory and stress. Although the spatial and temporal organization may be similar in all three, they each use a different energy, and therefore each has a different meaning.

Dance theorist Sandra Horton Fraleigh describes the inseparability of movement from its energy both in the performance of the movement and in the perception of it.

> The dancer's movements are workings of her mind, will, intuitions and imagination. ... The audience perceives her dance through her movement as it conveys her intentions. In short, they see what she does and see the thought in it—not behind it or before it. If she moves softly they see softness, if she moves sharply, that is what they see.[9]

This quote concerns the movement of a dancer, but the same method of perceiving movement intentions can also be applied to naturalistic movement of actors in a drama or characters in a documentary. For an editor, the implications of this are that she cannot just shape movement in time. She must also phrase its energy to make the rhythms of the film congruent with the intentions of the movement of the film. For a live dancer, actor, director, or choreographer, trajectory phrasing is simply shaping flows of movement energy and direction

---

PRACTICAL EXERCISE

Time, Space, and Energy: Part 2

Using the same scenario set up in Part 1 of this exercise in the previous chapter, a third person now has a chance to direct the scene. The only direction he is allowed to give is of energy, but he has the whole of the expressive range of energy, or "effort," as described above, to work with. The actions of the performers have to be the same—sit and read, walk in, look up, etc., but the director may now apply adverbs, words that describe actions, to the movements—as in "shake your head lightly, indirectly, with the intention of flirting" or "shake your head heavily, slowly, with the intention of resisting." Once again the emotion and the meaning of the scene will change and illustrate the way an editor shapes the meaning of an exchange through the selection and juxtaposition of various takes, performances, or shots with different energy qualities.

At this point in the exercise everyone will notice that time, space, and energy are really difficult to separate. In fact, they work cumulatively. You can manipulate time fairly discretely, but any manipulation of space will necessarily also change time because it will take longer to go from point A to point B if you have set point B farther away. Or the character will have to travel more quickly. Either way, longer (duration) or more quickly (speed), time is being manipulated, too. Energy cannot be expressed separately from time and space, and changing the instruction to the performers regarding their use of energy will necessarily change their use of time and space. Looking away dejectedly might involve just a small shift of the eyeballs, whereas looking away furiously might be a fast twist of the whole spine.

The editor receives material, shots, that already contain some fixed aspects of time, space, and energy. Her job is to arrange and juxtapose these aspects, using timing, pacing, and trajectory phrasing, into sequences of affective rhythm.

during performance. For the editor, trajectory phrasing in film editing is the shaping of flows of movement energy and direction by choices of takes and cuts.

As with timing and pacing, there are a number of operations that constitute trajectory phrasing: linking or colliding trajectories, selecting energies, and stress.

Linking or Colliding Trajectories

Trajectory phrasing has a spectrum of possibilities from matching trajectories to colliding trajectories. The question, Should the connections be smooth or abrupt? is one consideration in the shaping of trajectory phrasing. Or, to paraphrase the argument that went on between the Soviet montage theorists Eisenstein and Pudovkin, should the edits create "linkages" or "shocks"?

Practically speaking, the smoothness or abruptness of a movement trajectory shaped by cutting depends on the relationships created by juxtaposing visible aspects of movement such as screen direction. For example, a smooth cut is one in which movement from right to left in one shot is matched with movement from right to left in the next shot. A cut in which movement from right to left is "collided" with movement from left to right, or simply *unmatched* in spatial organization and energy, is a little shock. Eisenstein includes graphic directions, scales, volumes, masses, depths, close and long shots, darkness and lightness in his list of visual elements that can be collided (or, as Pudovkin might perhaps prefer, smoothly linked).

Selecting Energy Trajectories

The phrasing of the movement energy is also a matter of selecting shots for the qualities of energy they contain and thus choreographing a sequence of energy flows.

In a contemporary film that has Hollywood-style coverage, a cut may be a "match cut," a "match on action," or a collided cut, but it is not

FIGURE 3.7

Joel Grey in Cabaret *(Bob Fosse, 1972). In the film* Cabaret, *Editor David Bretherton often makes very hard cuts between scenes, slamming together the energy in images to make surprising connections between ideas and create a physical jolt or shock for the audience that underlines the film's themes and makes them palpable experiences of the motion and emotion of life in Berlin in the 1930s. [Photo credit: ABC/Allied Artists; The Kobal Collection]*

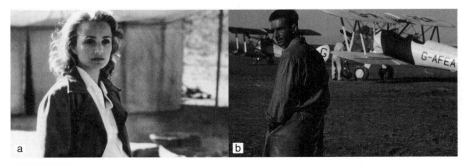

FIGURE 3.8

Kristen Scott Thomas and Ralph Fiennes in The English Patient *(Anthony Minghella, 1996). Editor Walter Murch favors smooth linkages of movement energies in* The English Patient, *which help him to underline the lyrical aspects of the film and the connectedness of the central characters to each other on a nonverbal level. [Photo credit: Tiger Moth/Miramax; The Kobal Collection; Phil Bray] just* a choice between linkage and collision; it also contains choices from among an array of *energy quality* possibilities.

For example, here is a scenario in which the editor is choosing to match cut: a man and his wife sitting on the sofa have a small disagreement over a book they are reading together. She gets up and moves to the kitchen, he follows. We will call the "getting up and moving to the kitchen" the movement trajectory of each character, and the two of them getting up and moving to the kitchen will be the movement trajectory of the scene. Imagine that in this particular example the coverage includes a shot of the woman moving with a degree of hesitancy and one of her moving with a greater degree of confidence. Same movement, different energy or attitude behind it. The coverage also includes shots of the man getting up with difficulty and other shots of him springing off the sofa. Any of these shots can be cut together to match (link smoothly) but the rhythm of the scene is shaped by the choice of juxtapositions of movement energy. Is her move to the kitchen hesitant, whereas he springs off the sofa to follow her? Or is her move confident, whereas he moves with difficulty? Or perhaps her hesitation and his difficulty will be cut together to create the trajectory that best expresses the movement of emotions in the film.

These same principles apply in cutting of, for example, documentaries, in which there is no Hollywood-style coverage. Cutting the movement energy of events, information, colors, textures, ideas, emotions, and so on is a process of shaping the flow of energy found in the various shots into the single flow of movement and energy over time known as "rhythm".

Stress

"Stress" is emphasis created in rhythm by the use of the energy in a shot as an accent. Choosing where to place the stresses or the accents by use of energy is part of trajectory phrasing. It is the punctuation of the cine-phrase. As it says in *The New Princeton Encyclopedia of Poetry*

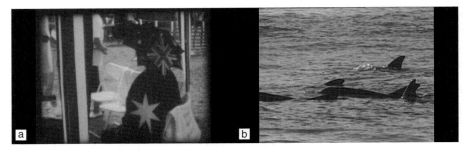

FIGURE 3.9

In this cut from the documentary Island Home Country *(Jeni Thornley, 2008), the raucous movement, colors, and framing of an Australia Day celebration picnic (a) collide with the flow and grace of the dolphins in the sea (b). Cutting these two shots together creates an idea through visual collision; in this case, the idea that colonization and nation building conflict with nature and First Nation peoples.*

and Poetics, "Accent in the sense of emphasis is the more general term, 'stress' is the more precise … stress can denote intensity as opposed to pitch or length."[10] The definition of rhythm in music in *The New Grove Dictionary of Music and Musicians* doesn't cover everything about rhythm in film editing, but it does explain the importance of stress when it says, "duration and stress—in other words constructions in time and gradations in strength—are the central determinants of rhythm, its constituent factors."[11]

Stress refers to the rise and fall over time of intensity of energy. Accents of stress arise from patterning of energy. In a choreographically shaped phrase of edited material, a 2-second shot may either be a 2-second close-up of a scream or a 2-second wide shot of a sigh. The shots are of equal duration, the rates of movement or change within them are comparable, but the stress (effort) they contain and the stress (emphasis) they create are different. Both the shot size and the energy being expended within the shot contribute to the energy accent it makes.

Trajectory phrasing is something spectators feel in a very immediate way. We feel the movement flows that are created across shots without conscious processing of smoothness or abruptness, hesitancy or confidence, stress accents or patterns of accent, because the recognition of

USEFUL QUESTIONS

In a situation in which the flow of movement energy doesn't feel right for an editor, she may be able to ask herself some questions about the trajectory phrasing she is creating. Examples of these questions may include: What are the flows of movement energy that are inherent in the shots available to work with? Where along the spectrum of matching versus colliding should these energies cut together? What is the "story" in terms of energy flow? (For example, after the little dispute on the sofa, is the wife confident and the husband struggling, vice versa, or some other configuration?) What point should be accented or stressed? Should it create stress by repetition, duration, or selection of energy? The answers to all of these questions will determine the trajectory phrasing that the editor designs.

flow of movement energies is done by the spectator intuitively, using his mirror neurons and kinesthetic empathy (as described in Chapter 1). The spectator's immediate feeling of a trajectory phrase is the result of many hours of intuitive work by the editor in which she cuts the flow of movement energy into one trajectory or another until her own mirror neurons and kinesthetic empathy light up with the feeling of the "rightness" of the flow.

SUMMARY

Timing, pacing, and trajectory phrasing are the tools that an editor employs when cutting rhythms. Each of these three is actually a term covering at least three editing operations to do with choices made in shaping movement and energy over time. The creation of rhythm in film editing will generally rely on all of the tools or operations described herein being employed simultaneously or in close alternation because, as Laban and Bartenieff suggest,

> ... rhythm is not just a duration of time, accented by stresses. It is also the result of the interaction of Effort combinations with variations in spatial patterns.[12]

Having looked at the sources of knowledge about rhythm, some of the choreographic processes at work in creating it, and the tools an editor has for shaping it, I will turn now to the purposes of rhythm in film.

ENDNOTES

1. Durr, W., Gerstenberg, W., and Harvey, J., "Rhythm," in *The New Grove Dictionary of Music and Musicians,* p. 805. The quote is from Jaeger, W., "Paideia," p. 174f.

2. Interested readers will also find expansive discussion of the idea of repetition as an expressive motif in *Film Editing: the Art of the Expressive* by Valerie Orpen.

3. Bordwell, D., and Thompson, K., *Film Art: an Introduction,* p. 197.

4. Durr, W., Gerstenberg, W., and Harvey, J., "Rhythm," in *The New Grove Dictionary of Music and Musicians,* p. 806.

5. In his book *Film Style and Technology: History and Analysis,* Barry Salt includes a study of average shot lengths in narrative drama films over time. David Bordwell picks up on his findings and develops them in an article published in *Film Quarterly* in 2002. Bordwell says, "In 1999 and 2000 the ASL (average shot length) of a typical film in any genre was likely to run three to six seconds." Bordwell, D., "Intensified continuity: visual style in contemporary American film—critical essay," in *Film Quarterly,* p. 16.

6. Stein, J., and Urdang, L., editors, *The Random House Dictionary of the English Language,* p. 1503.

7. For a thorough explication and contextualization of Effort, see Bartenieff, I., with Lewis, D., *Body Movement: Coping with the Environment.*

8. "Physicists recognise the existence of a universal interaction of forces such that the separation of entities into discrete and autonomous units is called into question, and explorations of the microscopic constituents of matter suggest (*sic*) that there are no irreducible bodies in the world, simply 'modifications, perturbations, changes in tension or energy and nothing else' (1959, 337; 1911, 266), no things but only actions (1959, 705, 1913, 248) or movements (1959, 707; 1913, 249–50)." Bogue, R., *Deleuze on Cinema,* p. 16.

9. Fraleigh, S. H., *Dance and the Lived Body: A Descriptive Aesthetics,* p. 169.

10. Preminger, A., and Brogan, T. V. F., editors, *The New Princeton Encyclopedia of Poetry and Poetics,* p. 1068.

11. Durr, W., Gerstenberg, W., and Harvey, J., "Rhythm," in The New Grove Dictionary of Music and Musicians, p. 806.

12. Bartenieff, I., with Lewis, D., *Body Movement: Coping with the Environment,* p. 75.

CHAPTER 4

Tension, Release, and Synchronization

All of the tools, the choreographic processes, and the editor's sources of intuitive knowledge about editing a film's rhythm are used by editors in service of fulfilling rhythm's purposes in film. The question in this chapter is: What *are* the functions of rhythm in film? The following discussion suggests that the functions of rhythm are to create cycles of tension and release and to synchronize the spectator's physical, emotional, and cognitive fluctuations with the rhythms of the film.

TENSION AND RELEASE

One function of rhythm in film is to shape, modulate, stimulate, and elevate the movement between tension and release. This movement is particularly crucial to drama, as John Sayles, American independent film director, reminds us:

> ... movies depend on tension and release for their impact. ... The audience is made to expect something, the event draws nearer and tension builds, then the thing happens and the tension is released.[1]

The shaping of tension and release is also a function of rhythm in documentaries, in which tension may be created about, for example, the outcomes of events or the answers to questions, and in films other than dramas and documentaries, which might rely on a more directly visual, aural, or kinesthetic mode of tension and release.

FIGURE 4.1

The physical movement in this image from John Sayles's film Matewan *(1987) poses a question that creates tension, which is: Will the character catch up with the train? James Earl Jones's performance helps the story to create stakes—we empathize with the movement of his face and body and hope he will get on board, and fear he won't, and worry about what is at stake if he doesn't. The shaping of the rhythm of this sequence in editing would involve shaping the duration for which we are held in suspense about those questions and the timing, pacing, and energy of the way the answers unfold. [Photo credit: Red Dog/Cinecom; The Kobal Collection]*

Rhythm shapes cycles of tension and release by shaping time, energy, and movement through the film in patterns designed to provoke and modulate particular qualities of empathetic response. I emphasize *empathetic* here, because rhythm is a felt phenomenon; the spectators' experience of rhythm, just like the editor's, is an embodied, physiological, temporal, and energetic *participation* in the movement of images, emotions, and events in the film. Empathy is feeling *with* (rather than feeling *for*). So whereas it is the job of narrative, information, or images

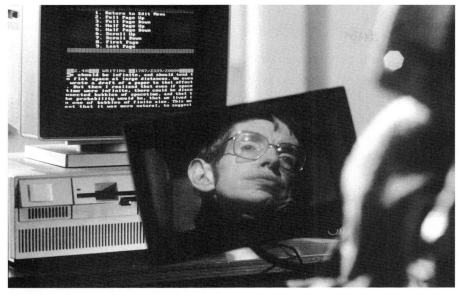

FIGURE 4.2
In the documentary A Brief History of Time *(Errol Morris, 1993), editor Ted Bafaloukos, who has cut all of Morris's highly original and engaging documentaries, shapes tension around the big questions: Where did the universe come from? Will time ever come to an end? And the more personal questions of scientist Stephen Hawking's life, health, ambitions, and thoughts. [Photo credit: Triton; The Kobal Collection]*

to cue and provoke thoughts and emotions, it is the job of rhythm to modulate the rate and quality of the spectators' participation in or feeling *with* the movement of these elements in the film. Rhythm does this by modulating the cycles of intensity and relaxation of the movement of images, emotions, and events in the film. The spectators perceive this intensity and relaxation of time, energy, and movement *directly* as forms of tension and release in their own bodies.

To elaborate on the notion that rhythm is perceived directly, I will briefly recap the points made about how rhythm works with the physical movement visible and audible in films, and the physical processes by which our bodies perceive and understand movement. Chapters 1, 2, and 3 of this book are about the *editor's* perceptions of rhythm, her processes and tools. But they also cumulatively point to the functions of rhythm in creating cycles of tension and release and synchronizing the *spectator's* rhythms to the film's pulse and its fluctuations.

Chapter 1 discussed mirror neurons through which, neurologically speaking, one participates in the intentional movement one sees. That chapter also discussed the notion of kinesthetic empathy, which is the felt recognition of movement that is seen or heard by a body that has comparable experiences of the physics of motion. These two significant modes of perceiving movement—mirror neurons and kinesthetic empathy—are both physiological. Their presence in our physiology means that the movement we *perceive* activates our knowledge of that movement's significance. Furthermore, this activation is an immediate, empathetic experience—we experience physiological tension and release virtually simultaneously with perception of movement patterns of intensity and relaxation.

Chapter 2 determined that the art of shaping rhythm is a choreographic art in that it involves shaping physical movement for affect. The core unit of this choreographic art is the pulse. A pulse is, in itself, a minute fluctuation of tension and release. The pulse is the energetic emphasis (tension) placed on one syllable or part of movement in a "measure" of two or three syllables or parts of movement. The de-emphasized part of movement in the measure is the release of the tension. Thus, whereas Chapter 1 established that movement in film has a physiological effect on spectators, Chapter 2 determined that editors shape movement pulses and phrases choreographically to modulate their affect. Cumulatively, the implication of these two chapters is that pulses and phrases of movement in film are choreographically manipulated into rhythms by editors.

Chapter 3 discussed the tools an editor has for shaping rhythms, which are also attributes of rhythm itself. These tools—timing, pacing, and trajectory phrasing—are used by editors to determine the qualities, rates, and intensities of movement in a film's rhythm. Connecting Chapter 3 back to Chapter 1, we can say that these qualities, rates, and intensities of movement are experienced by the spectator as the rise and fall of their own physical responses to the film. When time, energy, and movement are choreographically shaped by timing, pacing, and trajectory phrasing, they create cycles of somatic tension and release.

Rhythm's physical effect on the spectator is also often experienced as emotional affect. Because rhythm is direct address to the body, it is also, to some extent anyway, direct address to emotion, because "feelings," in the sense of emotions, are physical, too. Torben Kragh Grodal talks about this in his book *Moving Pictures: A New Theory of Film Genres, Feelings and Cognition,* and reminds us that story gives us cues about how to feel, but the strength of feeling relies on how the images, sounds, and movement are shaped to impact on us physically. He says an important part of the experience of emotions

> … relates to involuntary body reactions. … These involuntary reactions are controlled by the autonomic nervous and endocrine systems, which regulate the viscera, the heart, stomach, lungs, liver and skin, and which play a major role in the constitution of emotions. The connection between "viscera states" and emotions has been known for centuries, because everybody experiences strong changes in the viscera when excited: tears, salivation, change of respiration, butterflies in the stomach, a pounding heart, blushing, sweating.[2]

In other words, emotions are, at least in part, physical experiences of movement in the body through rises and falls of intensity of activity. Grodal continues, "When a viewer chooses to watch a film, he thereby chooses to be cued into having constant *fluctuations* [my emphasis] of heartbeat, perspiration, adrenalin-secretion and so on."[3]

The editor is trying to create an appropriately felt rhythm of these fluctuations in the audience. The questions are: How long to keep the heart racing at one rate? When, how, and with what to slow it down? It is not just a matter of finding the right amount of time to build tension or hold off release of story information, it's a carving of the qualities of that time, also, through timing, pacing, and trajectory phrasing. A film's significance is not just "this happened and then that happened" (although that is a rhythm, too—this, then that). A film's impact is in the *way* that this, then that, happened, including how fast or slow or bumpily or smoothly or forcefully or limply. As Professor

PRACTICAL EXERCISE

Murderer in the Dark

Murderer in the Dark, sometimes called Murderer's Wink, is a game for experiencing tension and release. Gather together six or eight people to play; a classroom of between twelve and twenty is also an excellent amount. Everyone sits in a circle and closes their eyes, then the game moderator walks all the way around the circle and, while walking, taps one person on the shoulder. That person is the murderer, and no one except the moderator and the murderer knows who he is. The murderer's objective is to "kill" everyone off without being discovered; his weapon is a wink. If the murderer catches the eye of another player and winks, that player has to count slowly to 5 while looking around the room and then "die"; the more theatrically, the better. To discover the murderer you have to see him wink at someone, but not at you.

The game is great fun to play, but the interesting part is the discussion afterward, which concerns time, the release of information, and tension. How much information do you have at the beginning of the game? You know there is a murderer but you don't know who—you are asking yourself questions: Who is the murderer? Will I be killed? When will someone be killed? With each death there is a shift both of tension and of information—you experience, in rapid succession, shock or surprise depending on how theatrically the death has been performed, then relief that it is not you, then escalating tension as the number of possible victims diminishes. So you could be next, and the tension, fleetingly released, begins to build again.

In working with rhythm, the editor is working with exactly these devices: time, energy, and the release of information to create tension. How long can a question go unanswered before interest is lost? If the murderer in your game is not

bold and no one gets killed, the interest diminishes very quickly, because the tension of the questions "who" and "when" is answered by "no one" and "never"!

The release of information is not just a matter of timing, but also of energy—if a victim just shrugs and says, "I'm dead," there is very little impact. If he suddenly stands, shrieks, and falls writhing to the floor, there is, perhaps, overkill. Modulating the intensity or energy of a performance to release and rekindle tension is part of the editor's job, too.

The tension is a combination of these three things—timing, energy, and release of information. Tension is in the unanswered question; rhythm is the time, energy, and movement that modulate its build and release.

FIGURE 4.3

A classic wink: Bob Hope and Dorothy Lamour in Caught in the Draft *(David Butler, 1941). [Photo credit: Paramount; The Kobal Collection]*

van Leeuwen says, "rhythm plays a crucial role ... in the *way* the story is told, in the game of revealing and withholding story information from the viewers to maximize both their active involvement in anticipating the events and their passive abandon to the story's events."[4]

So, whereas characters, images, or stories trigger specific emotions, expectations, and ideas, the rhythms of these modulate the rise and fall of the tension—the "resonance of bodily reactions"[5]—with which we follow them.

By modulating tension and release, rhythm acts on the spectators as a generative aspect of their acceptance and comprehension of a film. Rhythm refines the rides you take with a film—the rise and fall, the speed of the curves, the sense of balance or danger in the stability or suddenness of movement in the world of the film. It doesn't matter if the film is a thriller or a romance, narrative or abstract; the editor works with the "life of the object visibly recorded in the frame"[6] to determine the timing, pacing, and trajectory phrasing of its movement, and spectators' bodies respond to this rhythm.

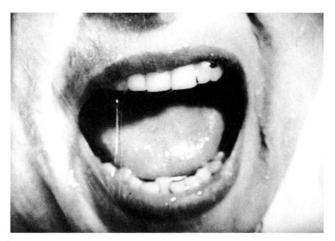

FIGURE 4.4

One of the reasons that the murder in the shower of Janet Leigh's character in Psycho *(1960) is so shocking is that it is so unexpected. Director Alfred Hitchcock, master of subverting our expectations, does not develop tension in the conventional ways, and so when the shower scene comes, our heart rates and other visceral responses jump very rapidly from a state of calm to a state of extreme activity. [Photo credit: Paramount; The Kobal Collection; Bud Fraker]*

SYNCHRONIZATION

Riding the rise and fall of tension and release when watching a movie, the spectator's body rhythms and the rhythms of the film to some extent sync up into a physiological phenomenon of *feeling with*. The "ride," rhythmically speaking, is the movement of the film composed in such a way as to influence the spectator's pulse, breath, attention, and other bodily rhythms.

As discussed earlier, rhythm is part of our biology, and to survive we oscillate with the rhythms of our environment, our planet, and our solar system. Similarly, to survive socially, we coordinate our rhythms with those of other humans. For example, we meet the energy and pace of others in conversation, and we synchronize with them to have an effective transaction. If, at a gathering, everyone is talking in hushed tones and with terse gestures, we match these to understand and connect with the people. If those in the gathering are laughing uproariously and flinging their words and gestures freely, speaking in hushed tones and with terse gestures won't coordinate and will either cause those in the gathering to change and converse to a new rhythm or cause you to be left out. "As we act together we synchronize. The rhythms of our actions become as finely attuned to each other as the parts of different instruments in a musical performance."[7]

The implications of this social synchronization, for film spectatorship, is that the film becomes a rhythmical partner in a social exchange to which the spectator synchronizes. This physiological syncing function of rhythm in film is a significant source of affect. As philosopher Gilles Deleuze says in *Cinema 2: The Time Image*, "It is through the body ... that cinema forms its alliance with the spirit, with thought."[8]

Deleuze goes on to suggest that cinema forms this alliance by making the body pass through a sort of "ceremony."[9] This ceremony to which

Deleuze refers is, I believe, a ceremony of synchronization. The film's rhythm synchronizes the body, influencing the spectator's physical and cognitive fluctuations to follow its own. My own description of this ceremony is of movies as a form of meditation for the unquiet mind.

SYNCHRONIZING WITH THE DIRECTOR

Sometimes tensions arise between directors and editors who "feel" things differently, and the editor has some tricky judgment calls to make in these situations. If a director feels the rise and fall of tension and release or the flow of movement in a different way from the editor, it could be because he is not seeing what is really there, but what he hoped would be there, or what he intended to have captured but didn't. In these cases, it is up to the editor to bring the director around to a new way of seeing the material. This may mean working without the director present for a while and shaping something that has its own integrity. Then, when the director sees it, there is an opportunity for him to say, "That's not how I intended it, but it really works."

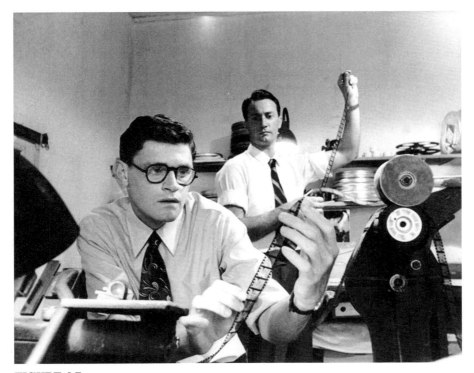

FIGURE 4.5
Working collaboratively in the edit suite under pressure, as seen in Phillip Noyce's classic Australian drama Newsfront *(1978). [Photo credit: Palm Beach Pictures; The Kobal Collection]*

On the other hand, sometimes directors and editors feel things differently because the director is deeply tuned to the material and the performances, and the editor doesn't yet see its potential to go in a particular direction. In these cases, it is really important to try to synchronize *through* the director. Use his sense of how things flow rather than your own—see with his eyes, feel with his heart rate, tune your kinesthetic empathy to his feeling for the rise and fall of tension in a scene or across the whole film.

In either case, it's essential not to make too big a deal of things too early. Much will change over the course of an edit and if there is a showdown over who is right about a given moment, then that moment will always be a sore point, no matter who wins. Furthermore, both the editor and the director actually lose in these showdowns because their experience of the contentious moment shifts from being a direct experience of the material to an indirect one: instead of seeing the moment, they remember the argument and impasse it caused and see it as a problem. Diplomacy skills are emphasized in the teaching of editing, and this is one example of where those skills can be used to good effect. If no standoff is created by the editor, then, later, when things have cooled down, it will always be possible to come back and have another go at the moment in question.

A cautionary note for both editors and directors: Editors hate it when directors snap their fingers or hit the table to indicate where they want a cut because these gestures, as well as expressing a kind of dictatorship or distrust of the editor's intuition, can actually jump between the editor and her own feeling for the material. On the other hand, these directorial gestures are very immediate physical responses and could save lots of time and discussion about how the material should be shaped. If the editor can just step back and not take them personally, the director's gestures can be a great guide to how he feels the material. My advice to directors is: Try not to snap your fingers, as that seems imperious, but do make the gestures that will clue the editor in to how you feel the material; that way, at least she'll know what she's working with.

Meditation is a practice that, through concentration, frequently on some rhythmically repetitive phrase or chant or breathing pattern, stills the fluctuations of the mind. The various objectives of this practice, from inner peace to complete enlightenment, are not what make it comparable with movies. What is comparable is the syncing or bonding that occurs through rhythmic connectivity in meditation. This aspect of meditation is imitated by the functioning of rhythm in film.

By shifting the spectator's physiological rhythms into sync with its own rhythms, film organizes the body's fluctuations into a single, focused, undistracted attention. The objects of meditation can only be realized when "the fluctuations of the mind cease."[10] The objects of rhythm in film are realized when the fluctuations of mind are subsumed into the fluctuations of tension and release in the film. Much of this work is done by story, structure, and performance, but some of it is done by shaping movement and energy over time to create the cycles of tension and release to which the spectator's mind and body synchronize.

CASE STUDY IN TENSION, RELEASE, AND SYNCHRONIZATION: *BROADCAST NEWS*

There are hundreds of sequences that could be chosen to illustrate the movement of tension and release in films. I have chosen this sequence from *Broadcast News* (James L. Brooks, 1987), not just because it works so well, but because it is a scene about the rhythm of the editing process. In it, there is a brief moment in which the synchronization that happens between the director and the uncut material is dramatized, revealing and illustrating the activation of mirror neurons and kinesthetic empathy (as discussed in Chapter 1). The other especially useful aspect of this sequence for talking about shaping movement into cycles of tension and release is its overtly physical expressions of emotion and events. The director, James L. Brooks, takes delight in shaping the physical expressions of rhythm to draw us, physically and psychologically, into the tensions of the situation.

Broadcast News is about the shift in the culture of television news coverage from serious journalism to entertainment. It is told through the stories of three central characters: Jane Craig (Holly Hunter), a producer who believes passionately in journalistic integrity; Tom Grunick (William Hurt), a handsome, airheaded news anchor who performs well but doesn't really understand what he's saying; and Aaron Altman (Albert Brooks), an intellectual reporter who is too earnest and can't compete with the smooth, self-confident Tom, even though he's a better reporter.

At the beginning of an early sequence in the film, there is a tight cut to Jane Craig, the producer, in the edit suite, working to a deadline, commanding her online editor, Bobby (Christian Clemenson), to run the

FIGURE 4.6
Richard Marks, editor of Broadcast News *(James L. Brooks, 1987), cuts to this scene in the middle of Jane Craig's (Holly Hunter) phone conversation and edit. She is multitasking, talking rapidly into the phone, watching the rushes, and barking orders at the online editor (Christenson Clemenson) all at once, which immediately establishes the base pulse and energy of the scene—this is as calm as things are going to get.*

story they are editing one more time (Fig. 4.6). He protests mildly and she overruns him with overlapping dialog and a much more forceful tone. Immediately, with the timing of these first cuts and the energy of the exchange, a tension is created. Most particularly it is Holly Hunter's portrayal of Jane's physical tension that is driving the scene. Her tone, speed, and attack express a furious will to keep control, overlaid on an edge of panic. The editor of *Broadcast News*, the extraordinary Richard Marks, cuts between Jane and Bobby in such a way as to highlight, extend, and physically impress this tension upon us as we experience the flow of the story. Marks cuts back to Jane as she grabs her water bottle and drinks abruptly, and to Bobby as he stabs the keys of his console with in rapid-fire staccato. Even though they are both just doing their jobs and nothing too dramatic is happening, we experience these punctuations and emphasis points as a rhythmic volley that lifts the energy and attention.

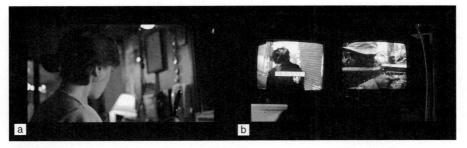

FIGURE 4.7

In (a) Holly Hunter is speaking the same line as the character in the news story she is cutting (b; character on the left). She imitates his cadence and says the words with him, essentially singing along with him to immerse herself fully in his intent and the rhythm that expresses it. She has raised her pen in a gesture like a conductor's and waves it sharply at Bobby, the online editor, to indicate where she wants him to cut in to the shot.

At this point in the scene, Holly Hunter's character, Jane, actually enacts the synchronization that takes place between the material and the people working on it in the editing suite. As the voice in the videotape she is editing says a line, Jane says the line, too, aloud, mimicking the videotaped character's intonation and intent (Fig. 4.7a). Holly Hunter perfectly plays out the way that Jane, as the person cutting the film, would mirror the video image, embodying it physically, as a quick and direct way of giving herself the physical feeling of the uncut material. This physical imitation of the material is like blinking or breathing with it, or as will be discussed later, "singing" with it. As the timing, pacing, and energy of the material inhabit the body of the person cutting the film, she has a direct physical feeling of where to cut. She knows what the phrasing should be because she can feel it, in her body. This moment gives a succinct insight into the action that directors and editors do over and over again in shaping the rhythm of a film; whether they are shaping it at their leisure or under the bone-crushing pressure of a broadcast news production, they physically imbibe the rhythms they see and hear, and shape them to feel right in response to the feelings they have for them in their own bodies.

As the scene in *Broadcast News* progresses, more characters enter the tiny cutting suite, each bringing with him or her a contributing rhythm. First is Tom Grunick, who, as played by William Hurt, is a placid, accommodating presence. His rhythmic function is as a "rest." Shots of him, bemused and observing quietly, are dropped in between shots of other characters to give us breath, a contrast, and a bit of distance from the escalating tension. The entrance of Blair Litton, played by the inimitable Joan Cusak, brings with it the question at the heart of the tension of the sequence. Everything that happens for the rest of this sequence, both rhythmically and narratively, refers back to this question. Blair says, or rather insists, urgently, "We don't have enough time!" (Fig. 4.8), thus planting the most classic, oft-used, and reliable tension creator in motion pictures: the time pressure or the question: Will they make it in time? It is important to note that time pressure is not just a narrative device; it is, of course, a rhythmic device, because

FIGURE 4.8

Holly Hunter and Joan Cusak play their characters' relationships and intentions, the subtext of the scene, physically. Holly Hunter is shutting her eyes to try to shut out Joan Cusak's manic intrusion, with the realities of time, on her vision for the piece, while Cusak thrusts her energy and anxiety forward at Hunter with every muscle and intonation.

time is a key element of rhythm. The time pressure almost acts as another character or voice in the rhythmic composition being constructed here, because each character's rhythmic propensity is played out against it. Jane's tight, terse gestures get tighter and terser, for example. And when Bobby makes a little mistake, it triggers a major movement into another gear.

By the time this little mistake occurs, much has happened: new narration has been recorded, new relationship tensions have been revealed, we've cut away and come back to the edit suite, and we're down to 2 minutes before the story is due to air. Bobby fumbles (offscreen), says "whoops", and everyone shifts (Figs. 4.9a and 4.9b). The actors move into position like a string quartet or a corps du ballet, and the director, James L. Brooks, begins to have some fun with the tensions and rhythms he has set up. Holly Hunter's character, Jane, the producer, takes the lead—her voice is the strongest and she has the most to lose here. She starts chanting, "Bobby, Bobby, Bobby, Bobby," at a rate and consistency designed to move our heart rates up a couple of notches. Her friend Aaron, the intellectual reporter who has come in to support her, plays the viola to her first violin. He punctuates her chant with low moans and a steady rocking. Jane's adversary in this scene, the hysterical timekeeper played by Joan Cusak, takes up the counter-melody with a steady stream of high-pitched squeals or grunts as though she is under torture of some kind, and William Hurt's character Tom, the cello in this quartet, grinds his teeth steadily, his eyebrows working contrapuntally to the hysteria around him. This is a staged bit of physically and aurally expressed rhythmic tension, and it gets me every time. I know it is coming, and yet when the rhythm begins, I still sync up to it. The rhythm acts on my body, and my conscious knowledge of its purpose, direction, and outcome is irrelevant to its physiological effect on me as a rhythm.

The moment ends abruptly with three shots: (cut) Bobby pops the tape out of the machine, (cut) hands it to Blair, and (cut) Tom says "GO!"

FIGURE 4.9

(a) When Bobby says "whoops," all of the characters assembled in the edit suite in Broadcast News *reveal their panic about the time pressure they are under. They move into position (b) and start a rhythmic chant that has the function of probably driving poor Bobby, the online editor, crazy, and of raising the spectators' heart rates and blood pressure as we get caught up in the rhythm the characters create.*

But the release is minimal—the tension of the little rhythm ballet described above is capped off with the punctuating three cuts and the word "GO," but the tension of the scene's big question—Will they make it in time?—is not resolved; in fact it, is rekindled with the force of Tom's "GO!" And so ensues a beautifully cut madcap physical comedy sequence as Joan Cusak's character, Blair, all flying hair, flopping limbs, and flinging exclamations, dashes from the cutting room to

FIGURE 4.10

Three shots in less than 2½ seconds conclude this part of the Broadcast News *sequence. In (a) Bobby pulls the desperately needed tape from the machine; he passes it to Blair in (b), nearly knocking Tom out with it; and in (c) William Hurt, as Tom, uses his energy to throw the tape and Blair into a headlong hurtling trajectory toward the newsroom with one word: "GO!"*

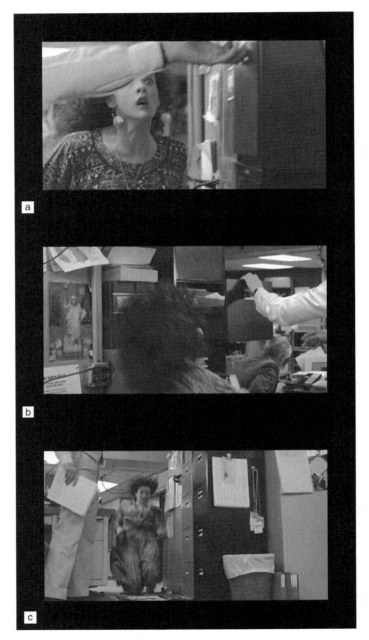

FIGURE 4.11
Broadcast News *Editor Richard Marks cuts together three shots to make a dazzling trajectory of Joan Cusak's move as she dodges a file cabinet drawer in her mad dash to the newsroom with the tape that is due to go straight to air in 15 seconds.*

the newsroom (Fig. 4.11). Every possible visual and physical obstacle, encounter, and energy in this sequence is shaped by the editor, Richard Marks, to have maximum impact in their trajectory and inspire the gravest and funniest kinesthetic empathy in the spectator. We *feel* every one of the great Joan Cusak's galumphing moves in our own body, and although it feels as though it is happening to us, it isn't; it is happening to her, and is therefore madly funny.

I find it interesting that my students consistently find this sequence both tension filled and humorous, even watching it twice in a row. The first time I screen it, I just let them watch and laugh. The second time, I break it down into all of the points articulated above, but, piece by piece, they still find it funny, and they are still filled with tension. I attribute this phenomenon to the power of rhythm over information. As we mirror and empathize with the movement of images and sounds, emotions and events on the screen, our hearts, pulses, breaths, and bodies get caught up with these movements even though we cognitively know where they will lead. If the film's movements are directed and cut so that we feel with them, then we synchronize to them, and their rhythms move us through cycles of tension and release.

SUMMARY

The function of rhythm in film is to create cycles of tension and release, which the spectator "rides" physiologically, emotionally, and cognitively. The ride is felt as variations on the pulse of a temporal world that is created in the process of editing the rhythms of the film. By syncing the spectator's rhythms to the film, rhythm functions in a way that is comparable to meditation; it provides a "restriction of the fluctuations of consciousness."[11] This "meditation for the unquiet mind" is not a path to enlightenment, but it activates a physiological focusing effect similar to that of meditation to carry the spectator along on the ride of the rhythms of the film.

This chapter on tension, release, and synchronization also connects the findings of the first three chapters to propose specific ways that the editor's various intuitions, processes, and tools shape the spectator's experience. The ideas about mirror neurons and kinesthetic empathy, about the choreographic shaping of pulses and phrases, and about the timing, pacing, and trajectory phrasing of rhythm have been looked at in the light of their impact on the spectator's experience of rhythm in film. The result of this discussion can be summarized in an aphorism frequently repeated by filmmakers: *The editor is the film's first audience.* The movement that the editor shapes into rhythm must first affect the editor in order to become the cycles of tension and release and the synchronizing force that move the spectator.

The conclusion at the end of the first four chapters of this book is that rhythm in film editing is shaped by editors through an intuitive knowledge of the rhythms of the world and of their own bodies as informed by the functioning of their kinesthetic empathy and mirror neurons. The same physiological rhythm detectors are, of course, present in the spectators, who imbibe the edited/shaped rhythms of the film physiologically. The editor's knowledge and experience of rhythm are gathered through participation in movement, so movement is the material that is choreographically manipulated to have the desired effects on the spectator. One could say that rhythm in film editing is this shaped movement or, more precisely:

Rhythm in film editing is time, energy, and movement shaped by timing, pacing, and trajectory phrasing for the purpose of creating cycles of tension and release.

The rest of this book will look at different kinds of movement and rhythm and how they work in the processes of film editing.

ENDNOTES

1. Sayles, J., *Thinking in Pictures: The Making of the Movie "Matewan"*, pp. 114–115.
2. Grodal, T. K., *Moving Pictures: A New Theory of Film Genres, Feelings and Cognition*, p. 42.

3. Ibid.

4. van Leeuwen, T., *Introducing Social Semiotics*, p. 186.

5. Grodal, T. K., *Moving Pictures: A New Theory of Film Genres, Feelings and Cognition*, p. 4.

6. Tarkovsky, A., *Sculpting in Time*, p. 119.

7. van Leeuwen, T., *Introducing Social Semiotics*, p. 182.

8. Deleuze, G., *Cinema 2: The Time Image*, p. 189.

9. Ibid., p. 190.

10. Gannon, S., and Life, D., *Jivamukti Yoga*, p. 26.

11. Feuerstein, G., *The Yoga-Sutras of Patañjali: A New Translation and Commentary*, p. 26.

CHAPTER 5

Physical, Emotional, and Event Rhythms

As discussed in Chapter 1, the movements of actors, on however large (whole body) or small (blink) a scale, are the explicit expression of their internal rhythms and emotions. Leisurely strolling and frenetic pounding have different rhythms. The timing and energy of the movement within them is their emotion made explicit, and this is the material being composed into the film's rhythm.

The movement available to choreograph into meaningful patterns of time is not limited to the human body. Movements in the world of the rushes are that world's explicitly stated rhythms. Water, for example, has certain properties of movement that have various meanings. Rushing, trickling, boiling, and freezing water all contain different qualities of time, space, and energy, and these properties, when brought to the rhythmic composition of a film, extend their emotional meanings across the images.

Movement as a material from which edited rhythms are shaped is not limited to movement of images. It includes movement of sound, emotion, ideas, and stories. As Linda Aronson, author of *Scriptwriting Updated*, writes:

> In fact everything about film—about *moving pictures*—is connected with time and movement in time, that is to say action, in every sense. Film consists of movement in all ways, physical, emotional and spiritual. In screenwriting, story is movement and our characters move through their own mental landscapes.[1]

Aronson makes distinctions between different kinds of movement, when she refers, for example, to "physical, emotional and spiritual" movement. Making distinctions between these kinds of movement creates the possibility of articulating subtly different approaches to the shaping of each kind of rhythm. Below, I define and describe three kinds of movement that editors work with and look at the some possible approaches to them.

THREE KINDS OF MOVEMENT

One experience the spectator has of movement is the sensory experience of physical movement—of the purely visual and aural aspects of shaping of time, space, and energy. In this kind of experience, there is kinesthetic empathy with the rise and fall of the energy of the physical movement by itself, its freedom or boundness in space, its velocity, its curves, lines, grace, awkwardness, and so on, through a myriad of movement qualities. Following along with the arcs and flows of movement is a kind of ride in and of itself, in which the contraction and expansion of dynamics in time, space, and energy are a physical experience. The term I will use for the rhythms an editor shapes in response to physical trajectories whose meaning is direct, rather than representing something else, is "physical rhythm" (Fig. 5.1).

The next sort of engagement is barely separable from the first, and in many cases will have precisely the same source, but is experienced slightly differently. It is the experience of the trajectory of the *emotions* in relation to the trajectory of the movement. Performances and juxtapositions convey emotions and provoke emotions. The editor's attention when cutting psychological exchanges is not so much on the motion of the images as on the "dance" of the emotions. The editor is still shaping the physical movement (that's all she has to work with), but she shapes it with her focus on how it conveys emotion, not on how it conveys pattern or spectacle. The movement patterns created by an editor *could* be understood as physical experiences, because

FIGURE 5.1
Bernadette Walong in No Surrender *(Richard James Allen, 2002). Dance films and scenes are driven by physical rhythm. Rather than representing something else, the physical movement is the meaning. [Photo credit: The Physical TV Company/Dominika Ferenz]*

the emotions are being physically expressed, but in fact, the editor is watching for and creating a pattern of the dynamics of emotions seen on the screen. The term I will use for the rhythms an editor shapes from movement experienced as emotional movement is "emotional rhythm" (Fig. 5.2).

The third kind of movement that I wish to distinguish for the purposes of this discussion is the movement of *events.* An event is the release of new information or change of direction for characters as they pursue their goals. Each significant change in a story or structure is an event. Some events are big and have repercussions for the whole plot; others are minor and change the direction of the plot a bit. In some films events occur rapidly, even dizzyingly; in other films there may be little change over the course of the whole, and the story may consist of just

FIGURE 5.2

Tom Wilkinson and Sissy Spacek in In the Bedroom *(Todd Field, 2001). The movement of emotion is the primary currency of this intensely felt drama. The spectator's ride is almost exclusively with the emotions being conveyed by the actors and shaped by the editor. [Photo credit: Good Machine/GreeneStreet/ Standard Film; The Kobal Collection; John Clifford]*

FIGURE 5.3

Bruce Willis in Live Free or Die Hard *(Len Wiseman, 2007). Almost everything in this action-packed film is an event that changes the course of the plot or story. The actors are not known for the emotional strength of their performances, but that's not the point of this sort of film, in which the thrills for the spectator come not only from the fireworks of the visuals but also from the rapid-fire change of events. [Photo credit: 20th Century Fox; The Kobal Collection; Frank Masi]* one substantial event. In either case, an event is a perceptible change at the level of story or structure. It is what happens in a story as distinct from the emotional exchanges (which may, of course, be the source of story changes) and image flow (which expresses and reveals the events). "Event rhythm" is the shaping of time, energy, and movement of events—the rate and strength of change over the course of the story or structure as a whole (Fig. 5.3).

These three types of rhythm—physical rhythm, emotional rhythm, and event rhythm—are cumulative. The physical rhythm sets up a kinesthetic empathy. The emotional rhythm relies on the physical, which is reframed as emotionally laden, to have its impact. And the event rhythm relies on both the movement of image and sound and the movement of emotion to communicate or convey its information.

All three kinds of rhythm are ultimately just strands of one rhythm—that of the edited film—but making distinctions does have practical uses for the editing process. Distinguishing between kinds of rhythm allows us to identify more precisely where a problem may lie or where the attention needs to be focused to make a rhythm work. It gives us something specific to look at and describe in our consultations about the progress of an edit, as opposed to trying to look at what has often been called "invisible."

Distinguishing between the kinds of movement an editor is shaping is useful for the judging of editing, too. It is a way of describing what we know or mean when we say something feels right.

When the Australian Screen Editors Guild was trying to start up its annual editing awards, there was a lot of discussion about the difficulties of judging editing and the lack of shared language for describing good editing. We wanted to institute awards to give editors the credit they deserve, but the question of how to judge the editing almost sank the process. The distinction between the movement of events, of emotions, and of physical images and sounds proved very useful to me in putting forward a set of judging criteria for the awards. The guild steering committee adopted these criteria, and I am reprinting them here as an example of how the distinctions between kinds of movement and rhythm can be helpful in judging the whole.

---

australian | screen | editors

Australian Screen Editors Guild Awards Judging Criteria

(Judges assign a score from 1 to 10 for each criterion; the highest score out of 50 wins.)

1   Movement of story
Is the story clear? On a scale of 1 to 10, how well organized is the flow of information or plot events to convey the film's intentions?

2   Movement of emotion
Is the film compelling? How well shaped are the performances and interactions in the film to convey feeling and provoke emotional responses?

3   Movement of images
Are the film's images shaped effectively? From cut to cut and over a sequence or series of cuts, how well has the editor shaped the flow of images to create a visually engaging experience?

4   Style
Whether obvious or unobtrusive, has the editor established and sustained an approach to cutting that is appropriate to the production and supports the ideas and themes?

5   Structure and rhythm aggregate
This criterion addresses the integration of the other four, story, emotion, image flow, and style, into a whole that is well paced, timed, and organized to convey a compelling experience.

To elaborate on how an editor shapes physical, emotional, and event movement, the next three chapters will each focus on a particular type of rhythm. Chapters 6 and 7 each have a case study to demonstrate the practical applications and outcomes of focusing on a particular strand of rhythm, and Chapter 8 has case studies focused on bringing all three types of rhythm back together to look at rhythm as a whole as "... indispensable in fusing together the meanings expressed ..."[2]

GOOD EDITING IS *NOT* INVISIBLE

People often say that good editing is invisible; that if it's good, it lets you sink into the story so that you don't see the edits. But good editing is not invisible. True, you don't see the edits, but you *do* see the editing. In fact, saying "editing is invisible" is like saying films or videos are invisible.

So what do you see? You see movement. Movement shaped by editing.

You see physical movement. Watching the visual images is one level of seeing a film or video, and the flow, the pattern, or the movement from one image to another and over a sequence is created in editing.

You see (and hear!) emotion. Performances and interactions convey emotions and provoke emotions. Just like the movement of images, there are lots of ways that these can be spun in the editing suite. The flow of emotion doesn't shape itself, and when you experience it, you are experiencing editing.

All of these images and emotions are governed by structure or the movement of events. What happens? How is information released? The flow of the story is also shaped in editing. You definitely don't see structure when you see a good film, but if you experience a good story, one that moves along in a way appropriate to its subject matter, that doesn't confuse or bore, then you've seen the editing.

I propose that editors stop perpetrating the myth that good editing is invisible. Instead, when someone says good editing is invisible, editors can say, "Well, you can see movement, can't you? Editing shapes the movement that you see." If the images fall into a compelling visual pattern, if the emotions engage, if the story makes sense and keeps moving, the editing has shaped these three kinds of movement.

It would be easier, of course, not to argue. But this is not just a theoretical issue for editors; it's practical, political, and cultural. If we keep letting the myth that good editing is invisible slide by, it's an easy step from there to not knowing the difference between good editing and not-so-good editing, and an even easier step from there to just having the director or producer cut it himself.

When we say that good editing *is* visible, we can say how a good editor's talents are vitally important to the success of a production. A good editor has a talent for shaping movement. And this talent is distinct from the talents required for directing, producing, or shooting. It is a sensitivity to the movement of shots, performances, and story; a facility for shaping the flow of movement for an audience beyond itself; and a creativity with combining the movement of images, emotions, and events laterally, to come up with something that is much more than any one of those things on its own.

ENDNOTES

1. Aronson, L., *Scriptwriting Updated: New and Conventional Ways of Writing for the Screen*, p. 40.
2. van Leeuwen, *Introducing Social Semiotics*, p. 182.

CHAPTER 6

Physical Rhythm

In the late 1920s Soviet filmmaker Dziga Vertov made a strong argument, in words and through his films, for editing being a means of showing the truth of the movement of the world:

> To edit; to wrest, through the camera, whatever is most typical, most useful, from life; to organize the film pieces wrested from life into a meaningful rhythmic visual order, a meaningful visual phrase, an essence of "I see."[1]

If one is concerned with physical rhythm, one is concerned, as Vertov proclaims above, with "meaningful rhythmic visual order," not as a means to something else but as a revelation in and of itself.

"Physical rhythm" is the rhythm created by the editor when she prioritizes the flow of the visible and audible physical movement in the film over other types of movement (such as emotional interactions of characters or larger patterns of events in stories). As we will see when looking at emotional rhythm and event rhythm, both of these types of rhythm crafting also rely on the shaping of the visible and audible, but physical rhythm is made when the visible and audible movement and energy are the primary concern of the sequence, the initiating rhythm.

In physical rhythm, movement patterns create meaning directly. Dance scenes, fight scenes, chase scenes, and action scenes are usually examples of this in narrative film. In abstract films, physical rhythm is often the only kind of rhythm being shaped, as these films are made exclusively of abstract flows of color, line, shape, etc. In physical scenes and abstract films, form and content are one: the spectator is watching the movement patterns, and the movement patterns are the meaning and metaphor.

If an editor is working primarily with physical rhythm, she is working primarily with physical movement's size, speed, force, direction, and other visible or audible elements. Her cine-phrases are made by shaping arcs of movement in the frame, of the frame, and across the joins of two or more shots. Her choices pertain to linkage or collision, to the rise and fall of energy, to the rate and concentration of movement, to the pulses and cycles of tension and release of *physical* movement.

When prioritizing the shaping of physical movement patterns, the editor's intuition makes use of a range of techniques and approaches, four of which are described below.

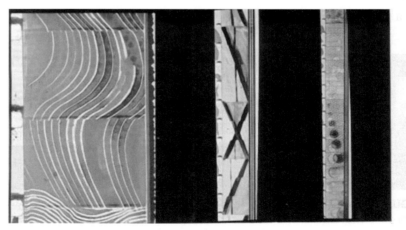

FIGURE 6.1
Frames from Len Lye's Colour Box *(1935). New Zealand filmmaker and "motion artist" Len Lye scratched lines and patterns directly onto the film—he was not using the movement of light, color, and shape to represent anything but the movement of light, color, and shape. Lye's short, abstract "ballets" are compelling for their surprising and humorous patterns and crafting of physical rhythm.*

RECHOREOGRAPHING

Rechoreographing involves changing the sequence of movements, or the emphasis points in phrases, even modifying the pulse by extending or contracting arcs of movement to create the movement *feeling* the original choreography or blocking created. When doing this, I sometimes imagine how the series of shots would constitute a waveform pattern if their accents were charted on paper. Then, from this imaginary chart I decide if the dynamic wave's peak is too sharp or too shallow, too broad or too narrow, or otherwise distorting the flow of movement trajectories beyond a range that expresses the scene's intentions. I then alter the actual sequence of moves or pauses or gestures accordingly, to change the shape of the dynamic wave. One method of doing this is to redesign the movement phrases using shots that allow one character or image to finish another's move. In other words, have a movement impulse start in one shot and then continue or complete its trajectory in the next shot. For example, a soldier shoots an arrow in one shot, and in another shot, the arrow plunges into the enemy's body. Or a wave crests in one shot and crashes in the next. Rechoreographing

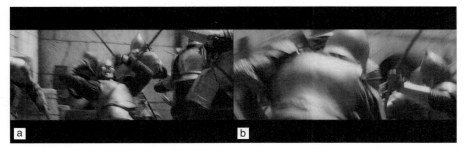

FIGURE 6.2

Battle scenes such as this one from Lord of the Rings, Return of the King *(Peter Jackson, 2003) may be choreographed in real life to unfold in real time, but they are rechoreographed in editing to make the most dynamic use of movement, energy, and time. In shot (a) the editor, Jamie Selkirk, has chosen to show us the peak of the movement curve as a warrior is slain. We don't see him fall to the ground, though; instead the editor cuts to a complementary movement in shot (b) that picks up the arc of the first shot's movement trajectory and shifts it in another direction, moving our eye to another action in the battle.*

allows the editor to use the most dynamic bits of each shot and also to lengthen or contract the arc of the movement to make the most effective use of its energy, speed, and direction. The screen can flatten three-dimensional physical movement and rob it of expressive energy, but this technique returns the fullness of that expressive energy by putting the camera, the body in motion, and the edits into a complementary choreographic composition shaped by the editor.

PHYSICAL STORYTELLING

This method involves asking the question, What is a particular movement communicating in emotional or narrative terms? When cutting a dance scene or a fight scene, for example, ask yourself or the director: Where are we now in the movement's "story"? Where have we come from? The answers guide the direction of the editing. If the fight starts between equally matched opponents, you may start by looking for shots in which their movement energy in the frame is equally strong. If one fighter then gets the advantage, it is important to know where in the movement story that happens, on this punch or that fall, or this jab or that stumble; otherwise, you risk emphasizing the wrong energy for telling the physical story. It is possible to shape the movement of time and energy in physical rhythm to tell innumerable different physical stories, and it is often the case that the editor changes the story or how it unfolds, because particular shots have more impact, beauty, or energy and so the physical story she cuts unfolds different from that which may originally have been intended. This an excellent way of working, and very common, but not the only way. It can also be creatively stimulating to get the director to make a narrative translation of the physical movement, which may otherwise be quite abstract—to tell you the movement's story. Either knowing the director's version of the story in movement quality/energy terms or building a version of the physical story based on what the material is asking for informs decisions about how long to stay with things, how quickly to build or to establish them, and where their development is leading.

FIGURE 6.3

Editor Thelma Schoonmaker and Director Martin Scorsese had a different physical story for each of the many fight scenes in Raging Bull *(1980), and each is cut accordingly to be a pure physical expression of what is going on narratively and dramatically. The fights don't represent other ideas; their composition in movement, frame, and cuts is the meaning, the story, physically told. [Photo credit: United Artists; The Kobal Collection]*

DANCING EDITS

As discussed in Chapter 2, editing is a form of choreography. An edit is a way of limiting or shaping the flow of movement, creating a smooth connection or a shock. The edit is the join in movement arcs or the accent that creates a phrase. To "dance the edits" means to use the edit point as an expressive element of the physical action. This approach creates a choreography of shots that makes the fullest possible use of the potential of cinema to create impact with physical movement. Shaping physical rhythm involves using the cut as an element in the

FIGURE 6.4

Audiences sometimes complain that in dance films like Chicago *(Rob Marshall, 2001), the editing is too fast or there are too many close-ups, so that they can't "see the choreography." No one would ever say this about a fight scene or a chase scene. That's because the choreography of these cinematic scenes is always created in the editing, and has been since the earliest days of cinema. Fred Astaire would not let directors edit his dance scenes because the entire rhythmic composition within them was created by him and his dancing partner. Without in any way diminishing the greatness of Fred Astaire, it is possible to say that cinema has other things to offer in an experience of physical movement than just recording the dancer's moves. In contemporary dance film, it is not that you are missing the "dance" by seeing only one dancer or one body part or by seeing a rapid hit–hit–hit of cuts. This is a* screen *dance, whose ultimate choreographic form is created with the cuts. What you see in the moves, the shots, and the cuts is, cumulatively, the action or the dance, not a version of the action all cut up. In these four shots from* Chicago, *Editor Martin Walsh makes a dance by editing together four moves into a rhythmically coherent phrase.*

dynamic of the sequence. In a physical rhythm, the movement phrases, experiences, and actions are created with the cuts, which are themselves part of the action, part of the storytelling, part of the dance.

SINGING THE RHYTHM

During the cutting process, movement trajectories shaped by cuts can "sound" in the editor's head. This phenomenon draws on a kind of synesthesia that I think a lot of editors have. As the editor Tom Haneke says, "I hear spaces."[2] This may also be one reason editing is so often compared with music. The movements "sound" in editors' heads (bodies), with their timing, pacing, and trajectory phrasing making a kind of song. It is very hard to vocalize this song, and I'm not much of a singer. So when I say "sing," I often mean just tuning my awareness to the song in my head. I sing my cuts, too, not just the movements in a given shot, but the phrases that I make with edits, listening to breath, intensities, tensions, and releases of the flow of energy, time, space, and movement to see if I've hit a false note. It is not just because my background is in dance that I also "dance" as I cut. I have heard other editors speak of this phenomenon, too, wherein they notice their head, shoulders, eyebrows, blinks, or breaths moving sympathetically with the movement phrases being cut together, tracking their rise and fall of energy, and noting their punctuation points with a short sharp nod.[3] Singing the rhythm is an embodied manifestation of thinking rhythmically as described in Chapter 1. It is tuning one's own physical rhythms to the rhythms being perceived in the rushes, and it is a process at work in every single rhythmic decision I make.

In sum, when creating physical rhythm, editors often contend with the movement patterns visible in the raw material by *rechoreographing*. They find out the intentions of the director or the story and practice *physical storytelling*. They exploit the possibilities for using a cut as a form of movement; for example, as a link or a collision, with *dancing edits*. And editors tap directly into the innate rhythms of their own physical presence, their own body rhythms, by *singing the rhythm*.

What follows is a brief analysis of the ways in which I used rechoreographing, physical storytelling, and dancing edits to cut a dance scene in the Physical TV Company production of *Thursday's Fictions* (Richard James Allen, 2006). As noted above, singing the rhythm is an underlying constant through all of my work.

CASE STUDY: "NOW" SCENE FROM *THURSDAY'S FICTIONS*

Physical TV Company productions are stories told by the body. In other words, the movement of dance in these productions is embedded in the movement of narrative, and there are moments when the whole story is carried by the physical. The final dance scene in *Thursday's Fictions* is one of these moments.

The dance scene at the end of *Thursday's Fictions* is a roughly 12-minute sustained movement sequence. Because this particular dance scene was always intended to be realized on the screen and not on the stage, its problems and possibilities are similar to those presented by many physical scenes: the movement has exciting moments, but its overall shape must be constructed in editing to give it direction, flow, cycles of tension and release, and a rhythm to which the spectator can synchronize. This particular scene had some inherent shape, as would, for example, a choreographed fight scene or sex scene, but the editing challenge was not to realize that precise shape, but rather to find the rhythm that expressed its intention.

At the beginning of the sequence (Fig. 6.5), the character Wednesday (Richard James Allen) has just asserted himself forcefully to save the trunk full of dances from Saturday (Emma Canalese, voiced by Mêmé Thorne). Shaken, and barely recovered from his exertion, he opens the trunk, thinking the dances will come flooding out.

But the trunk is empty (Fig. 6.6).

FIGURE 6.5
Wednesday (Richard James Allen) shouts Saturday (Emma Canalese) out of his house. [Photo credit: The Physical TV Company; Simon Chapman]

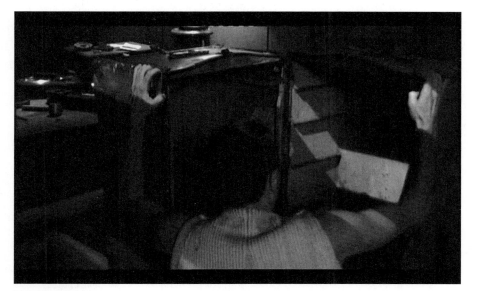

FIGURE 6.6
Wednesday opens the trunk. [Photo credit: The Physical TV Company; Simon Chapman]

Stunned, Wednesday moves tentatively out of his safe, warmly lit corner, into the cavernous, gray room where all of the furniture left over from his father's life is scattered about, covered in drop cloths (Fig. 6.7).

The dance sequence begins when Wednesday starts to uncover the furniture and realizes that under each cloth is not a piece of furniture but a beautiful dancer, frozen and lifeless (Fig. 6.8).

The movement journey of the scene is from frozen lifelessness to floating freedom. It does not move in a straight line; its trajectory moves forward in three waves, and each of these is a construction of movement phrases into a rhythmic cycle of tension and release within the larger construction of phrases and cycle of the whole dance.

The dancing starts with Wednesday doing an "unfreezing" solo (Fig. 6.9).

The physical storytelling in Wednesday's opening solo, after all of the drop sheets are off, is that like the dancers, but in his own way, Wednesday is frozen, too. He reels and catches himself and then performs a

FIGURE 6.7
Drop cloth-covered furnishings in Wednesday's house. [Photo credit: The Physical TV Company; Simon Chapman]

FIGURE 6.8
Wednesday pulls drop cloths from the frozen, lifeless dancers. [Photo credit: The Physical TV Company; Simon Chapman]

FIGURE 6.9
Wednesday moves creakily, unfreezing. [Photo credit: The Physical TV Company; Simon Chapman]

series of gestures that move from a Frankenstein-like circling of his arms to a flowing, generous hand gesture. In the cut I worked to create the feeling that sometimes Wednesday was moving and sometimes he was being moved by the energy and atmosphere around him. There is a 70-second tracking shot that leaves his movement and returns to it, de-emphasizing the effect of his movement and stressing the stillness in the room and the dancers. This long tracking shot is beautiful, and beauty is one of the reasons the dances need to live. But it is dead beauty. The long time that it goes on for creates desperation for changes, dynamic variations, and movement. Getting the audience to want and value these things seemed like a good idea because these things are about to be served to them in spades. Coming out of the tracking shot, the stress and trajectory connections of the cuts are the start of the character's physical transformation. The cuts here obey the rules of continuity cutting, but just barely, so they feel magical, and this begins to lead to the next bit of physical storytelling in the dance.

What wakes the dancers from their frozen, lifeless state? In the script Wednesday's warming warms them. His feeling stirs theirs. When he starts to move more fluidly, his energy spreads around the room and awakens the dancers' movement energy. But, in rough cut screenings, this didn't seem to be coming across to an audience unused to reading movement, because the screen flattened the movement energy that was apparent and legible in live dancers. So we rechoreographed, cutting in a couple more visible cause-and-effect shots to say that, literally, his movement stirred them.

Wednesday throwing his body creates a current of air that stirs the dancers' skirts, then their hands, then their breath. We did this to make the connection physically visible. His movement trajectory stirs them (Fig. 6.10).

Then the dancers start their movement journey by breathing. How much is needed to make that point? In the original choreography you could see the whole room come alive in just three long, visible inhalations and exhalations. (The movement exaggerates and shapes the in and out of the

FIGURE 6.10
Wednesday also throws one of the drop cloths he has removed to try to stir the air around the dancers.
[Photo credit: The Physical TV Company; Simon Chapman]

breath.) I thought at first I needed to go around the room to each dancer and see her take her breath, to show the breaths of each dancer awakening. (We have to stay close to feel breath—moving to a wide shot to show them all breathing just reads as bland.) But once we had the "stirring/waking" working better, we found we needed far fewer breaths—in fact, it was now back to the original three. Inhale in one shot, exhale in the next—I rechoreographed so that the dancers finished one another's breaths.

In the next moments the dancers come shuddering to life in a sequence that stops and starts haltingly. The same problem occurs as with the breaths—when you see the whole room live, you see that only three dancers are moving, and it looks like a little spike that shudders to a stop. The whole group has not yet coordinated, but the little spikes spark once, twice, three times around the room. But if we go out to the wide shot to see the three moving dancers isolated in a still room, their spike has no spark. The solution here was in rechoreographing to get the feeling intended. Instead of a whole room going still for 1 second, we ended up prolonging the stillnesses by cutting around the room on

FIGURE 6.11
Dancers Terri Herlings and Linda Ridgway begin to catch the spark of life and disperse it around the room. [Photo credit: The Physical TV Company; Simon Chapman]

the dancers so that the beginning of each movement spike, coming out of stillness, can be seen. The movement story is that the spikes spark around until, by the third one, everyone takes off (Fig. 6.11).

A sequence follows in which the dancers' energy is a bit frenetic, all over the place (Fig. 6.12). The physical storytelling is that they are coming to life awkwardly, struggling to break the ice and to get coordinated. To make this visible onscreen, we use a lot of dancing edits. We have gestures colliding, only peaks of energy being used, no full movement arcs until they stop.

In the next sequence, high-energy twists, leaps, spins, and dives are cut together with respect for screen direction and energy, not real time (rechoreographing). This montage of individual gestures travels first from screen right to screen left (Fig. 6.13a), then back from left to right (Fig. 6.13b), as the dance did. In the live dance this happens three times. In the cut it occurs only once, but the dancing edits create

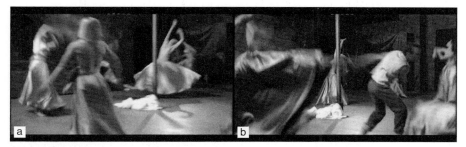

FIGURE 6.12
The dancers moves and energy go wild. [Photo credit: The Physical TV Company; Simon Chapman]

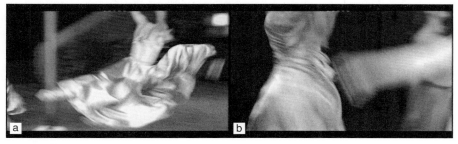

FIGURE 6.13
Leaps and twists cut together to create a flow. [Photo credit: The Physical TV Company; Simon Chapman]

far greater intensity of juxtaposed movements. The composition of a series of short stabs, each one triggering the next, makes the same feeling as was on stage but through a different approach.

As pioneering dance film maker Amy Greenfield says:

> Filmdance energy is produced through editing as well as the camera. Movements can be shortened, interrupted, and put together in such a way as to heighten the perception of energy. An extreme example of such an energy is obtained by interrupting movement at its climax.[4]

At 11½ minutes into the scene comes the penultimate sequence of the dance (Fig. 6.14). Called the "tribal" sequence, it is designed to emphasize the peak of unity and power of the group, as it reaches the climax of the dance's story. The dancers have come fully to life. They have explored different configurations of fractured movements; of solos, duets,

FIGURE 6.14
Unison energy for the first time in the dance. [Photo credit: The Physical TV Company; Simon Chapman]

and trios; and now they finally come together in a unison of powerful downward stomps and elongated stretches. The visual rhythm is complicated by the fact that the whole group starts the beat and keeps the beat, but individuals split off to dance in counterpoint and then return. Given the complexities of the physical rhythms and their importance to the physical story, I sang this one out loud as I cut, making sure I knew where the downbeat was on each cycle of stomping, stretching, and circling. I stretched the beat sometimes, which worked better visually but created difficulties for the composer. The downbeat then became a discussion point between myself; the director/choreographer, Richard James Allen; and the composer, Michael Yezerski. Michael was eventually able to find a continuous and urgent rhythmic pattern through this climactic section.

The physical storytelling of the last section, known as the final float, is that the dancers, their beauty, breath, life, time, space, energy, and movement are all dissolving into one another (Fig. 6.15). The final digital effect returns the dancers to their state of light, but out of the trunk, where they can shine.

FIGURE 6.15

Dancers dissolve into one another—an editing device functioning narratively. [Photo credit: The Physical TV Company; Simon Chapman]

FIGURE 6.16

Dance becoming light. [Photo credit: The Physical TV Company; Simon Chapman/Mark Woszczalski]

SUMMARY

Working with the physical movement of dance in *Thursday's Fictions* gave me the opportunity to work directly on shaping physical rhythms. In this case, rhythmically complete phrases of movement were devised by the choreographer, but the timing, pacing, and trajectory phrasing of any movement are always somewhat altered when movement is framed and captured by a camera. Therefore, the editor's job is to re-create not the precise choreography, but the feeling of the original choreography. The same is generally true of most scenes in which physical rhythms dominate. Chases and fights, for example, must have their rhythms created in editing to *feel* like chases and fights. This involves shaping the relative timing, pacing, and trajectory phrasing of movement visible and audible in shots. I have named the processes I use to accomplish the shaping of physical rhythm: rechoreographing, physical storytelling, dancing edits, and singing the rhythm. Each of these is a name for a method of activating my intuitive rhythmic thinking in service of the choreographic shaping of physical rhythm. To some extent, because the visible and audible movement of a film is the material the editor has with which to shape any rhythms, these same processes occur in the cutting of emotional and event rhythms, too.

The next chapter will look at emotional rhythm and articulate some ideas about seeing and shaping the movement of emotions in the physical movement of performers.

MUSIC, SOUND, AND PHYSICAL RHYTHM

Dances in musicals are cut using the music to which they were choreographed, but the final 12-minute dance scene of *Thursday's Fictions* was choreographed in silence, with the dancers creating a strongly rhythmical bond between themselves to keep in time. It was done this way on purpose. One of the core principles of Physical TV Company productions is that rhythm in the final film is created in the edit suite. The composers I work with don't like temp music because it boxes them into a corner when the director gets attached to it. I don't like it because it defeats the point of the whole exercise. If you cut according to some external rhythm, what happens to the rhythms inherent in the movement? And what happens to the rhythms the editor sees, imagines, or dreams of bringing into being by the choreography of cuts? They get no opportunity to exist, never mind be brought to life.

Some physical scenes will very often benefit from the use of temp music, particularly if they have no choreographed shape and the editor has to invent the structure of the rhythm. In this case editors may use some music to help them find a first cut or direction, but they are wary of letting the music impose too much of itself on the images and will strip the music out periodically to check that the visual flow has integrity without the music.

Much more important than temp music for physical scenes are temp sound effects. Much of the rise and fall of emphasis and energy in an action, fight, or chase sequence is carried on the sound. So, the editor is wise to have a cache of punches, whooshes, thuds, and crashes handy to indicate the punctuation marks she intends to have in the phrasing of the movement of image and sound through the scene.

ENDNOTES

1. Vertov, D., *Kino-Eye: The Writings of Dziga Vertov*, pp. xxv–xxvi.
2. Tom Haneke, quoted in Oldham, G., *First Cut: Conversations with Film Editors*, p. 44.
3. In the documentary about editors and their processes, *The Cutting Edge: The Magic of Movie Editing* (Wendy Apple, 2004), there is a sequence in which Walter Murch demonstrates his version of singing the edits. He says he edits standing up to feel "sprung" and able to "hit the cut with my knees bent . . . this allows me to internalize the rhythms, the visual rhythms of what is happening."
4. Greenfield, A., "Filmdance: Space, time and energy," in the *Filmdance Catalogue*, p. 6.

CHAPTER 7

Emotional Rhythm

This chapter is about shaping emotional arcs. It will look at the variations on the use of a choreographic approach when the priority is not the visible movement values *themselves,* but the emotions that the movements express.

Emotional tension and release are shaped by the timing, pacing, and trajectory phrasing of emotional energy. Practically speaking, this means that performance guides the cutting. For editors, "performance guides the cutting" is a much-used and well-favored axiom and offers a very useful starting place for considering the principles involved in the crafting of emotional rhythms. Being guided by performance means focusing attention on the intentional movements made by actors and, in documentary, by non-actors telling their stories.

In *In the Blink of an Eye* Walter Murch discusses using one intentional movement that can be observed in performances: the blink. He says an editor could look at when the actor blinks to determine the rise and fall of the character's emotional dynamic:

> … our rates and rhythms of blinking refer directly to the rhythm
> and sequence of our inner emotions and thoughts … those rates
> and rhythms are insights into our inner selves and, therefore, as
> characteristic of each of us as our signatures.[1]

The blink is just one of a range of visible movements of thought or emotion. The performers' faces and bodies make a dance of emotions—of

FIGURE 7.1
Documentary generally uses non-actors, but the same rule applies: people convey emotions through intentional movements. In the documentary Thin Blue Line *by Errol Morris, this character, Randall Adams, who is on death row for killing a police officer in Houston, conveys his innocence and sincerity to the audience through his movement and intonation, his upright posture and direct gaze to the camera, as much as his words. He was, as a result of this documentary, acquitted of the crime. [Photo credit: American Playhouse/Channel 4; The Kobal Collection]*

impulses, responses, and responsive impulses fluctuating over their physical presence. Their pauses, hesitations, shifts of position, glances, swallows, twitches, smiles, sobs, sighs, starts, shakes, affirmations, denials, and so on are all contractions and releases of feeling, all energetic motions written all over the screen. Similarly, the rise and fall of intonation, the pauses and stress points, are the movement of emotion and intention through sound.

In cutting emotional rhythm, a performance that has a movement rhythm within it is given to the editor and the editor has to work with that rhythm by making choices about it. The choices might be described as running along a spectrum from respecting it completely and not cutting at all to cutting in such a way as to disrupt it utterly and create a new rhythm. There is a lot of room for rhythmic creativity and decision making along the spectrum between these two poles. There are tandem considerations at work in making these decisions. One consideration is the strength of the performance—a strong performance is more likely to be used and to be respected. It will also shape the emotional rhythm by prioritizing the emotions it conveys, which is the other consideration in cutting emotional rhythm: Which emotion is being conveyed, for how long, and at what level of strength or intensity? This question will be answered in the editing process, and its answers may respect the intentions of the original script, or they may be swayed by the strengths and weaknesses of performances and shots.

In editing, the decisions about where and when to cut emotions are decisions about how to throw the emotional energy from one shot to another. I use a dance improvisation exercise called Throwing the Energy as a metaphor for what an editor is doing when shaping emotional rhythm.

In the Throwing the Energy dance game, the first dancer pretends she has a ball of energy in her hands. The ball is invisible, but she articulates its outlines by shaping and moving her hands around it. She plays with it for a while, letting it travel through all parts of her body, and as she does, we get to see what kind of energy she imagines it to be. If it is crackling, snapping energy, her limbs slash and jab; if it is calm and floating energy, her limbs sail and glide. Once she has played with the energy for a while, she passes it on to the next dancer. She throws the energy to the next dancer, who picks it up, *as it was thrown,* into her body. If the first dancer slams the ball of energy at the second dancer's head, the second dancer will instinctively reel as though hit. If the first dancer dribbles drops of energy into the second dancer's palm, the second dancer will crouch around the drops protectively, gathering them before they slither away. In other words, the kind of energy the first dancer throws, combined with the force, speed, and direction of her throw, equal the kind of energy that the next dancer receives.

FIGURE 7.2

One of the earliest things children learn is to respond to emotional energy. As infants, although we cannot understand words, we still understand the energy with which they are spoken. For example, we shrink from anger or embrace delight, because the energy communicates the emotion on a nonverbal level. In this sequence from Down Time Jaz *(Karen Pearlman, 2002), I used the children's innate capacity to respond to energy qualities in movement and got the child performers to dance very convincingly by playing the Throwing the Energy game with them. [Photo credit: The Physical TV Company; Dominika Ferenz]*

Throwing the energy is what an editor is doing with cuts. An editor chooses the first shot's duration and frame to throw a certain kind of energy. This shot is then juxtaposed with another shot. The second shot receives the energy the first shot throws. The editor is creating an impression of cause and effect, an impression that the energy and action in the first shot causes the responsive motion seen in the next shot.

Because the energy thrown creates a cause-and-effect relationship with the energy of the next shot, the editor has begun to shape a trajectory phrase of emotional energy. For example, if a character smiles gratefully in one shot (the gratitude being the energy or intention that propels the movement of the smile), and another character shrugs awkwardly in the next shot, the gratitude appears to have caused the awkwardness. The timing, pacing, and trajectory phrasing of this exchange are a little piece of emotional rhythm built from the rhythm of the performances.

In the Throwing the Energy game, we watch the energy course through the dancer, changing and expressing her Effort, or intention. This is also what we are watching when we watch a character's emotion move. We are watching, on a much more minute level, the play of emotional energy in his body, how slowly he smiles, how awkwardly he shrugs. These are the

PRACTICAL EXERCISE

Playing the Throwing the Energy Game with Nondancers

Playing the Throwing the Energy game with editing or filmmaking students gives them a very immediate experience of how this concept works in the filmmaking process, and I have found, over years of teaching, that it works equally well with any kind of students—they certainly do not have to be actors or dancers.

Get together a group of five or more people; a small classroom of ten or twelve students around a central table is ideal. If there is no central table that everyone can sit around, try clearing some space and getting everyone to stand in a circle. Start the game off by pretending you have a ball of energy in your hands. Shape your hands around the ball, shift it from one hand to the other, and then toss it, as you might toss a tennis ball to someone else in the room. The person you throw it to will catch it. And not only will he catch it, but he will raise his hands to catch it in the air along the trajectory in which it was thrown. I have seen students raise both hands overhead and stumble backward five steps to catch a wildly thrown pitch that is sailing overhead. I have even seen students duck when they think they will be hit by the energy and then turn around and run to the spot where it would have fallen, had it been a real ball, and retrieve the invisible, imaginary substance, the energy that was thrown.

When all of the students have had a chance to throw and catch the energy, there are two things to point out to them.

1. They all catch the energy the way it was thrown. Make an example of one or two who made particularly responsive catches by describing the motion they did to receive the energy they imagined was being thrown. Then draw the metaphor explicitly by explaining that this is what an editor does. She throws the energy from one shot to the next. She chooses the shots, their placement, their duration, and the frames to make an emotional arc from one shot to the next, so that it appears that the emotional energy thrown in one shot is the energy responded to in the next shot.

2. The next thing to point out is that the energy is invisible. This always gets a laugh, because of course everyone knows the energy is invisible. But the interesting thing is that, even though it is invisible, they all watch it. No one's eyes stay on the person who has thrown the energy, all eyes *always* follow the invisible ball to the next person. And this is exactly what the editor is doing to create emotional rhythm. She is catching your eye with the emotional energy and then throwing it to the next shot with exactly the right timing to keep you watching the invisible movement of energy as it travels between the performers.

expressions of emotion in movement. Seeing the emotional energy work its way through an acting performance is more subtle than seeing energy in a dance, but there are some specific things that actors do in creating their performances, which, if an editor knows to watch for them, can help her shape the energy and arcs of emotional rhythm.

PREPARE, ACTION, REST

One useful idea about actors' movement comes from the Russian theater director Vsevolod Meyerhold, who was a direct influence on the seminal Soviet director, editor, and teacher Sergei Eisenstein. Meyerhold's influence on Eisenstein had a significant influence on the development of editing and film form.

Meyerhold developed a system called biomechanics through which he "tried to help his actors find the right pose, the right gesture or business, to figure forth their interior states as economically as possible."[2] One of his ideas is that every movement has three phases: a preparation, an action, and a recovery.[3]

Leaving aside, for the moment, how this theory manifested itself in Meyerhold's actual works, what is interesting for the editor of emotional rhythm is that it provides a way of seeing a trajectory through an actor's movement. It implies a phrasing in every complete action that can be marked off, with a conceptual grease pencil, as a possible place for a cut. If an editor can watch an actor picking up a cup of tea (or throwing a bomb) and see these three phases of movement, then the editor can ask herself: What do I need from this movement to throw the emotional energy to the next character or event? Do I need just the preparation? Is it enough for the audience to know that the first character does pick up the tea, and it is the way he goes for the tea that causes the other character's disapproving glance? Or do I need to see it all the way through to the first character's obvious enjoyment of the tea, and that becomes what causes the disapproving glance? As the name biomechanics implies, this is quite a mechanical way of breaking down an actor's movement. But if it is mechanical in the sense of "how it works" rather than mechanical in the sense of "machine-like," it can be useful to editors. By watching for the prepare, action, recovery arc of a given movement, whether by an actor or by a non-actor, editors can find an optimal point to cut in the trajectory of the emotional energy to convey the force and quality of emotion required by the scene.

Biomechanics was developed by Meyerhold to some extent in opposition to the technique of actor training that his contemporary,

Konstantin Stanislavski, was developing. However, two concepts that are also very helpful to editors in training their eyes to see emotions move come out of Stanislavski's "method."

THE ACTOR'S ACTIONS

One important concept Stanislavski introduced to the training of actors is the idea of "actions." An action, in actors' terms, is the actor's psychological intention spelled out as a verb. The reason for making his intentions into verbs is to give the actor something to do rather than to be: doing is active, being is passive. Most importantly, for the editor, the action, being a verb, implies movement of thoughts or feelings.

Actions in this sense make the text or the subtext into emotional movement. If an actor has the line, "May I have some cake?" his subtext may or may not be the same as the text. He may be saying the words that ask for cake, but the subtext is asking not for cake, but, for example, for affection.

Actors will try to make their actions as active and emotionally accurate to their subtext as possible. "To ask" is one possible action, but depending on what the actor thinks is his real objective in the scene, "to ask" might turn into "to plead," "to manipulate," "to distract," "to deceive," "to declare love for."… Whereas some of these may seem outlandish with reference to a simple piece of cake, it is important to remember that unless all the character really wants is cake, he could be asking for any number of things—love, time, respite, engagement, or forgiveness, for example. His objective is what he really wants; his action is what he is doing to get what he wants. His action is the energy that propels his movement.

An editor can look at the actor's movement (including the sound movement of the voices rather than the words) and see what an actor is doing subtextually. If the editor can see the action, for example, pleading, behind the words, then she can discern a point at which the action has reached its optimal energetic point for the throw. The editor can perceive the action as a movement phrase, see where its cadences, breaths, stress points, etc., are, and make the cut at the exact point at which she wants to throw the energy to the next actor for precisely the impact she wants it to have.

If we look at an actor's action as what he is *really* doing, then we can explain why cuts that don't match perfectly in continuity still work. When the emotional energy is being shaped, we don't notice little continuity errors or mismatches because we are not watching the character reach for cake; we are watching him reach for affection. Our attention is not on the movement patterns in and of themselves, it is on their emotional meaning. If the cut throws the emotion well, then our eye follows the emotion, not the cake. The emotional movement is visible, as Murch tells us, in the rate and quality of blinks and also in the breath, the tilt of the head, the purse of the lips, the raise of an eyebrow, etc., and all of these movements, especially seen in close-up or medium close-up, are effective ways of throwing the emotion. So if an actor reaches for cake with one hand and then picks it up with the other, this continuity gaffe will go unnoticed if the actor is truthfully inhabiting the body of the character. If the actor is playing his action and throws his emotion to the other actor with movement such as a hopeful raise of his eyes, then, as his eyes lift up, the editor sees the emotion move and cuts to his girlfriend. Does she reassure or turn away from that hopeful pleading? The editor has thrown the movement of the emotional energy and opened the questions, "How will it be caught?" and "What will be the effect this emotional cause has?"

Throwing the emotion well is not just a case of deciding on the cadence of the emotion being thrown but how it is going to be received. If we go back to the dancers' improvisation, the dancers receive the energy as it is thrown, so what they are reacting to is not just the energy but where it is directed. If it slams at their head, they don't shake it off their fingers. Film actors are not improvising; even if they were on set, now that they're on filmstrips, they are not any longer. So, the editor can look both at the available range of reactions and at the available range of throwing actions before choosing exactly where to cut. The editor's job is to shape the movement of the emotion by shaping a movement that feels as though the actor who catches it is responding to what was thrown. It is the actor's performance that draws our "eye-trace"[4] to the emotional movement; it is the editor's cut that determines the trajectory of the throw.

BEATS

The Stanislavski "method" has another word that could be very useful for editors in shaping emotional rhythm, which is "beats." There are a number of possible interpretations of this idea, but for our purposes we will say that the beat is the point at which an actor changes or modifies his action.

For example, if a character named Joe wants affection but asks for cake, his girlfriend might say, "Help yourself." But if his girlfriend is withholding affection and her action is "to ignore," then Joe, having failed to achieve his objective (getting affection) with his first action, "to ask," will then shift his action to any number of other actions as the scene and the director require, such as "to demand," "to inspire," or "to insist." The change of action, or change of what Joe is doing to achieve his objective, from asking to demanding is called a beat. There may be any number of beats in a scene until objectives are achieved (Joe gets affection) or thwarted (his girlfriend breaks up with him). Keep in mind that, in the real world of a documentary or in a well-crafted drama, the other person, the girlfriend in this case, will also have objectives. She will have actions she is trying to do to achieve them and beats as she changes her action to accomplish her goals. The emotional energy is thrown between the two characters, back and forth. If Joe throws his request for affection gently, by asking, and the girlfriend throws back a block by ignoring, then the change of Joe's action to demanding is caused by the emotional energy his girlfriend threw. This is a cause-and-effect chain. Asking causes ignoring, ignoring causes demanding, and so on. Emotion moves back and forth, like a tennis ball in play. But it is the editor who shapes the rhythm of the game. She shapes it by choosing the shots for the energy they contain, juxtaposing the shots to make a dynamic and credible emotional arc and trimming the shots to the frames on which the energy is optimally thrown and caught.

What is important for the editor is that a beat gives her the chance to see the end of one emotional energy trajectory and the rise of another. The energy of the actor's movement will change according to the actor's intention, and editors who sensitize themselves to these changes can see beats as little movement phrases. For some it may be useful to articulate the change verbally, to pinpoint the movement on which the actor changes from asking to demanding. For others it may be just as useful to detect movement changes more abstractly, to see energy shift, to detect changes in timing, pacing, and trajectory, and to know that these are beats. Seeing beats in either way gives the editor the chance to see the rhythms inherent in the actor's movement. For example, if Joe's action is to ask, his eyes will move directly, and he is likely to blink at the end of his request, throwing it to his girlfriend with a simple and direct energetic motion. If his girlfriend throws back hostility by ignoring him, Joe will have a beat, a responsive shift of his action to this new emotional development. Possibly that beat can be seen as he looks away, blinks a few times, maybe bites his lip or sighs, possibly not. Either way, the beat will occur as he shifts into his new action, in this case to demand, and his eye, breath, head, and face movement will change again. The editor uses all of these moves as potential cutting points, because they are the movement from which she will shape the rhythms inherent in and constitutive of the *meaning* in the actors' exchange.

In sum, editors throw the emotional energy of one shot to the next by choosing which shots to juxtapose and the frames on which to juxtapose them. When the throw is caught and the response is thrown back, the editor has shaped a cause-and-effect chain. To shape the cause-and-effect chain effectively, the editor watches for the movement of emotion across faces, gestures, and sound. The ability to see Meyerhold's preparation, action, recovery arc and Stanislavski's actions and beats gives editors the ability to see emotional energy move and ways of cutting emotional movement into rhythms.

CASE STUDY: *THE HOURS*

What follows is a case study on the cutting of a scene from *The Hours* (Stephen Daldry, 2004), a drama scene in which the emotional rhythm is shaped from the energy thrown between two characters as each tries to achieve her objectives.

There are, of course, thousands of scenes that could demonstrate the principles involved in shaping emotional rhythm. I chose this scene from *The Hours* in the first instance because of the brilliance of Toni Collette's performance as Kitty, the neighbor who comes to call on one of the central characters of the film, Laura, played by Julianne Moore.

Toni Collette has an astonishing capacity to reveal the layered symphony of emotion moving through her character's soul through the energetic movement of her face, head, and body. But her performance in this scene had to be balanced against the elegant performance by Julianne Moore, whose character is tentative and uncertain compared to Toni Collette's brassy extroverted Kitty. The editor, Peter Boyle, does an extremely effective job of balancing the two performances, shaping Toni Colette's to just the right amount of expressive activity and providing respite from the intensity of her energy with well-measured interjections of the restrained Julianne Moore.

This scene, with its surprising climax, is played almost entirely on subtext, and the richness of that subtext is experienced in the emotional arcs shaped by the editor. Boyle has been guided by the performances, but also shaped them to give balance between them and continually renew the questions of how each character's utterances will affect the other. If, for example, Kitty confesses, what does Laura do? If Laura probes, what does Kitty do? These questions, as discussed in Chapter 2, are not consciously asked. They are created and understood immediately by the movement that expresses emotion, movement that we experience directly through our mirror neurons and our kinesthetic empathy. The shape, rate, and intensity of emotional movement, the tension and release of the emotional questions it raises, are in the hands of the editor.

This scene between Kitty and Laura is complex and traverses, in the course of the 5 minutes it takes to play out, an escalating series of character objectives, actions, and beats. It starts with Kitty coming in on Laura at a vulnerable moment, when Laura is cursing her own incompetence at baking; her cake has turned out lumpy and lopsided. Kitty's objective at the beginning seems to be to boost her own confidence, to compare herself to her neighbor and come up favorably. Laura just wants to appear to be a proper homemaker or, on a more basic level, to survive, to keep her head above water in this competition.

Kitty notices that Laura has baked a cake and walks over to inspect it. Cut to Laura getting coffee spoons from the drawer as though she wishes she could just crawl into the drawer and hide (Fig. 7.3a). We see just enough of her tension to know she feels Kitty's inspection keenly and then cut back to see just enough of Kitty's tinkling, mocking laugh to know that her good humor is laced with scorn (Fig. 7.3b). Too much of Laura's anxiety in this exchange would make her look hopelessly neurotic. Too much of Kitty's mocking would make her look cruel. The balance that Boyle has achieved in the time spent on each of them and the timing of cuts onto their gestures gives the relationship complexity—there is friendliness, helpfulness, good cheer, and irony at the same time there is neurosis, mocking, and gloating.

FIGURE 7.3
The emotional rhythms of this scene from The Hours *(Stephen Daldry, 2004) are beautifully modulated by editor Peter Boyle. In this exchange he balances Laura's (Julianne Moore's) discomfort, visible in her tense shoulders and back, with Kitty's (Toni Collette's) friendly mocking to give the exchange a bit of sharpness but not draw blood.*

Once Kitty is seated at Laura's table with a cup of coffee, there is a series of shot–reverse shot cuts of the two women in conversation. (Shot–reverse shot meaning seeing Laura from Kitty's point of view and then reversing to see Kitty from Laura's point of view.) This is a very common configuration for a two-handed scene, and the emotional rhythm is shaped by choosing when to cut from one character to the next. In this case Kitty's flirty self-confidence bounces energetically against Laura's quiet, self-effacing comments and inquiries. Until Laura says something that Kitty doesn't really understand (Fig. 7.4a) and Kitty reacts, first defensively (Fig. 7.4b) and then by withdrawing her attention from Laura and looking around the house irritated and bored. When Kitty's eye lights on a book Laura has left on the countertop, there is a cut to a wide two-shot. Cutting out of a shot–reverse shot sequence and into a wide two-shot (a shot with both characters visible in it) is usually a signal that the emotional objective of a scene has either been achieved or thwarted. In this case Kitty's objectives have been achieved—she is confirmed as commanding and vivacious—and Laura's have been thwarted—she has lost Kitty's approval by her clumsy introspection. Up until now, we have been watching the emotions being thrown between the two, watching first one character, and then the other, receive the emotional energy and bat it back. When the emotional question has

FIGURE 7.4

After some chit-chat, Laura throws an idea toward Kitty that she doesn't really understand (a) and Kitty reacts by closing off her charm and openness (b).

been resolved, cutting to a two-shot gives the audience a more objective view of the state of play. The two-shot serves as a punctuation point, closing one question and opening another.

In the wide two-shot, a book, *Mrs Dalloway* by Virginia Woolf, is in the foreground, in focus, and the two characters are out of focus in the background (Fig. 7.5a). The cinematographer pulls focus (shifts the focal point from the foreground to the background) in the middle of Kitty saying the line, "Oh, you're reading a book." This line is an accusation. If the subtext were written as text it might read, "That's a very strange thing to do; no wonder you're so strange." Kitty gets up, covering

FIGURE 7.5

Editor Peter Boyle comes in on this two-shot as a way of changing the subject and tone of the scene. The shot starts with the book in focus and Kitty's attention on it, out of focus and in the background. Then the focus shifts to Kitty, who takes charge of the dynamic of the conversation once more and sashays over to have a look at the book.

her distaste for books with a teasing inquiry and swinging her hips in a mix of officiousness and flirtatiousness as she goes to pick up the book, asking, "What's this one about?" (Fig. 7.5b). Laura, left in the background of the wide shot that Kitty now dominates completely as she rifles through the book, starts to explain, haltingly.

The spatial dynamic and performances create tension—is Laura going to manage to stumble through an explanation or dissolve tongue-tied in the path of Kitty's effusive handling of the conversation? Laura manages. She looks inward and draws on the strength she's gotten from the book to say, "Well, it's about this woman who's incredibly, well, she's a hostess and she's incredibly confident...." Here Boyle cuts to a reverse shot of Kitty in time to see Kitty's expression change from boredom and distaste to apparent interest and delight as the key character in the book is described as "confident" and "giving a party." Seeing Kitty shift from boredom to engagement is important because it allies Kitty with the confident character in the book.

Boyle then cuts back to Laura, who gently delivers a blow to Kitty, a velvet-covered hammer that cracks Kitty's façade. We are on Laura, who looks more glowing and energetic than she has yet in the scene; she says, ostensibly about the main character in the book, but clearly also about Kitty, "Because she's confident, everyone thinks she's going to be fine. But she isn't." (Fig. 7.6a). This is an emotional throw to Kitty,

FIGURE 7.6
Laura is gently cracking open Kitty's façade by describing the plot of the book, Mrs Dalloway. *She throws her energy gently but confidently, and it hits its mark, making Kitty slow down and reflect.*

and Boyle cuts to her to let us watch the whole arc of her receiving and responding to the emotional energy. Toni Collette, as Kitty, speaks volumes with her facial expressions, even the way she flips through the pages of the book, by slowing down and absorbing the impact of this blow to her façade (Fig.7.6b). She closes the book with a degree of deliberateness that says, I don't want to be like this character anymore, but I can't just dismiss her.

Laura's action now is to expose Kitty; Kitty's is to keep control. This moment is sustained by the cutting. Kitty closes the book; cut back to Laura, watching; back to Kitty as she puts the book down; back to Laura, who says "So," quietly; back to Kitty, who gathers herself together and tries for a perky smile but breaks it off to look away. I say that this series of five shots sustains the moment rather than being a volley or a series of throws and catches of emotional energy, because nothing changes between the two characters. It is as though the moment is holding its breath; they are both holding the energy, filled with the question of how Kitty will deal with this sudden revelation about who she really is.

Holding the moment in this way is a very delicate operation and needs to be done fluidly and lightly. All too often one sees a strong emotional scene become heavy-handed by sitting too long on the emotionally laden shots with no change or variation. But Boyle's handling of this moment is both fluid and light. He cuts very fast: all five shots in under 15 seconds. But because the characters are both concentrating intently, the very fast cutting does not draw attention to itself. In fact, if ever cutting could be called invisible, this is it. We see the movement between the two characters as though it is utterly "natural", when of course, it is anything but! The sense that it is natural comes from the perfectly judged timing of the cuts. It feels as though, if we were standing in the room with them, we would look from one character to the other at exactly this rate, to see what would happen. I believe that this is an example of the editor's internal body rhythms at work in shaping the emotional arc of the scene. He is watching and cutting to coincide with the way the question sits in his own body, as though he has placed himself in that room as our proxy, watching and wondering, moving from one shot to the next, on behalf of us, quietly—without disturbing the energy of the scene, but quickly, so that we don't miss a beat.

The scene now moves through another series of beats: Laura has watched Kitty trying not to be like the woman in the book, the one who seems fine but isn't. Now Laura probes and Kitty confesses that she is also not fine. In the exchange that follows, there is a series of escalating revelations by Kitty about her fears and feelings of inadequacy. The cutting comes back to a shot–reverse shot pattern, and Boyle makes a series of very effective choices about where to place the cuts. As Kitty speaks, her sentences are punctuated with bright, fake smiles. Boyle uses these smiles as throws and catches of the emotional energy. He leaves a shot as Kitty begins to smile and pull her façade up (Fig. 7.7a) and cuts to Laura listening or nodding (Fig. 7.7b). Then he comes back to Kitty as the smile disappears (Fig. 7.7c) and she speaks the truth once more. Starting to smile throws the energy to Laura; Kitty is begging for reassurance. Laura's sympathetic nods throw the energy back to Kitty, and Boyle cuts back just in time for us to see the last few frames of Kitty's smile disappearing as Laura's probing sends her deeper into her pain.

The emotion escalates and Laura stands up, coming into Kitty's shot to hug and comfort her so that once again we are in a two-shot, when the objectives of the scene are achieved.

Laura kisses Kitty tenderly, lovingly, on the mouth. Kitty returns the kiss willingly. Laura has achieved her real objective; she has expressed her true desire, her love, her forbidden sexual longings. Kitty has also achieved her real objective, to get respite from her pretence, to be loved for who she is, not for the act she puts on.

But the scene doesn't end there. Kitty at first seems to accept what has occurred; she says to Laura, "You're sweet," and then Boyle cuts in a

FIGURE 7.7

At the end of shot (a) Kitty starts to smile again. She is moving away from her pain by putting on a happy face, but Boyle doesn't let her get away with it. Instead he cuts to Laura, nodding gravely (b), and doesn't come back to Kitty until he can come in on the shot just as her smile starts to fade (c).

long close-up on Laura so that we can see the dawning of revelation on her face. The time spent on Laura's reaction also gives Kitty time to pull herself together. It is a long beat for each of them as they adjust their objectives and actions to respond to what has just happened, with Laura moving toward her feeling and Kitty turning sharply away from what has passed between them.

Kitty interrupts Laura's reverie, and Boyle gives us just enough time on Laura to see her respond to the interruption before cutting back to Kitty so we can see her grabbing the energy back from Laura and changing the subject completely. Now Boyle uses Toni Collette's performance differently than when her character was on the back foot, needing help. Each of the succeeding shots of Kitty shows the full smile, the complete preparation, action, and recovery of each smile and gesture functioning as a barrier deliberately thrown up between her and Laura, a rejection of Laura's comforting her, a denial of any need to be comforted. So the scene ends at the door, where it started, the relationship apparently unchanged. Kitty is confident, swinging her hips, click-clacking along in her high heels; Laura is disheveled, teary, and vulnerable. But as an audience we witnessed everything changing between them, because the scene was cut on subtext and emotional movement, and we are utterly changed by the intensity of the emotional ride we have just been on.

SUMMARY

In the cutting of emotional rhythms, editors make decisions about the extent to which they manipulate and alter a performance or leave its rhythms intact. The strength of the performance and the relative importance of various emotional moments in the story are each a consideration in the editor's decisions in this process. In shaping the emotional movement the editor throws the energy or intention of one performance across a cut to create the appearance of a cause-and-effect relationship in the movement of emotions. If an editor can see the performers prepare, action, rest movement arcs, or their actions and beats, the editor can use these physical movements as guides for phrasing the emotional movement, its optimal cutting points, and its rhythm across an exchange.

The next chapter will look at the movement of events and inquire into the processes and problems of shaping event rhythm.

ENDNOTES

1. Murch, W., *In the Blink of an Eye,* 1992, p. 62.
2. Schmidt, P., "Introduction," in *Meyerhold at Work,* p. xiii.
3. Pitches, J., *Vsevolod Meyerhold,* p. 55.
4. Murch, W., *In the Blink of an Eye,* 1992, p. 62.

CHAPTER 8

Event Rhythm

Event rhythm is the timing, pacing, and trajectory phrasing of the movement and energy of events over the course of a whole film. It is found in the temporal, kinetic, and energetic flow of story or structure, of sequences, or of a series of two or more scenes. Each scene in which a problem is initiated and resolved or a question is raised and addressed is an event. Sequences in which a series of scenes opens and explores problems, questions, or ideas are events. A series of events collected and shaped into a cause-and-effect relationship is a plot. Shaping the rhythms of events and plots involves balancing the flow of information, ideas, unanswered questions, or character journeys so that enough is happening to engage the interest, but not so much is happening that there is confusion. If at any point the film loses the audience's curiosity, its willingness to stay and find out what happens next, it has lost the momentum and energy of event rhythm.

The process of shaping event rhythms takes into consideration practical factors such as the required length of the finished project, the number of story or informational points that need to be included, and the relative importance or emphasis of these events. In some productions—for example, narrative drama for a 1-hour commercial television slot—the parameters within which editors have choices about these things are very narrow. For these productions, a formula will have been set that dictates a certain amount and flow of information, a certain amount of tension and release. There will be a set number of

FIGURE 8.1

In this sequence from Episode 2, Series 3, of The West Wing *(series creator Aaron Sorkin, 1999 to 2006), flashing lights, moving cameras, emotional tensions, competing points of focus, and multiple agendas crowd the frames of eleven shots (with only one setup repeating) as they race by in under 30 seconds. But there's only one question that has been asked and answered: Will the president run for re-election? The series makers sustain our attention on that question while reminding us of all the stakes and keeping the question in motion, like a fast-moving soccer ball, around the array of stakeholders. The editor, Bill Johnson, A.C.E., organizes the motion of that ball in play, revealing the president in close-up only when he reveals his answer. Using this kind of classical patterning, even with the very contemporary movement feeling in most episodes, the physical and emotional movement of the* West Wing *series matches the movement of plot in significance and energizes the viewing audience with concern for the characters as much as for concern with the issues or events.*

story beats or plot points between each commercial break, and each of these sequences will end with a high-stakes, open question to be resolved after the break. In art films, conversely, there are rarely such constraints, and the event rhythm may well take precedence over any other consideration in the structuring of a film.

The process of shaping event rhythm is not just a collection of practical considerations; it is also a storytelling process. It shapes the ebb and flow of tension and release and the synchronization of attention over the whole, and it takes into account the audience's cultural experience and expectations with genre and form. The editor relies on implicit or explicit information about who the audience is for the project when shaping its event rhythm. Movies, like people, are variable in their rhythms. Film rhythms, especially their overall event rhythms, are designed for particular audiences, and an editor needs to know her audience to make the rhythms that will sync up with theirs. In commercially driven cinema, it is implicitly understood by film studio executives and their marketing experts that people within a given target market will share rhythmic propensities—their bodies, paces, energies, attention spans, and cycles of tension and release are different from those of people in another target market. Teenage boys can sink into sync with some rhythms, middle-aged women with others. Rhythms for one target market will of course have some commonalities with rhythms designed for another target market because all spectators have beating hearts, inhalations and exhalations, spans of attention, mirror neurons, and other physiological rhythms that are the "target" of the film's rhythms. But different audiences have different rhythmic propensities, and this includes methods and rates of assimilation of information about events.

Plots are designed differently for different audiences. Their genres and subject matters inherently contain different flows of energy and tension and release. An action film designed for a mass audience might, for example, be about saving the world in a hurry from a cyber terrorist. This is not a plot that can dawdle, reflect, or ruminate. The action must not only continually move forward, but it must do so with enormous energy and conviction, fighting its way through escalating physical and psychological obstacles, under pressure of the threat of imminent collapse of civilization as we know it. On the other hand, for a small-scale drama that is, for example, a psychological study of mourning, the time and energy are treated commensurately with the subject. They are measured and introspective with very few plot events that would require a change of energy, a renewed attack on a problem, or a hasty retreat from danger. These plot examples are not only designed in content for very different audiences, but they are rhythmically shaped for these different audiences' propensities, and their flow is given a form defined both by their stories and by the feeling states that their audiences seek and expect from these stories.

When I began researching this book, many people asked me if it would include a study of the rhythmic expectations in different cultures. While this is a fascinating area for consideration, it is not included in the book in the end because my purpose is not to say a particular culture has this or that kind of rhythm, but to offer some ideas about what rhythm is and how it is shaped, that can be used effectively for the analysis of any rhythm and applied to the process of shaping any rhythm. Certainly cultures have different rhythmic propensities, and these are shaped by a large number of variables, including the sense of time, space, and the appropriate use of energy that define social interactions, languages, and stories of a culture, the history of storytelling in the culture, and the specific artists that have emerged from the culture and shaped its understanding of what is a good screen story experience. The plots are different—the very idea of what constitutes a plot may be quite different—and the physical, emotional, and event rhythms that could be said to characterize different cultures will demonstrate distinctiveness and diversity, at least for as long as cultures remain diverse. The principles put forward in this book could be used on a case-by-case basis to develop an understanding of the kinds of expectations and synchronizations that different national cinemas create or sustain.

It would also be possible to apply these principles of shaping rhythm to the strictly constructed "restorative three-act structure"[1] found in many Hollywood films. But it is perhaps not necessary to make that analysis in this book, because the rules of shaping these rhythms have been prescribed in many screenwriting manuals.[2] The points in time at which climaxes, crises, and reversals are supposed to take place in these structures are well known both by the filmmakers and by their audiences. The editor's job is to add freshness to these well-worn structures with their shaping of the flow of emotions, images, and sounds, their feel for the timing, pacing, and trajectory phrasing of moments and stories, but not to stretch the structure beyond a point where audience expectations can be met and satisfied. Very often, if an editor is shaping a drama script, the work is not to invent some new pattern of rise and fall of tension and release, but to cut away the extraneous, or build up moments so that the overall shape of event rhythm and plot can conform to the expectations audiences and filmmakers have for a restorative three-act structure. This process of shaping event rhythms to conform to a known pattern of cycles of tension and release is a process of using intuition accrued through the experience of many screen stories to make a film "feel right."

SHAPING THE RHYTHM OF EVENTS

If an editor is working with scripted material and has shaped it according to the script's structure but it does not yet "feel right," it may be worthwhile for her to think about the cycles of tension and release she is shaping and how they are built around open dramatic questions. A dramatic question is a question with something at stake and an action implied. A dramatic plot will have a number of these questions at play. There will probably be an overarching question of the story; for example, a mystery will pose the question, "Who dunnit?" Within that question there is a series of other questions, often about relationships, motives, and the process of discovery of the answer to the larger question. The energy of these smaller questions is the energy that propels the viewer's interest forward. The editor has some tools available to her for shaping the flow of questions and answers if the plot as written doesn't feel right when cut together. She can, for example, use timing, in the sense of when she puts events in relation to each other, shifting around the sequence in which they unfold to reshape the plot so that questions are posed by events and resolved in a more satisfying flow. She can also employ the tool of the ellipsis, which is strategically pulling out bits of the action that resolve the questions of scenes or events and cutting to a scene in which the answer has been accepted and assimilated by the characters and they are in the process of acting on it. This creative ellipsis on the part of the editor activates the viewer's mind in piecing together the cause-and-effect chain, and this activation has an energizing effect.

Throwing the energy, as discussed in Chapter 7, is an idea about shaping the energy of an emotional exchange into a meaningful cause-and-effect chain that can be repurposed for shaping the large arcs of events in relation to each other. The flow of energy in one scene or sequence has to be "thrown" to the next one so that events feel as though they are in response to one another, and the cause-and-effect chain of the whole holds together. If events are given too much emphasis by duration or by stress accent, they may feel disproportionate to the events which follow them. Similarly, if they whip by too quickly, they may not have the impact needed to make what follows them feel related. The useful question for an editor here is: What is this scene, sequence, or event about? This may at first seem obvious, but the answer is not always so obvious and needs to be considered not just in relation to itself, but in relation to events that preceded and that follow. A scene may appear to be about a car crash, for example, but really be about rebuilding trust between two characters. If the event is cut only for the text and not for the subtext, then events later on, where the trust is at stake, will lose their links in the cause-and-effect chain.

Sometimes scripts are overwritten because things that are in black-and-white print don't have the same energy, impact, or information that is present in sound and moving image. One of my first editing teachers, Sara Bennett, tells a story that neatly sums this up. She had a job where there were ten pages of script setting up a character's social and economic status. On-screen, the ten pages were cut down to one shot of him slamming the door of his Mercedes, which said it all. Directors may easily have the same thing happen when shaping a performance. When the performance is in little bits being shot over hours, days, or weeks, it may be hard to tell when an emotional moment has been stated. Once the editor starts shaping these moments into sequences, though, she can see when an emotional event has already occurred. Leaving in moments in the unfolding of an event that are emotional repeats will dull the impact and break the momentum of the audience attention or interest in what happens next.

The creation of event rhythm relies on knowledge about when and how the spectator has assimilated the import of one event and can use his understanding of that information when assessing the next. If a film meets the requirements of subject matter or form to engage the interest of a particular audience, but that audience is then found to not want to know, to already know, or to not care "what happens next," then the event rhythm has been misjudged. The editor, in this case, can ask herself: What changes are taking place at a given moment that justify the duration, emphasis, and placement of a particular event? Soviet film director and theorist Vsevolod Pudovkin articulated this principle as early as 1929. His notion of "transference of interest of the intent spectator" applies at the level of shot-to-shot relations and event to event. Just as pulse is the smallest unit of rhythm, it is also, in a way, the largest unit, as the events in a film pulse between posing questions and answering them, between creating tension and releasing it:

> If the scenarist can effect in even rhythm the transference of interest of the intent spectator, if he can so construct the elements of increasing interest that the question "What is happening at the other place?" arises and at the same moment the spectator is transferred whither he wishes to go, then the editing thus created can really excite the spectator.[3]

Since 1929, the methods and rates of assimilation of information by audiences may have changed. Certainly, according to studies done by Barry Salt and by David Bordwell, the average shot lengths in films have been cut in half.[4] However, the practice of creating the question in the spectator's mind and then simultaneously resolving that question and creating it anew is still salient to the creation of event rhythm.

CREATING STRUCTURE AND RHYTHM SIMULTANEOUSLY

Before the advent of digital nonlinear editing systems, editors were taught to cut "structure first, then rhythm." Editors working on actual 16 mm or 35 mm celluloid strips of film had to take care not to mangle the work print by excessive handling. So they would make assemblies of all of the good takes laid end to end. Then choices would be made about which take of a given shot to use. That choice would be loosely cut, or rough cut, into a structure so that the editor and director would then be able to view the structure, or the events that would occur, and the order of the shots that would convey them. The choices made in the refining of the cut (from rough to fine cut) were, in this particular process, the rhythm choices I have discussed under the headings of physical and emotional rhythm. The processes of creating assemblies and rough cuts were considered processes of creating structure. Although these story structure cuts would have event rhythm inherent in the placement of events in relation to one another, that rhythm would not have been refined to include shaping of relative durations or emphases. This would happen in the transition from the rough-cut to the fine-cut stage.

With the advent of digital nonlinear editing technology, editors no longer have to worry about mangling film and can make and unmake and remake edits without harming the actual film print. This freedom to manipulate the precise timing, pacing, and trajectory phrasing of shots and cuts has changed the expectations that directors and producers bring to the first screening of a cut. It is now very unusual to make an assembly and rough cut of structure without an articulated rhythm. Instead, the first presentation of a structure will have been given some rhythmic consideration at the level of the individual cut, the scene, the sequence, and the whole. Then, the process is to refine, adjust, or completely change structure *and* the rhythm of the structure simultaneously. In the contemporary process, the shaping of rhythm is part of the shaping of structure. Throughout the cutting process, from the first cut forward, events are restructured and rhythms are refined simultaneously.

USING KINESTHETIC ANTIPATHY

One pitfall that needs to be avoided when cutting structure and rhythm simultaneously is becoming attached to lovely individual cuts or moments and trying to keep them in the film even if they do not really have a place in the structure. To avoid this, I have developed a particularly useful awareness of kinesthetic empathy, which is actually a skill at pinpointing my kinesthetic antipathy.

During cutting processes I am, as most editors are, under pressure, working long hours, and juggling schedules, expectations, deadlines, technology, egos, and so on. When I find, at certain points in the process, that I am getting very tired, I usually just imbibe more tea and M&Ms and chalk it up to the wear and tear of daily life. Soon, however, I begin to realize that, although I'm tired, I'm not always tired *in the same way* in the edit suite. I begin to tune my awareness to the particular kinesthetic experience of watching the film and find that I can observe myself "taking the ride" and pinpoint quite precise moments of ennui, particular moments when I stop physically attending to the trajectory of the film's movement and tune out. Once I realize that my tiredness is being triggered at precise points, I am able to use this pinpointed kinesthetic antipathy to ask myself questions, such as: What is the information being conveyed in this passage? How is it being conveyed? When has it been assimilated? When am I ready to know what happens next? This is a way of looking at the visually lovely material and polished cuts and asking myself if I am being seduced by beauty that worked well on its own but actually doesn't work in the structure.

Cutting documentary and cutting scripted drama diverge somewhat in their processes for shaping event rhythm. The bulk of the editor's work on a documentary is in finding and shaping the story at a structural level, whereas, in scripted drama, although an editor may make some pretty radical changes to the way the story unfolds or even what the story is, she is working from a base that has been determined before it is shot. In documentary the shooting may have been determined—that is, decisions would have been made about where to shoot, what events, confrontations, interviews, archival material, and so on to capture—but the story probably has not been finally determined.

The story in a documentary gets written from the raw filmed material. It is made from the response of subjects to questions and unfolding situations being revealed in the process of shooting, not necessarily before it. So the bulk of the cutting time is spent on shaping unscripted material into a structured experience, a story. The editor's first concerns are clarity of perspective, coherence, and creating a compelling experience or convincing set of ideas from the events, images, and sounds of the chaotic real world. This process of structuring material involves figuring out what's in and what's out based on the ideas that the events, images, and sounds convey when juxtaposed. So shaping rhythms is a part of shaping structure. The energy and pace of material will influence what stays in and what goes out as the information gets structured because meaning is understood as much through *how* information is conveyed as through *what* facts are given or statements are made. Timing dictates where to place shots, ideas, and the reveals of information in relation to one another. The ordering, weighting, and shaping of the movement, time, and energy of events, ideas, images, and information are part of the process of telling the story. Rhythm is not the whole of the range of concerns editors are grappling with in the documentary cutting process, but it is a substantial influencing factor in the choices editors make about how meaning will be created as story events unfold.

Editing is often compared to sculpting, and the two aspects of the metaphor are debated in this way: Is editing more like chipping away bits of stone to reveal the sculpture or adding bits of clay to construct the sculpture? Because editing is not *exactly* like sculpting, it is possible to say "both." The shaping of event rhythm is, in the first instance, like chipping away bits of stone. It is a matter of working with the script and determining where along the spectrum between respecting it absolutely and altering it radically the cut will fall. I have never yet met a script that was a perfected sculpture. All of them, when translated into moving images, require carving to realize the shape within them. As that shape begins to reveal itself, in the contemporary model in which structure and rhythm are formed almost simultaneously, editing becomes more like adding bits of clay, as in using material to soften curves or changes in the story or to heighten emphasis or extend duration. The process of sculpting event rhythms relies on knowledge about the film's audience and its rates and methods of assimilation of events. So the editor continually has to put herself in the audience's position, refreshing her own kinesthetic empathy and antipathy to feel *with* the rise and fall of the event's cycles of tension and release.

REINTEGRATING RHYTHMS

In most productions, physical, emotional, and event rhythms are all three at work, all the time, to create the movement and energy of the film, realized in time. The physical moves emotions, the emotional moves events, and the events move visually and aurally. In this way, the rhythm of the film is experienced as a whole, greater than the sum of its parts.

Delineating distinctions between kinds of rhythm is useful as a method for understanding aspects of the whole. Separating physical, emotional, and event rhythms is a way of talking about strands of rhythm that may always, or at any given point, be present in any two shots. One place where the distinctions can be useful is when an editor needs to know what dominates the movie she is cutting: What kind of movie is it? What kind of sequence or scene or cut? What are its priorities? The questions that each kind of rhythm poses can be asked of the raw material. The answers will point clearly to the film's priorities. But the awareness that at any given point all three kinds of rhythm may be present will be helpful in making the cut that much more subtle and articulate in its rhythms.

A film is like a living body in that it has physical movement, emotional movement, and changes in circumstances or events all occurring, balancing, being assimilated, and working in a cause-and-effect relationship with one another almost all of the time. The editor, who shapes the film's rhythms by using knowledge of the rhythms of the world and the rhythms of her own body, knows that there is not much life in a film without all three rhythms counterpointing, energizing, and shaping each other. To shape rhythms with a balance of physical movement, emotions, and events, intuitive editors draw on their own internal balancing act of physical, emotional, and event rhythms. The particular approaches to each kind of rhythm discussed herein can be employed at moments when a production clearly prioritizes one kind of rhythm, as, for example, *Thursday's Fictions* does in the "Now" scene or *The Hours* does in the scene between Toni Collette and Julianne More. But once physical rhythms and emotional rhythms are shaped in a given passage, they still need to be integrated into the rhythm of the whole.

The shaping of event rhythm takes into account the aspects of physical and emotional rhythm that audiences respond to and weaves them into an integrated, rhythmically articulated structure. Accomplished storytellers will set up these rhythmic patterns from the outset. The openings of their films establish time, place, characters, and dramatic questions; they also establish the rhythm to be developed, the feeling of the story that will unfold. The following case studies focus on the beginnings of two films and how they set up the films' overall event rhythm. From the openings, we can tell that each film has a radically different rhythm because, although they are both stories of Italian mobsters in America, they are told from radically different perspectives and are set in radically different worlds. Each one's rhythm is an integrated experience of the movement of images, sounds, and emotions that conveys the significance of events in a direct and immediate way, letting us feel something's impact and move on to what happens next. These patterns of time, movement, and energy are established in the first minutes and then developed and woven over the whole of the structure to convey the story rhythmically.

CASE STUDY: *THE GODFATHER* (FRANCIS FORD COPPOLA, 1972)

The core rhythm of *The Godfather* is stated in the first shot, established in the first scene, developed in the first sequence, and consistently maintained as a storytelling element conveying the themes and attitudes of the film. There is another countering rhythm in the film that is set up in the second scene and appears at intervals throughout the film until, 2½ hours later, in one of the most famous scenes in editing history, the two rhythmic qualities are intercut to bring the film to a climactic and complete realization.

The first shot of the film is a 2½ minute pull back from the face of a middle-aged Italian man, Bonasera (Salvatore Corsitto), telling a harrowing story of his daughter's abuse at the hands of callous young American boys. The shot slowly reveals the silhouette of the Godfather (Marlon Brando), who is listening. The physical movement of time and energy in this shot starts out being concentrated in Bonasera's face and eyes as he states his beliefs (beliefs that set up one of the central tensions of the film, the tension between the new life and ways of America and those of Sicily, the old country). But as the frame widens out and pulls away from Bonasera's face, the darkness around him becomes more engulfing, his expressions less visible, his stature and energy diminishes, until the silhouette of the Godfather fills a third or more of the frame. The stillness creates physical tension by holding the question of who will disturb this physical space and energy with movement and how.

The emotional rhythm in this shot is in the tension between the movement of Bonasera's voice, his cadence of outrage, counterpointed by the movement of the camera away from him, pulling back evenly, dispassionately. It is as though Bonasera is throwing his emotional energy into a growing void. This handling of emotion is also thematic for *The Godfather*. The shaping of the time, movement, and energy of emotion in this shot speaks directly to the spectator about how emotion is handled in this world: the outrages and blood feuds are kept at a distance, handled deliberately; they are "just business," not personal (Fig. 8.2).

The first scene of the Godfather is an event that will be repeated four more times in the first sequence: someone will come into the Godfather's office and ask him for a favor, which, on this day of his daughter's wedding, he cannot refuse. Each time the supplicant achieves his objective, but so does the Godfather, who makes a business of placing others under obligation to him. The rhythm of this first scene—stately, controlled, sustained, void of any physical or emotional violence—establishes one of the two initiating rhythms that work in counterpoint to each other to make the overall event rhythm of the film.

FIGURE 8.2
Amid somber colors and stately movements Bonasera whispers his request into the Godfather's (Marlon Brando's) ear. [Photo credit: Paramount; The Kobal Collection]

The other rhythmic quality of the film is established in the second scene, the scene of the Godfather's daughter's wedding party (Fig. 8.3). This buoyant party is filled with effusive gestures, bright colors, crowded, busy frames, and movement in all directions. The brightly jagged physical movement of people, voices, patterns of leaves and dresses, and songs are the meaning, just as, later in the film, the bright, jagged movement of extreme violence will carry the meaning

FIGURE 8.3
Al Martino and Talia Shire in the raucous movement of bright colors and sounds in the wedding party scene of The Godfather
(Francis Ford Coppola, 1972). [Photo credit: Paramount; The Kobal Collection]

of the physical energy that disrupts and punctuates the dispassionate rhythm of the other transactions.

The first and second scenes of *The Godfather* establish the pattern that the event rhythm of the film will have: grave deliberation occasionally jarred by energetic outbursts. In the climactic scene, known as the Baptism Scene, the two qualities are brought together. The stately, composed shots of a Catholic baptism in a cavernous church, a holy place of exalted worship, are intercut with the sudden, shocking brutal murders of five of the Godfather's enemies. By pulling the sound of the liturgy and the church music across the shots of the murders, the editors William Reynolds, A.C.E., and Peter Zinner, A.C.E., impress the stately, sanctifying sounds of the family's beliefs across the images of the horror they are committing. By timing the cuts to convey the clear culpability and knowledge the Godfather has of the violence he is perpetrating, and slicing through the peaceful baptism with countering thrusts of the ferocious energy of vengeance, the editors create a masterful dance back and forth that encapsulates the meaning of the film: the clash is what shapes the character of a man destined to be a powerful "Godfather."

In *The Godfather*, as in all great films, physical, emotional, and event rhythms are integrated. Together they are the shape of time, movement, and energy that express the meaning of the film. In *The Godfather* the shaping of the rhythm creates our understanding, at an immediate, visceral level, of the grave and ceremonial world in which honor and family sanctify, contextualize, even justify the chaotic and jarring acts of extreme violence that both disrupt and fuel it.

CASE STUDY: *GOODFELLAS* (MARTIN SCORSESE, 1990)

The two driving forces that structure the events of the entire film *Goodfellas* are set up in the first scene: a murder and a lifelong desire. The first is the murder. A guy in a trunk is stabbed and shot. We don't know who he is or why he is being killed so cold-bloodedly until an hour or so later, and we don't know the consequences of that murder until yet another hour after that. By organizing the story events in this way, to play out at intervals over the whole film, the writers, Nicholas Pileggi and Martin Scorsese, and the editor, Thelma Schoonmaker, create a story arc that functions the way that pillars might function in a building, supporting the roof at regular intervals but not cluttering the space between them. They also start off the film with a blast of physical activity and an insight into the emotions of this story.

When the guy in the trunk is well and truly dead, having been stabbed nine times and then shot four times, the narrator and central character of

FIGURE 8.4

In Goodfellas *the first introduction to the protagonist Henry Hill is as a slightly dazed man, buffeted by events, but also complicit in them, as he helps out with a routine murder and stays on track with his lifelong ambition to be a gangster.*

the story, Henry Hill (Ray Liotta), steps forward to close the trunk as his voice-over tells us, "As far back as I can remember, I always wanted to be a gangster." This introduces the film's other through-line of events: the story of Henry Hill's life and his rise and fall in the underworld. The voice-over is ironic. The killing is ignominious; there is nothing great or even courageous about it. Is this what young Henry, even from childhood, aspired to? Henry's statement is punctuated by another irony: a freeze-frame on him looking detached but slightly dazed (Fig. 8.4). Freeze-frames are a convention often used in cheaply produced dramas. In soap operas they hang in the air, directing the audience to sustain the emotion and recognize the importance of an event. But in *Goodfellas*, the freeze-frames emphasize the ignominious. They place weight and significance by stilling the constant motion and creating an accent. But the accent is almost random, resting on off-key compositions, occurring mid-action rather than at the climax or resolution, offering us a chance to examine something in detail in such a way as to actually undercut its potential importance. They freeze emotion and action and let us look at it dispassionately, make our own judgments about the lives it is framing: Are they fast, fun, and sexy, or meaningless, immoral, and nasty? Or both?

The film's first freeze-frame, accompanied by the raucous trumpet of an upbeat jazz song, plays with the conventional use of the freeze-frame, using its implication that this is a significant moment, to place emphasis on the ordinariness of Henry closing the trunk and the coolness of being a thug. It indicates that anything could be significant in this world, and the insignificant, the closing of the trunk, can be given as much weight and emphasis as murder.

The details of this scene are important because they set up the physical and emotional cadences that are repeated in macro by the rhythm of events throughout the film.

In *Goodfellas* murder is not more or less important than pasta. The film is not about the Godfather or the boss of a Mafia gang, who is the still center of the whirlwind of death and life around him. It is about the guys who do the boss's bidding, the guys who are in the vortex, flailing, swinging, drinking, laughing, cooking, killing, and never ratting on their friends. These guys are in constant motion, and the weight and gravity of events in their lives are not measured by the same standards as the weight and seriousness of events in other people's lives. This lack of moral compass is a central theme of the film, which is expressed (as it is in all great films) as much through the form of the telling as through the information being told.

The rhythm of *Goodfellas* is characterized by fluid and continuous motion and the ironic counterweighting of events in life with events of crime and death. Some of the most startling, momentous scenes of the film are of ordinary events, such as entering a club by the back door or telling a funny story around the dinner table. These events are accented in the unfolding of the film by the physical or emotional movement within them.

The scene in which Henry and his girlfriend (Lorraine Bracco) enter the Copacabana (a popular and exclusive nightclub in New York in the 1960s) through the back way is told entirely in one dizzying, sweeping glorious steadicam shot, which, through its intricately choreographed time, movement, and energy, synchronizes us with the girlfriend. We share her physical experience of being dazzled and swept up in the glamour of the back-alley life.

The scene in which Henry's friend Tommy (Joe Pesci) tells a funny story and then lashes out at Henry for laughing is filled with an extraordinary tension and fear about Tommy's paranoia and ability to turn on his friends. Nothing much happens in this scene; it turns out Tommy was just teasing Henry. But the emotional tension it creates colors the rest of Tommy's story so that, later, when Tommy casually shoots a waiter and kills him, there is very little fuss—it's just Tommy being Tommy.

The event rhythms in *Goodfellas* build to a cataclysmic sequence in which humor, motion, trivia, and passion bang into each other across hard cuts of stinging rock-and-roll music, perpetual cocaine-induced manic movement, and the basso continuo of paranoia, embodied in a helicopter buzzing overhead, following Henry through his harried day.

The sequence starts with a title card announcing the date and time: May 11, 1980, 6:55 AM. Rock and roll slides in under the title. There's a cut to a close-up of cocaine being inhaled, guns being dropped into a paper bag, and on the next shot the lead guitar kicks in as Henry exits his quiet, brick-fronted suburban home, wiping the traces of coke from his nose. The combination of music, camera moves, and cuts that follow in the next four shots set up the whirlwind ride that's coming over the next 10 minutes:

- Close-up of paper bag full of guns into the trunk, fast pan up to Henry's squinting up at the sky;

- Cut to helicopter flying between the trees;

- Cut back to a quick pan past Henry, glimpse the bag, the trunk slams down;

- Wide shot tracks in on Henry as he hurries into the car;

- Jump cut, he's driving and smoking.

Then in comes the relatively laconic voice-over, counterpointing the wildly erratic movement of the cuts, and adding a layer of irony. "I was going to be busy all day. . . ." Henry explains he has to sell guns, pick up his brother, deal drugs, and cook the pasta sauce.

The time of day appears on the screen at irregular points in the recount of Henry's day; it has an objective, distanced quality, as though labeling the evidence as in a police report, but so erratically it would mock any jury's desire for an orderly, clear, evidentiary report of the events leading to Henry's arrest. And what exactly is relevant as Henry hurtles toward his demise?

8:05 AM: Gun sale unsuccessful, Henry hatches a new plan and narrowly avoids a car accident. The series of preposterously repeating cuts from his foot on the brakes to his face as he screeches to a halt is entirely in subjective time—this is what it feels like to Henry, not necessarily the facts of what really happened.

8:45 AM: He picks up his brother, gets forced into having a checkup, the doctor is jovial, but Henry is sweating. He pops a calming Valium but the rock and roll is screaming. Voice-over: "Now my plan was . . . "

11:30 AM: Henry has yet another new plan; he's creating dinner and a sense of order, but at least one of these isn't going so well.

About 4 minutes into the sequence, 12:30, 1:30, and 3:30 all appear in 30 seconds of screen time, highlighting the sense that time is erratic, careening past wildly and then sticking on a detail. Music cuts in and out suddenly but exultantly, emphasizing the energy and anarchy of the movement through the day. The hard-driving rock and roll gives flow, direction, and energy to an action and then deserts it abruptly, only to slam in at another moment, another screech of tires or hit of cocaine.

Two minutes later, it's 6:30 and Henry is running out of the house again. "I told my brother to keep an eye on the stove. All day long the poor guy's been watching helicopters and tomato sauce. See, I had to get over to Sandy's, mix the stuff once, and then get back to the gravy." The "stuff," of course, is the cocaine, not the sauce, but even though one can get you arrested and thrown in jail for life and the other cannot, they both have to be stirred.

Fifteen seconds later, it's 8:30 PM, more coke, a complicated love affair, and back in time for dinner, which, suddenly (at 10:45 PM, the on-screen time tells us) is ending. Henry doesn't look happy; nothing's amounted to much, the family is annoying to be with, and he has to get on the road to get rid of the coke. Leaving the house, Henry is arrested.

This climactic sequence, as with the Baptism Scene in *The Godfather*, brings together the rhythms of the whole film and their meanings to create a sense that Henry's destiny is defined by the way he lives, and the rhythms of his life have spun out of his control. These rhythms have sucked us in, too, so we feel with them how fun it is to be constantly in motion, fleeting, dodging, ducking, and sliding over precipices to land on our feet. We're with Henry on his wild ride, exulting in the spin and whirl as long as it stays in motion, reflecting only when we're forced to see the consequences, the debris left in the dust by the tornado of this kind of life.

SUMMARY

Physical rhythm creates tension by posing the question of win or lose, catch or escape, or, at an even more subliminal level, by creating a pattern that the spectator participates in and wants to see fulfilled. Emotional rhythm creates tension or questions at the level of every cut. Each throw of a character's emotional energy, each emotional maneuver he tries, is a question being asked: What will be the response or the emotional effect of this action? Event rhythm is working at the level of the scene, the sequence, or the whole film. Each scene is a question in a drama: Will the character achieve his objective or be thwarted? It is actually impossible to separate the experience of event rhythm from the experiences of physical and emotional rhythm because the three kinds of rhythm are cumulative. Event rhythm is the flow of both the physical and the emotional through scenes, sequences, and structures that release information in a way that supports and conveys the sensations and emotions of the film.

ENDNOTES

1. Dancyger, K., and Rush, J., *Alternative Scriptwriting, Writing Beyond the Rules*, p. 16

2. The 1988 book *How to Write a Movie in 21 Days* by Viki King (Harper & Row, New York) not only proposes that the structure of a film has a very definite, required rhythm for its unfolding, but that a writer also has a rhythm for writing it. This book was recommended to me by my first film teacher, Pablo Frasconi, who warned that although it may be possible to write a film in 21 days, they would have to be 21 very good days, and these good days, may be just as likely occur over a period of three years as three weeks, which illustrates the difference in requirements on the internal rhythms of the editor to those of a writer! For a diagrammatic layout of the rhythm of events prescribed by King, see p. 40.

3. Pudovkin, V., "Film technique," reprinted in *Film Theory and Criticism*, p. 87.

4. See Bordwell, D., "Intensified continuity: Visual style in contemporary American film—Critical essay," *Film Quarterly,* p. 16.

CHAPTER 9

Style

The word "style" in editing refers to an aggregate of choices. It's a tricky word in that it can be quite amorphous, but it's useful in the discussions between directors, producers, cinematographers, and editors, because it allows them to imagine the whole production as a coherent rhythmic construction and discuss what the final will look and feel like.

To talk about the range of choices available in determining editing style, it is useful to break down the possibilities available, what they are, and what effects they create, so that these conversations between creatives can have some common terms of reference.

Editing style is generally determined by the director when they work with all of the collaborators on a production to manifest their vision; that is, to choose what shots, décor, sounds, music, and digital effects will be generated. The editor is the collaborator in charge of bringing these materials together. What she has to work with is the material at hand, and ideally, editing style will have been a core consideration, either implicitly or explicitly, in the generation of the material to be edited. Editing will have implicitly been a consideration in writing the script, as the writer juxtaposes scenes and images to tell a story or articulate a structure. It becomes an explicit consideration when the words in the script are made into shots and everyone has to think about how these shots will cut together.

In this chapter I propose two ranges of choices editors make that can be used to discuss and analyze editing style.

One range of choices editors and directors have to make about material generated and how it will cut together can be placed along a spectrum running from montage to decoupage (Fig. 9.1).

I am borrowing and adapting these terms for my own purposes in this discussion and will explain their origin briefly, below, before describing my usage of each and how I think they function as elements of editing style.

The second range of choices editors and directors make runs along a spectrum from what I will call collision to linkage (Fig. 9.2).

"Collision" and "linkage," words borrowed respectively from Eisenstein and his contemporary, Pudovkin, were the subject of heated debate and much animosity between these two key figures in the development of film in the Soviet Union in the 1920s. Eisenstein and Pudovkin each approached editing and ideas about film form differently, but the passage of time has softened the ideological distinctions between these two approaches to such a degree that we can now consider them as points along a spectrum of choices about style.

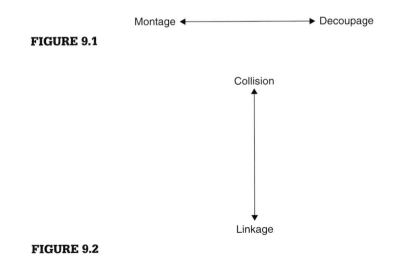

Montage ←———————————→ Decoupage

FIGURE 9.1

FIGURE 9.2

I will first discuss montage and decoupage, and then I will briefly outline some of the key ideas behind collision and linkage before I bring them all together to look at some case studies of their possible combinations.

MONTAGE

"Montage" is the word the French use for editing; it would literally translate into English as "assemblage" or "assembly." The implications of montage in French are both technical and creative. Technically, the editing is assemblage of pieces into a whole. Creatively, montage is assembling of images and sounds into relations that generate rhythms, ideas, and experiences of a whole.

My use of the word montage, however, is going to be slightly different from the French usage, which refers to the whole of editing operations. Instead I will draw on the common understanding of the term among English-speaking editors, who use "montage" to mean a particular kind of editing. To make a montage in an English-speaking country generally means to bring together images and sounds that are unrelated in time or space to create an impression, an idea, or an effect.

Films such as *Koyaanisqatsi* (Godfrey Reggio, 1982) and *Baraka* (Godfrey Reggio, 1992) are examples of montage in this sense. They are constructed from a wide range of images collected at different times and from all over the world and associated together to give rise in the viewer's mind of an impression or idea about the relations of humans to nature and the direction our cultures and civilizations may be heading in. There is no narration that explicitly states these themes, but the power of montage is such that these ideas arise most vividly in our minds—we as viewers make connections between the images that have been assembled together to reach an understanding of the meaning of their overall composition.

It is quite unusual to have entire feature films constructed in this way; more typically, there will be montage sequences within a feature film.

Often montage, or assembly of images unrelated in time and space, may be used in realist narrative feature films as a device for suggesting the inner, subjective mental state of a character who is hallucinating, dreaming, on drugs, or so overcome with emotion or sensation that he is outside of ordinary time and space.

This sense of montage as the close juxtaposition of disconnected images is a mainstay of advertisements, music videos, and those title sequences that summarize and introduce the themes and structure of the whole film. In these contexts, montage is a technique that allows audiences to surmise a message through their very powerful experience of making associations—an experience that is carefully modulated and shaped by rhythm.

DECOUPAGE

Decoupage is another term that I have appropriated from the French and am slightly changing or reinterpreting for the purposes of discussing style. In French, "decoupage" means, roughly, cutting something up with the intention of putting it back together again. It is used in the French film industry to describe the process of marking up a script to show the shots that will be used to cover each scene or action. The script is in a sense "cut up" into shots, the intention being, of course, to put these shots together in the edit suite to make the whole.

I am once again altering the French use of the word and using decoupage in English to describe a very specific kind of cutting up with the intention of putting back together, which is the cutting up of something that *could* unfold in real time and space into shots that will be put back together to create the *impression* of the events they contain unfolding in real time and space. Films that employ the Hollywood continuity style use decoupage in this sense as a primary mode of organizing the shots to tell the story.

The important question about using decoupage in this sense in a film is: Why would you do it? Why shoot something that could simply be done in one shot, in real time and space, and cut it into many shots that may have to be taken at many different times and in different configurations of the space, so that you can then put them back together to create the impression of one time and place?

One answer, of course, is rhythm. What the multiple shots provide an editor with is a much finer degree of control over the shaping of time, energy, and movement. Each shot and take of a scene that could have unfolded in real time and space will contain its own unique potential for contributing to rhythm. Performances will have different uses of time: faster or slower, shorter or longer. Shots will have different uses of space: close-ups, two-shots, wide shots, or other configurations. They will also each contain their own movement—movement of camera, characters, or composition, and the near-infinite range of energies with which these kinds of movement can be executed.

So, for the purposes of this discussion, montage is the association of things unrelated in time and space, and decoupage is the cutting up of things that could have unfolded in a single continuous time and space. These two approaches are being placed at either end of a spectrum, and the style of an edit may fall at one end or the other of that spectrum, but may also fall in the area between the two edges of the spectrum.

POINTS ALONG THE SPECTRUM FROM MONTAGE TO DECOUPAGE

One editing operation that is somewhere between montage and decoupage on the spectrum is "temporal ellipsis." Using temporal ellipses simply means cutting out bits of time, along the lines of the well-worn aphorism "drama is life with the boring bits cut out." Although that does not really describe the whole of what drama is, it is useful to a writer or an editor, each of whom can cut out time between events to highlight special moments to sustain the tension of an open question or simply to make the story move along faster, more rhythmically, or without irrelevancies.

FIGURE 9.3

Humphrey Bogart as Rick and Ingrid Bergman as Elsa in a romantic moment, one of many from a sequence of elided romantic moments in a flashback of Rick and Elsa's early days together in Casablanca *(Michael Curtiz, 1942). [Photo credit: Warner Bros; The Kobal Collection]*

A classic example of a sequence that relies on temporal ellipses to tell the story of a whole relationship in just a few minutes is the montage sequence in *Casablanca* (Michael Curtiz, 1942), which tells the back-story of the two main characters when they were young and in love, in Paris at the start of the war. There are images of Rick (Humphrey Bogart) and Elsa (Ingrid Bergman) laughing and walking in the streets of Paris, on a boat on the Seine, in a restaurant, and so on. These images are not exactly unrelated in time and space; in theory they could have been shot continuously, but then this section of the film would have been several days long and jam-packed with irrelevancies. So there is strong reference to continuous time and space, pushing this sequence away from the pure end of the spectrum that we are calling montage. However, although they could have been shot continuously and then cut up, they do not *actually* present continuous time and space. The ellipses are there precisely for the purpose of showing time elapsing and to give rise to the impression of love deepening over time. This impression is something we surmise from the association of images. Therefore, it is also not pure decoupage. The temporal ellipses within this sequence fall somewhere on the spectrum between montage and decoupage. The choice to make the sequence a somewhat discontinuous association of images and to make it also refer strongly to a continuous unfolding of time and space is a style choice.

Temporal ellipsis *between* scenes is another point on the spectrum between montage and decoupage. There are very few examples of feature films, documentaries, or television shows in which the duration of the film is the same as the duration of the story. So almost every film has a montage of distinct times and spaces. A film may have scenes within it that are absolutely continuous in time and space; for example, Jim Jarmusch's 1984 film *Stranger Than Paradise,* in which every scene is covered in one long shot. But these completely continuous scenes nonetheless form a montage when they are cut together into the whole time and space of the story. Most films are less extreme than this example and use continuity cutting inside of scenes and then cut these scenes together into a montage in which we surmise the connection between the scenes and the passage of time in the story. The cuts between the scenes can be more or less extreme: they may be cuts between leaving the house and arriving at the office as in a sequence early on in *The Truman Show* (Peter Weir, 1998). Or they may be cuts that collapse nearly 15 years into 1/24 of a second, as in *Citizen Kane*, when the edit between Thatcher wishing Kane a "Merry Christmas" at the age of 10 jumps to a shot of him saying "and a Happy New Year" on Kane's 25th birthday. These two examples illustrate the use of the same technique—temporal ellipses between scenes—with radically different styles, *The Truman Show* using a style much closer on the spectrum to decoupage, whereas the *Citizen Kane* example would have to be placed closer to montage.

What then is the purpose of distinguishing between montage and decoupage? We can use this knowledge, that the editing of a film will sit somewhere on the spectrum from the association of images that are completely unrelated in time and space to the shaping of images to give the impression of continuous time and space, to discuss style. We can ask: What is this project's approach to time and space? Is it different from one scene to the next? Is there a montage sequence within it, and is that montage a wild hallucination or simply a way of running quickly through a series of events? Do the transitions between scenes just cut out the boring bits? Or are they extreme statements about the passage of time?

But the range of choices from montage to decoupage is just one style guide or spectrum. The other style spectrum concerns flow of images and could be described as the range from collision to linkage. We'll look at the spectrum from collision to linkage next, before examining how the two sets of ideas come together to describe editing style and the rhythms in stylistic choices.

COLLISION

Collision is a term borrowed from the great Soviet filmmaker and theorist Sergei Eisenstein, whose ideas and films have had inestimable influence over the development of cinema and in shifting editing from being a means of stitching things together to being an art.

One aspect of Eisenstein's use of the word "collision" is neatly summed up by Louis Giannetti in his book *Understanding Movies*:

> Eisenstein criticized the concept of linked shots for being mechanical and inorganic. He believed that editing ought to be dialectical: the conflict of two shots (thesis and antithesis) produces a wholly new idea (synthesis). Thus, in film terms, the conflict between shot A and shot B is not AB (Kuleshov and Pudovkin) but a qualitatively new factor—C. Transitions between shots should not be flowing, as Pudovkin suggested, but sharp, jolting, even violent. For Eisenstein editing produces harsh collisions, not subtle linkages. A smooth transition, he claimed, was an opportunity lost.[1]

The dialectical ideology behind this notion of collision has, for better or worse, not really survived into the twenty-first century as common parlance among editors and filmmakers. In Eisenstein's terms, collision made the world go round. Change was the result of two opposing forces colliding together, and the energy and explosion of their clash propelled the world's metamorphosis from one system to the next. This idea extends into editing and film form for Eisenstein when he puts together remarkable collisions of various forces within his shots and films to propel ideas and emotions forward.

I often ask my students, by comparison, "What makes the world go round?" and, as I usually teach in developed, democratic, capitalist countries, the students consistently, invariably, and without exception reply, "Money." What they mean is that money is the agent of change, money is the force that can influence the turn of events. It is not, therefore, surprising that collision as a force in editing has been assimilated into editing style as just one way of cutting. It is used to suit the subject matter, and the rhythm of the production at hand. Collision is part of style, not a means of inciting revolution, because the purpose of most productions made in these countries is not to incite revolution but to engage, enlighten, uplift, inform, or entertain a target market.

Eisenstein's aesthetic development of the notion of collision has nonetheless exerted great influence over the development of editing possibilities, and his explanations remain valid and useful ways of describing a way of cutting at one end of the spectrum of stylistic choices available to an editor. Eisenstein's idea of montage is collision of independent shots. And "the degree of incongruence determines the intensity of the impression and determines that tension which becomes the real element of authentic rhythm."[2]

But what does collision or incongruity actually mean for us in terms of how images and sounds are joined? Eisenstein identifies every aspect of image and sound, including light, movement, shape, direction, tone, shot size, focal length, contrast, dimensions, durations, speeds, performances, symbols, and so on, as possible "attractions" to the eye. Each of these is something that might draw our attention in a shot. So a collision is the juxtaposition of differences between these elements rather than, as we shall see in linkage, a juxtaposition of their similarities.

A collision might therefore be a cut that juxtaposes light and dark, close-up and wide shot, movement left to right with right to left, stillness with activity, religion with politics, and so on. Each of these is a little shock, a little challenge to congruity, evenness of flow, smoothness. Even now, when these juxtapositions are so common in our world, it still takes the eye and the mind a bit of time or effort to connect and make sense of things that conflict in these ways or present these little incongruities. Inciting this effort is a way of engaging the audience more actively in putting together the images and surmising the ideas of the film. It is harder work to make these associations connect; it requires a more active viewer. By thus energizing the audience, collision energizes the film. So sequences or films that employ collision as a style can feel more energetic, vibrant, angular, or aggressive.

Collisions of these kinds are routinely used in action scenes, fight scenes, chase scenes, music videos, and ads in which the energy of the production needs to be upbeat and active, even aggressive, to convey its meanings. It is tempting to say that any scene driven by physical rhythm relies on this kind of cutting, and scenes driven by emotional rhythm do not, but this is not the case. Dance scenes, for example, frequently make use of smooth, "uncollided" cutting, whereas conversations may use surprising juxtapositions of frame size, performance, character movement, or other collided elements to make a point or an emotional impact. It is also tempting to say that collision is the same as montage, but as we shall see in the examples below, this is not the case. Montage, in my definition, may be the bringing together of things that are unrelated in time and space, but it is not always a bringing together by collision; sometimes it is a comparison of similarities that gives a montage its driving force.

Collision, then, is about difference, and difference is, according to Eisenstein, what allows us to perceive rhythm in events, in images, in music or sound. If all was the same there would be no rhythm, just a continuous hum in a custard-colored world. Eisenstein's emphasis on the collision of aspects of difference shifts editing from a job of connecting shots to an art of making ideas, images, and sounds an articulated and affectively powerful dance, by creating rhythms out of juxtaposition of contrasting images.

LINKAGE

Eisenstein's less well known but deeply influential contemporary, filmmaker and theorist Vsevolod Pudovkin, put forward a different idea about the function of editing. His notion of linkage, I propose, is less well known because it has, in fact, been more widely assimilated. It has seeped into the culture of editing and filmmaking to such an extent that it is normalized. I have often heard students call smoothly linked editing "normal" cutting or explain that they are going to shoot "normal" shots to make a smoothly linked film. But linkage, like any technique of artistic construction, is, of course, not normal or natural. It has behind it an ideology and an aesthetic purpose, which define its usage and its usefulness.

Pudovkin saw editing as a means by which the filmmaker could "see through the confusion of history and psychology and create a smooth train of images which would lead toward an overall event."[3]

When talking about style, the emphasis in this quote will be on smoothness and how to create it, but the purpose behind smoothness must first be understood if the style is going to have impact and meaning. "Seeing through the confusion of psychology and history" is the aim behind the smoothness for Pudovkin. This means creating a clear and comprehensible image of the world, one that cuts out irrelevancies and focuses the viewer on the significant moments, exchanges, and events that shape history, ideas, and thinking. The film therefore must, to paraphrase Pudovkin, guide the spectator psychologically. Pudovkin's intention, it could be said, was not so much to incite or ignite the audience as to immerse, influence, and convince it. To achieve this, he put forward ideas about film being built up, constructed, brick by brick. This construction depends, for its efficacy, on sinking the audience into the story or ideas. Any brick that stands out, draws attention to itself, is of an excessively irregular shape, size, or movement disrupts the flow of the construction and therefore disrupts the audience's immersion within it.

This view of editing is normalized in the Hollywood continuity system (which began being used even before Pudovkin's articulation of the ideology of linkage). In classical continuity editing, shots are often designed and juxtaposed with the ideal of smoothness of transition, the least possible disruption of the viewer's sense of the flow of time in continuous space. But not always. It is possible to have continuity cutting with collision. Linkage is not the same as decoupage. Linkage is often used with decoupage, but, as we shall see in the examples below, the spectrum from collision to linkage is different from the spectrum between montage and decoupage, and some decoupage employs collision very effectively.

So continuity cutting is a technique, and I am using the term "linkage" to describe a style within that technique. It might be more appropriate to use smoothness than linkage, because linkage could describe something that is abruptly linked, but I have chosen to use the word linkage for this aspect of style to remind us of the purpose behind the style: to create a smooth train of images. With linkage, we are at no time shocked out of the world of the story or characters; we are smoothly guided by the film's construction to empathy with characters and easy agreement with ideas it contains.

Smooth linkage of shots involves the opposite approach to collision. Rather than colliding light and dark together, lighting values from shot to shot are similar. The same is true for shot sizes that don't jump from wide to close, but link smoothly from wide to mid to close. Movements right to left link smoothly with other movements right to left, rather than colliding with movement left to right. Match cutting, or matching on action, is a key operation in making smooth linkages of shots. An unmatched cut from one part of a movement to another is a jump, or distortion of a movement's continuousness in time or space, and therefore a little shock or collision. This aspect of smoothly linking movement shape and direction through match cutting is the cornerstone of an "invisible" editing style in which movement flow appears to be smooth and continuous. However, as discussed in Chapter 5, editing, even editing style that emphasizes linkage, is not invisible. What we see is movement flow, smooth or collided, shaped by editing.

POINTS ALONG THE SPECTRUM FROM COLLISION TO LINKAGE

The spectrum from collision to linkage is a spectrum of choices that describes whether difference or similarity is emphasized by the cut, and whether the intention is to engage the viewers energetically with a series of little shocks to the eye or the mind or to guide them seamlessly into empathy and understanding with a series of linked nuances that build up, piece by connected piece, into a clear image or idea. This spectrum offers a range, a playing space, for the shaping of each of the elements of rhythm: time, energy, and movement.

Time can be collided or linked in shots. Speed of movement can be connected with similar or different speed. Duration of shot can be connected with similar or different duration. Collisions can be created even when connecting similar uses of time by choosing to cut before the peak of a movement arc. Seeing a movement that is started but unfinished cut with movement in a different shot gives a sense of some collision even if the movements were originally designed to link, and simply holding a shot for longer would have allowed that linkage. Cutting quickly, before a spectator can assimilate the full content curve of an image, creates a collision somewhere on the spectrum between pure collision and pure linkage because it unsettles the viewer and activates tension about what is unseen in a shot that has flashed by.

Energy qualities can also be collided or linked. Energy qualities, which are visible or audible in movement, color, light, tone, intentions, proximities, and so on, can be collided with their opposite, or matched with their like, from cut to cut or in patterns across any number of cuts. These patterns have the full range from collision to linkage, and the field of play in between, to modulate the rise and fall of energy and tension in a film.

Movement, as discussed above, can also be collided or linked, and the shaping of patterns of collisions or linkage is one way of shaping the moment-to-moment rhythm and the overall rhythm of a film.

STYLE CASE STUDIES

As noted above, it is tempting to associate montage with collision and linkage with decoupage, because it would seem that montage is a tendency to collide together things unrelated in time and space, and decoupage has as its goal the smooth creation of the impression of continuous time and space. But in fact it is only when we separate and articulate these two ranges of possibilities for cutting that we can describe a full range of cutting style choices.

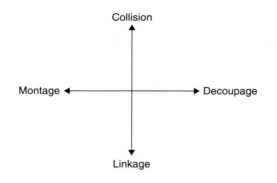

FIGURE 9.4

Each of the following four case studies pairs up a different combination of approaches, and the result is four distinctive styles.

Psycho—Decoupage and Collision

One of the best known scenes in editing history, the shower scene in which Norman Bates (Anthony Perkins) stabs Marion Crane (Janet Leigh) to death in *Psycho* (Alfred Hitchcock, 1960), is an example at the extreme edge of both spectra (Fig. 9.5). It is simple decoupage in that the scene could have been shot continuously in one take. The action could simply have unfolded in real time and space, but it was cut up into (many!) individual shots for the purpose of controlling rhythm and affect very precisely.

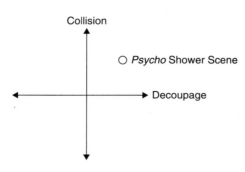

FIGURE 9.5

FIGURE 9.6
Anthony Perkins as Norman Bates collides with his victim in the decoupage of the shower scene in
Psycho *(Alfred Hitchcock, 1960). [Photo credit: Paramount; The Kobal Collection]*

The scene is also a very strong example of collision. The shots are designed, it seems, to collide in as many aspects as is possible, particularly screen direction and symbolic value, within the parameters of the action taking place. The butcher knife is sharp and dark, the skin of the victim is soft and white. The water pours from the shower head in dramatically angular directions, emphasized by strangely (within the context of the other shots of this film) tight close-ups. Janet Leigh's movements by contrast are soft and circular, particularly when masked by the filter of the shower curtain that diffuses light and form. And of course there is the music, by Bernard Herrmann, with its abrupt bursts of screaming strings, sharply staccato against the quiet that fills the space before and after the deed is done.

There are dozens of "setups" (placements of the camera in different spots) in this scene, and each of these is specifically designed to create a collision, a change, a difference from one to the next. By covering the scene in this way, Hitchcock gives the scene an energy of rapid, violent change, which does away with the need for explicit images. We never see the knife actually pierce the body; instead, we feel the tearing, stabbing qualities as we experience the extremes of collision between shots, their content, durations, shapes, sizes, angles, and symbols.

Apocalypse Now—Montage and Linkage

Francis Ford Coppola's *Apocalypse Now* (1979) is well known to have had a chaotic shoot riddled with problems ranging from a coup d'état in the country where they were shooting to the lead suffering a heart attack, an uncooperative star in a small but key role, the monsoons of the jungle, and simply scope and ambition beyond its budget. Once shooting had finally finished and cutting was in full swing, the editors found they did not have a satisfactory opening for the film. So they created one.

The opening sequence of *Apocalypse Now* is a smoothly linked montage (Fig. 9.7). It blends together long shots of a jungle, which at first appears peaceful and untroubled and then is slowly enveloped in the distinctive yellow smoke of napalm, with the close-up of a face (Martin Sheen as Captain Willard), upside down on the screen, eyes wandering restlessly (Fig. 9.8). It links the sounds of helicopter blades whirring with the image of a ceiling fan spinning, with the upside-down face, a gun, a domestic snapshot, a whiskey bottle, and the war machines flying over the jungle.

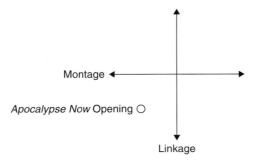

FIGURE 9.7

Linking all of these diverse images together and smoothly associating, even blending them into a single idea, is done by use of music and dissolves. The music, "The End" by the Doors, is much more than a quilt backing holding all of the pieces together. Its long continuous organ tones provide emotional values to the sequence at the same time as they provide linkage, through tonal similarity, from one image to the next. And the lyrics, also a low-pitched dirge-like drone, tell an aspect of the story in their words and their delivery. "This is the end," warns lead singer, Jim Morrison, both a peaceful oblivion to be longed for and a moment filled with dread. The music is part of the montage, built into the edit as images were being associated. It associates America, rock and roll, and hedonism with the jungles and war of Southeast Asia, connecting them via smooth linkage with the central image of Willard's head.

The connection of all images, sounds, and music through the mind of Willard is made visible through dissolves. A dissolve is a very soft cut that blends images together, softening their differences and linking their similarities. The longer it goes on, the softer it is, and these dissolves

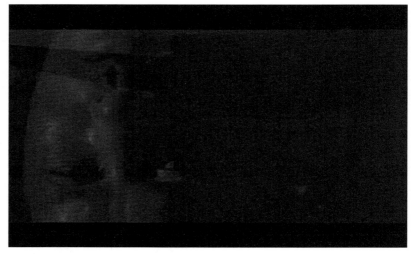

FIGURE 9.8
The montage at the opening of Apocalypse Now *(Francis Ford Coppola, 1979) links Captain Willard's (Martin Sheen) mind with the machines of war. [Photo credit: Zoetrope/United Artists]*

are very long. Dissolves are created by overlapping two pieces of footage and slowly fading one out as the other fades in, so that the images appear to blend or transform into one another. By dissolving together the image of Willard's head (upside down and therefore already somewhat out of kilter with the world) with the images and sounds of battle and home, these things are smoothly, seamlessly linked to give rise to the impression that the man's mind is whirring, spinning in circles with images of peace and war. The opening of *Apocalypse Now* sets up the character, his inner problems and his environmental problems, by using both linkage and montage to create an overlapping image of a chaotically integrated internal and external world.

Breaker Morant—Decoupage and Linkage

The decoupage and linkage in *Breaker Morant* (Bruce Beresford, 1979) does precisely what this smooth, unobtrusive style is designed to do: uses editing to subtly shape and modulate the story, cutting for dramatic purposes, emotional emphasis, and clarity rather than shock or association (Fig. 9.9).

The film is a flashback narrative, with the story in the present unfolding in a military court in South Africa during the Boer War and the flashbacks showing the stories the various witnesses and defendants are recounting. As it is a flashback narrative, there are substantial and very effective jumps

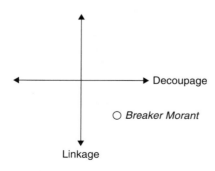

FIGURE 9.9

FIGURE 9.10

Edward Woodward and Jack Thompson play two Australians involved in a British court martial in Breaker Morant *(Bruce Beresford, 1979). This courtroom scene links images of the soldiers and officers, and their different cultures, under pressure in the continuous time and space of the interrogation. [Photo credit: S. Australia Film Corp/Australian Film Commission; The Kobal Collection]*

in spatial and temporal continuity between scenes, but within the scenes, the continuity cutting is seamless and supports the story subtly, with well-judged cuts matching actions and eye lines as a matter of course, but also heightening tension by shaping time and emphasis.

The coverage is spare in this beautifully directed, designed, and shot film, and this contributes to the sense of linkage. By repeating setups, similarity is enhanced and difference lessened. During the interrogation of the first witness, a repetitive pattern of use of coverage is established. Each new setup that is introduced is only one gradation of shot size up or down from the previous, and each is used at least twice before the introduction of a new shot. Until the first bombshell in the witness's testimony is dropped. Suddenly, the pattern of cutting changes and three new setups are seen in rapid succession. The moment settles down, and the editor (William Anderson) returns to a back-and-forth pattern of repeating shots until the next new damning revelation in the testimony, and again the pattern of repeating setups is broken and new angles are revealed.

All cuts, needless to say, are beautifully aligned to the principles of cutting emotional rhythm as described in Chapter 7, with the characters throwing the energy of their glances, sighs, questions, or lies from one to the other, motivating the cuts to show us reactions and actions in a revealing rhythm and steadily increasing pace. The linkage and decoupage function in seamless unity to create the impression of a continuous time and space with everyone present (there are 10 people in the room), intently focused on the same thing. The cutting lets us be swayed, just as the defendants and judges are, by the body language of the witness. It clearly reveals attitudes of all by cutting to reaction shots that are as responsive to subtext as they are to text (Fig. 9.10).

The coup de grâce is the timing. The British in the room hold themselves as though they are the very poles holding up the empire, and the edits on them are as clipped and neat as their moustaches. The Australians exchange uneasy glances and muttered comments framed and cut to reveal messy relationships and tensions. Their lawyer (Jack Thompson) makes a substantial piece of business out of shuffling papers noisily, and the editor extends the duration of each shot on him to include the maximum arc of each bumbling action so that when he finally does score a point, the contrast of the quick short shot on him in victory underlines the change. Most importantly, two moments, each after a sharply targeted question and before the damning answer, are suspended. These moments are extended by a series of short but still and close shots that each contain a tension of waiting in the balance of the question. At these two moments, without changing the style—each shot links smoothly to the next, time is not so exaggerated that it is implausible—it is as though the whole courtroom has suspended its breath, and the quickness of cuts, the stretching of time, and the stillness of bodies create emphasis with the minimum of collision.

Requiem for a Dream—Montage and Collision

Requiem for a Dream (Darren Aronofsky, 2000) makes use of montage and collision to convey the themes of the film in a visceral way (Fig. 9.11). The style synchronizes our physical experience of movement and energy with the protagonists' and sucks us down into the vortices of their stories.

Early on in *Requiem for a Dream* there is a quick, splashy, and stylish collided montage of cocaine use on the part of the protagonists (Harry Goldfarb, played by Jared Leto, and Marion Silver, played by Jennifer Connelly). The flashy and upbeat sound effects dance around the pristine framing of quirky shots of powder, money, pupils dilating, and bubbles splashing happily through the bloodstream. The sequence is so quick, the sound design such a funky music, that drug use looks fun

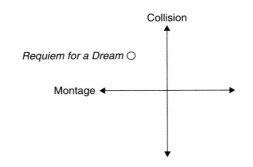

FIGURE 9.11

and playful. It's a bit alarming, but the collisions of these tangentially related images are more like percussion than concussion, and they have a rhythmic effect that is analogous to drugs themselves. Seeing and hearing these sequences is a bit of a buzz, a wake up, an aesthetic treat that makes you look forward to the next one.

And for a while these montages keep coming, but they grow a bit more harrowing and a bit more manic each time, soon mixing in Harry's mother's (Ellen Burstyn) growing addiction to diet pills and her subsequent hallucinations with the happy bubbling of heroin. As the film continues, the viewer experiences a kind of longing to return to the vibrant, surprising, upbeat little collisions of the early drug use, but instead, like the characters, we find ourselves increasingly bogged down in drug-induced hallucinatory nightmares. We stop getting the fun of using and start to experience the consequences. Montage images

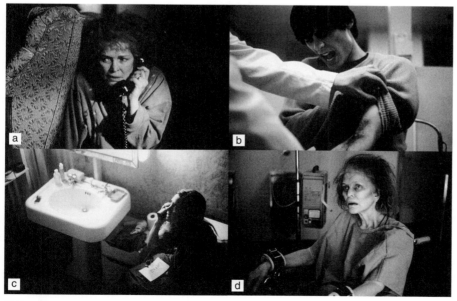

FIGURE 9.12

Ellen Burstyn, Jared Leto, and Jennifer Connelly in a colliding montage of each of their downward spirals in Requiem for a Dream *(Darren Aronofsky, 2000). [Photo credit: Artisan Pictures; The Kobal Collection; John Baer]*

still collide, but they are longer, more loosely framed, and altogether messier, until the final montage sequence (Fig. 9.12) in which the worst horrors imaginable befall each of the characters. This last montage sequence is neither quick nor pretty; it's not percussive or seductive. Instead, there is a relentless collision of images of pornographic rape, amputation, and electric shock therapy, each shot a sharp and painful degradation, all cut together an almost unbearable expression of the cumulative disintegration of life, human connection, and hope. This sequence mirrors the first sequence of drug use by being a collided montage, but it takes our pleasure in that stylish rat-a-tat of images and sounds and twists it into despair, thus using form and style to create the meanings of the film itself.

CONTEMPORARY STYLE: AFTER THE NEW WAVE

For this style rubric to have the flexibility needed to be useful in the long term, it must be able to take some contemporary cutting, which does not, on the face of it, appear to fall into any of the categories described above, into consideration. It must therefore contend with some of the unique arrangements and derangements of time, energy, and movement in film editing, from Jean-Luc Goddard's *A bout de soufflé* (*Breathless*) (1960) on.

After the strict rules of Hollywood continuity-style cutting had firmly reigned for so long, Jean-Luc Goddard opened a floodgate of new editing possibilities when he deliberately cut out chunks of time and space within an otherwise continuous action to make the jump cuts in *A bout de soufflé*. Goddard's intentions, like those of his forbears, the Soviet montage theorists Eisenstein and Pudovkin, were political. Fed up with the hegemony of the Hollywood style and its messages about orderly social behavior, the jump cuts "warn viewers that they are watching a film and to beware of being manipulated."[4] The idea of reminding viewers of this fact was indeed revolutionary. It took the most effective form of propaganda available at the time and rendered it toothless. Unless audiences are allowed the luxury of slipping into the story unobstructed, they are unlikely to be convinced of its message.

But whether these jump cuts succeeded in their purpose of disconnecting viewers from their unreflective engagement with story or not is debatable. They may have at the time, but now they have become part of style, or as Ken Dancyger, author of *The Technique of Film and Video Editing*, says, "The jump cut has simply become another editing device accepted by the viewing audience."[5] Even Cecile Decugis, the editor of *A bout de souffle*, reminds us that, "As Cocteau said, 'all the revolutionary ideas in art become conformist after 20 years.'"[6]

Jump cuts can indeed appear in the most mainstream of Hollywood films now. When Goddard shoots an action in a continuous time and space and then cuts a chunk out of the middle so that a continuous action jumps *out* of ordinary time and space, he turns decoupage into montage, or at least shoves the decoupage down toward the other end of the spectrum. The action was continuous in time and space when it was shot; in other words, it was covered as decoupage and then cut to be discontinuous montage. One could also say it was probably shot as linkage but then cut into collision. By dropping frames from within continuous shots, *A bout de souffle* is broken into discontinuous pieces, and those pieces are then reassociated without continuous flow so as to give rise to a new idea or understanding. Breaking temporal and spatial continuity creates what could be thought of as a jagged edge to each bit of action, which collides with the next bit's equally jagged, torn, continuity.

The question then is, stylistically speaking, why do such a thing? What is the purpose of discontinuous continuity and jaggedly collided linkage in a contemporary film (given that it is not the same as Goddard's original purpose)? I propose two possible answers: first, it's cool. It is cool to put in jump cuts in the same way that all harmless rule breaking is cool. Cool is defined in reaction to the establishment, though.

Therefore, it is cool to put in jump cuts if they fly in the face of the rules of continuity cutting, but only until such time as jump cutting has been assimilated into those rules, which I believe it has been.

The other reason to use a jump cut style is to present a state of extreme subjectivity. As with montage, a jump cut signifies that the perspective of the character has deviated far enough from normal or from that of the other characters around her so as to disrupt her sense of ordinary time or space.

In the very mainstream film *Erin Brokovich* (Steven Soderbergh, 2000), when Erin (Julia Roberts) gets bad news on the telephone, there is a series of jump cuts that convey her emotional distress at what she is hearing and, although all of the shots are objective, it is possible to understand from the jump cutting that her subjective experience is intense enough to have disrupted her ordinary feeling for time and space.

A far more extreme, revolutionary version of this intensified subjectivity occurs in Oliver Stone's *Natural Born Killers* (1994), in which Woody Harrelson and Juliet Lewis play characters who live so far outside of the rules of civilization that not only are they unstuck in time and space, but their subjectivities rule the construction of their worlds, which blink rapidly, almost compulsively, through colors, textures, framings, and media. There is, to quote Dr. Jane Mills, film scholar, "visual anarchy," as point of view and perspective bounce from the inner realities to the objective actualities of the central characters, and everyone they encounter, so swiftly and colorfully that the two soon blur and take on a new, mixed version of reality in which the continuity of time and space is creative and variegated in its contraction and expansion.

Natural Born Killers remains a watershed in the "in your face" editing style, paving the way for sequences and films such as *21 Grams* (Alejandro Gonzalez Inarritu, 2003) that come completely unstuck in continuous time and space even as they portray events that could be depicted in the Hollywood continuity style or even in single shots.

FIGURE 9.13
Woody Harrelson as the radically subjective Mickey living in his own perception of time and space in
Natural Born Killers *(Oliver Stone, 1994). [Photo credit: Warner Bros; The Kobal Collection; Sydney Baldwin]*

But the style rubric of the intersecting spectra of montage to decoup-age and collision to linkage remains useful for describing these "new" editing approaches, because their newness is in fact a variation on the old styles and develops in reaction to the concerns of the more traditional forms. To experience these editing styles as revolutionary, we have to experience them in relation to the traditions they disrupt, traditions that, of course, were at one point quite revolutionary them-selves. Perhaps Oliver Stone and the editors of *Natural Born Killers,* Brian Berdan and Hank Corwin, see a smooth linkage as a wasted opportunity, just as Eisenstein did, but take it to farther extremes.

CONCLUSION

If we say that style is the result of a set of choices and define those choices as sitting within a range from montage to decoupage and from collision to linkage, then it is possible to say that style choices are choices about the shaping of a film's time, space, and energy, three things by now familiar to the reader as core components of rhythm. In films from the 1920s to the present, style choices and their consequent editing rhythms shape the movement of images, events, and emotions to give rise to ideas and distinctive perceptual experiences in film.

ENDNOTES

1. Giannetti, L., *Understanding Movies*, p. 133.
2. Eisenstein, S., *Film Form: Essays in Film Theory*, p. 50.
3. Pudovkin, V. I., *On Film Technique and Film Acting*, p. 31.
4. Dancyger, K., *The Technique of Film and Video Editing, Theory and Practice*, p. 132.
5. Ibid.
6. Cecile Decugis as quoted in McGrath, D., *Screencraft: Editing & Post-Production*, p. 75.

CHAPTER 10

Devices

A device, for our purposes, is something that "complicates the formal patterning ... providing form with variations."[1] It is a way of constructing a moment or a passage that varies the unfolding of a story from direct linear cause-and-effect chains to more complicated and potentially formally more expressive patterns of telling. In particular, for editors, an editing device varies the form by playing with some of the unique capacities of cinema to shape time, space, energy, and movement to create experiences of tension and release.

Before talking about devices and their uses, it is important to note here something editors often say when trying to make generalizations about their work or working process, which is, "It depends on the story." These editors are, of course, absolutely right. Every decision made in the edit suite needs to be made with reference to the unique story being told, whether that story is narrative drama, abstract meditation, investigative journalism, or some other form. But devices, unlike individual decisions, styles, or processes, do have modes of construction that travel across stories and can be discussed out of the context of any particular production and applied to any story. This chapter looks at two devices, parallel action and slow motion/fast motion, and how they are constructed. It presents some case studies on how they have been effectively used and offers some principles about them that may be useful for any production. But ultimately it will be up to the individual editor to make use of them, and their particular applications will be unique to their stories.

One question that can be applied to almost any production is: How do these devices shape the audience's perception of story, or, how do they "show" story? One way that parallel action shows story is by allowing the audience to move ahead of the character in its understanding. As a spectator, we experience both sides of a parallel action sequence, but the characters do not. So our understandings and feelings for the story in these sequences are shaped by the device as much as by the performance or the events taking place. The device shows story, rather than saying it, by revealing events in two places at the same time and creating a space in which the viewer can surmise and feel more than just what is happening in each. The viewer's mind can juxtapose the two and draw conclusions, take sides, hope, and fear, without being told what to think. By the audience being shown more than the characters can see, and being shown it with a rhythmically shaped passage of time, energy, and movement, the meaning and the feeling of the story is conveyed cinematically. It is shown, not said.

Slow motion and fast motion are also cinematic story-showing[2] devices. They give audiences direct physical experiences of the ways in which characters are thinking or feeling. These time-manipulation devices can distort the flow of time's movement in the film to convey an inner world. They also create an image of time that becomes our experience of time; sometimes aligning us more closely with the character's subjective experience, other times commenting or creating an experience in us that is outside of what the character could know or feel.

The following case studies on parallel action and slow/fast motion discuss each of these devices in a craft sense, so that they are readily available to practitioners, and extrapolate principles from the specific examples given of how they might work affectively, or not work if they become clichés, and what thought processes they might be relied upon to convey or create in any screen production.

PARALLEL ACTION

Another way of saying "parallel action" is to say "meanwhile." "Meanwhile" is a literary device that was very fashionable in the early years of film. The grandfather of many film devices and conventions, filmmaker D. W. Griffith, says that he was heavily influenced by Charles Dickens, the king of plotting meanwhiles, but actually this use of meanwhile can be found all over literature.[3] Ironically, just as Dickens is credited as an authority for a device that is really "common to fiction at large," D. W. Griffith was later credited with devices that were common, even intrinsic, to the development of narrative film form at large.[4] Whether invented by Griffith or having evolved as the aggregate of filmmaking knowledge developed and spread from country to country, parallel action is one of the earliest cinematic storytelling devices to be explored and continues to be used as an extremely effective, efficient, and exciting way of moving story events, creating feelings, revealing information, and heightening tension.

As a film-editing device, parallel action essentially leaves one character or story in progress and turns to look at what is happening elsewhere at the same time. Why do this? One reason is, as Eisenstein said, to relieve boredom. But I would put that in the positive and say that one of the primary purposes of parallel action is to create excitement. From the point of view of shaping cycles of tension and release, the device of cutting parallel action opens questions. How will the two things that are happening in two different places at the same time impact each other? And, inherent within that question, how will these events impact each other, is the even more tension-filled question of *when* will they?

The nuances of "when" are the editor's domain. As editors, we know from the script that the two sides of the parallel action will eventually connect and that the plot events that are the result of their convergence will occur. Contemporary audiences are pretty well aware of this, too. If one were screening a dramatic film in which a fireman was racing to save a child in a burning building and paused the film midway through the action to ask, "Will the fireman get there in time?" the audience would be most likely to say, "Yes, probably." But audiences are not really in the theater just to experience the unfolding of events. They also come to the cinema to have the psychosomatic experience of *how* the events unfold. It is their empathetic experience with the characters on their journeys, and their feeling with the movement of image, sound, emotions, and events, that they also come to the movies for. They may be confident the fireman will save the child from the burning building but still come to the movies to enjoy the tension of the open questions. How close will he get to missing it? How much tension will there be? How well will the editor cut the parallel action sequence? How well will she modulate the rate and angle of convergence to create a satisfying tension, a satisfying unfolding of the action in time, a satisfying rhythm?

PRACTICAL EXERCISE

Parallel Action Part 1

You can directly activate the discussion of parallel action in the case studies that follow by setting up a practical exercise for yourself now and then adding to it after each case study reveals another aspect of parallel action.

The task is to write or imagine a parallel action sequence based on the premise that a detective is hunting for a fugitive.

First decide on the facts of the case: what, where, when, who, and why. There is no requirement that your characters or problem be of a particular type. Your detective might be the good guy or the bad guy. She might be a down-to-earth sheriff in Minnesota or he might be an adrenalin junkie secret agent in another galaxy. The device is useful in all genres, in all kinds of cinematic stories, even documentaries and associative films, if you can capture the image and sound in such a way that the story feels as if it had been shot at roughly the same time in two different places.

Next, decide on the story action in your first sequence of shots. Describe what is happening in one place and time; for example, where and when the fugitive begins the story, and "meanwhile," what is happening in the detective's location.

Now, before going on to read the case studies, decide how your sequence is going to end. Will the fugitive be caught or escape?

Once you've jotted some notes on all of these points, go on to read the case studies, and, if possible, see the films they describe. After each case study add another set of shots to your sequence, deciding on the shot sizes and contents and cuts. In other words, decide what the viewer will see and hear and when we will see and hear it using the cutting principle the case study reveals.

PARALLEL ACTION CASE STUDIES

The Great Train Robbery (Edwin Porter, 1903)

This first case study of parallel action is not a study of true parallel action but of an innovation in film form that is an important precursor of parallel action.

In 1903, Elliot Porter made *The Great Train Robbery*, a film that was innovative in length, subject matter, and structure. It depicts the story of a robbery and the subsequent escape and capture of the thieves, mostly in a linear timeline: first the robbers enter the train station, knock out the station master, and tie him up so he can't warn the train conductor; then they rob the train and escape. But as the robbers are

FIGURE 10.1

The Great Train Robbery *(Edwin Porter, 1903), at about 16 minutes, was roughly four times as long as almost any film up to then and told a tension-filled tale of the American frontier. [Photo credit: Edison; The Kobal Collection]*

escaping we see something that has not yet been seen in film in 1903: Porter cuts back to the train station, where we see the station master recovering and sounding the alarm. It looks as though Porter is saying, "The robbers are escaping, and *meanwhile* the station master is waking up." In *Film Editing, History, Theory and Practice*[5] Don Fairservice argues that this is not really a "meanwhile." In fact, he claims that what Porter is doing is more complicated: he is taking us back to an earlier point in time and showing us the continuation of action that would have happened earlier in the story. However, whether it is a true parallel action or not, for our purposes it does something that sets a precedent for parallel action: it cuts from the experience of one time, place, and character action in progress to another, revealing to us, as an audience, something that none of the characters could know. We move ahead of the characters in the story, knowing more than they do and experiencing the tension of the questions: How will these two strands of action impact each other? And when?

To contemporary eyes it is a bit tricky to see this story as tension filled, but this is not a fault of the plotting or the structure. Rather, it just takes too long, and it happens in long shots only, no close-ups. So the rhythm relies solely on performance and plot, the story showing

PRACTICAL EXERCISE

Parallel Action Part 2

The questions raised by Porter's structural innovation of cutting away from one action to see another are: How will these two events impact on each other? And when? When writing the ending or the scenario about the detective chasing the fugitive, you wrote the facts that tell *how* the two sides of your parallel action will impact on each other. The opportunity now is to think about *when* the two sides of the action in the story will converge.

Will the convergence be prolonged by complications or come to a quick and decisive end? How much time will we spend with each character, getting to know him and care about him?

Make a decision about how long you would like your parallel action sequence to be, how long the overall production will be, and how much weight or emphasis this sequence has in the overall film. It could be the entire plot or only a small part of it. Now write the next series of cuts, adding in a complication to each character's objectives that could prolong the sequence. Later you will have to decide whether to keep this subplot, when you decide if you've got the rhythm of the sequence right.

is hampered, to our sensibility, by being out of sync with contemporary rhythms. However, it does serve as a useful example of how much the contemporary audience experience of story relies on cinematic aspects of editing and shooting to create understanding and empathetic engagement. And it also reveals the impact the editor can have on story experience by modulating the rate and angle of convergence of the two parallel events.

Strangers on a Train (Alfred Hitchcock, 1951)

The opening sequence of *Strangers on a Train*[6] is a close-range parallel action sequence. We see two pairs of feet, one with flashy two-toned shoes and one with sensible brown shoes and a tennis racquet, stepping out of taxis at a train station. The shoes' owners are unaware of each other but, as the editor (William H. Zeigler) cuts back and forth between them, we are aware of both walking on what appears to be a direct collision course toward each other. We are, consciously or unconsciously, caught up in the question: How will these two characters, about whom we have already made a series of judgments based on their shoes, impact each other? And when?

Hitchcock, being a master filmmaker, knows that these are the questions he has created and chooses to make use of our expectations to create a twist. The two pairs of feet walk toward each other (apparently) at an accelerating pace; the cuts also accelerate, and the music by Dimitri Tiomkin emphasizes the connection and tension between the two images as they appear to come closer and closer, faster and faster. Just when we expect them to collide, Zeigler cuts to a wide shot of the turnstile at the train track entrance, and the two sets of shoes walk in, one at a time, without noticing each other. It turns out that "brown shoes" was farther away from the entrance than "flashy shoes," but the tight framing and accelerating cutting played right into the expectations of the audience that they would crash into each other. Hitchcock uses his knowledge of the audience's expectations to set up some underlying themes of the whole film, that things don't unfold as you might expect, life takes unexpected pathways and can turn to the left or the right in an instant.

After the turnstile shot comes a dissolve to a shot of the train tracks diverging at a crossing. The train stays on the straight track until the last possible second and then moves onto the track that veers off in another direction, affording us another metaphor for the lives of the two key characters whose paths cross each other's on this journey. Only then does the parallel action between the two pairs of shoes come back into play; the shoes walk along the corridor of the train, sit, cross their legs, bump each other, and that's when faces are finally revealed: when the strangers meet.

In this example of parallel action we get some important information from the mise-en-scène: our judgments about the characters come from the style of shoes, our sense that they are going to crash comes from the screen direction and pace at which they apparently walk toward each other. But it is the cutting that creates the possibility for us to surmise story. The cutting is what creates the impact of the sequence because it makes us think that these two events will impact each other, and soon! This is an excellent example of cutting creating the story. It allows us to surmise things that in fact are not part of the plot; it gets us to, in a sense, tell ourselves the story by giving us the opportunity to make a connection between two things. The cutting allows us, as viewers, to think we know more than the characters, to think we are moving ahead of them, to feel tension about the impending collision, and it even creates the possibility for the viewer to learn that things are not what they seem.

Gallipoli (Peter Weir, 1981)

Parallel action is frequently about time pressure. As discussed earlier, the tension is not only about whether two people or events will intersect, but when, and if it will be soon enough. The audience's experience of how the time passes, how the pressure mounts, and how time,

Parallel Action Part 3

Hitchcock and Zeigler's parallel action sequence in *Strangers on a Train* demonstrates some valuable principles about frame exclusion and inclusion that can apply to the scenario you are writing: What will be seen in your fugitive/detective scenario? And what information will be withheld? It is also possible to extrapolate from this sequence that accelerating pace and cutting between things moving right to left and things moving left to right will create an expectation that they will collide. Further, on a more sophisticated level, it is possible for you to use that expectation in your sequence to give us the expectation that things are about to converge and then to twist that expectation to reveal something else.

Write the next sequence of shots in your scenario and give some attention to what is seen and for how long, and what is not seen but which we might surmise is just outside the frame. Note, also, screen direction. At this point in your scenario, do the characters appear to be moving toward each other or away? More quickly or less? What expectations can you create with timing, pacing, and trajectory phrasing?

movement, and events feel on each side of the action creates their understanding of the story.

Peter Weir's *Gallipoli* tells the story of Australian soldiers fighting in Turkey for the British Empire in World War I. This story occupies an interesting place in Australia's national mythology, being a horrible defeat and terrible loss of lives and, at the same time, a moment when Australians asserted their ability to stand up for themselves and not just be minions of the British. So the ending had to convey both. It had to make us care about the soldiers and mourn their loss, but not see it as a simple, ignominious defeat.

The ending of the film is a parallel action sequence in which one soldier (Frank Dunne, played by Mel Gibson) runs toward the trenches to deliver a message that could save all of the men's lives. The sequence starts 9 minutes before the climactic ending, but at first it doesn't feel much like classical parallel action. Frank leaves the trenches with a note for the officer in charge and we go with him, following him as he talks, first to one officer, then another, and cutting only occasionally back to the trenches to see what is going on there. The emphasis of time is on Frank's journey and his obstacles, actions, and emotions.

FIGURE 10.2
Mel Gibson as Frank Dunne, running, pressured by time and responsibilities, in Gallipoli *(Peter Wier, 1981). The other side of the parallel action in this sequence shows us what he is responsible for and increases our anxiety about his run. [Photo credit: Associated R&R Films/Paramount; The Kobal Collection]*

The questions are: Will he get killed on the way? Will the snobbish British officer defeat his initiative? Will the Australian superior officer do the right thing and stand up for his men? And, as Frank stands in the tent of the Australian general, holding his breath on a knife's edge of anticipation (a beautifully cut moment), we hold our breath too and silently wish for the general to make up his mind, be decisive, give the order in time!

But just as Frank gets the all-important message to delay the attack, the sergeant back in the trenches gets the opposite message by telephone, and now the emphasis of the cutting shifts.

Frank begins his run back up the hill, through the other soldiers, under enemy fire, and against the clock. But although his journey is action packed and filled with tension, there are only seven short shots of it between this point and when the film ends 4½ minutes later. The rest of the time is spent in the trenches, mostly in intimate, lyrical shots of the young men whose lives will be lost if Frank doesn't make it in time. The very sensitive and clever editor, William Anderson, understands that this is no longer just Frank's story. He has shown us how hard and important Frank's struggle is, but now the emphasis is shifted from Frank's journey to what's at stake. In other words, the emphasis has shifted from action to emotion. The editor makes a very well-judged choice to spend the balance of his time on investing our emotions and making us care, so that the ending is not just "oh, too bad, he didn't make it," it is a devastating experience of loss for the audience.

The lesson to take away from this sequence (once you get over its overwhelming impact) is that in a parallel action sequence it is often possible to identify one side of the sequence as "action" and the other as "emotion." In other words, one side might be under time pressure or pursuing a goal or moving events along in some way, whereas the other side is what's at stake. In this case the men in the trenches are at stake, and the editing is structured in such a way as to immerse us deeply in feeling for and with them. It favors emotion over action and consequently, when they are gunned down, we feel loss.

So the question an editor can ask herself when cutting parallel action is: Where is action and where is emotion? And what is the balance I need to achieve between them?

PRACTICAL EXERCISE

Parallel Action Part 4

The question for an editor is sometimes whether to create parallel action if it didn't exist in the script, but more often there are likely to be questions of emphasis, as in: Which side of the story do I show, when, and for how long? Which actual cutting points will slant the stories in the way I want? These questions also lead us back to, Whose story is it? As in: Who do I want the audience to care about and sympathize with, and who do I want them to hope wins?

In the scenario you are creating, it might be possible to say that one side is action and one is emotion or to say who is driving the action and what is at stake. If your detective's job is at stake and the fugitive keeps out-maneuvering her, then action is with the fugitive and emotion is with the detective. It could just as easily be the opposite, or it could be that the detective is trying to catch the fugitive to warn him of the great danger he is in. No matter what the plot events are, the question of balancing action and emotion could be available for the editor to play with.

The next question for the editor is: If one side is action and one side is emotion, how much time do we need to spend in each place to raise the stakes and the tensions? If one or the other side were seen for longer, how would that change the balance? These are not just questions of emphasis by duration, of course. Sometimes great emotion or furious action can be seen very quickly because it is contained in the energy or movement of the shot. As you sketch out the next part of your parallel action sequence, try to makes notes that reveal the balance of action and emotion you will create to elicit the response you want from the audience. It is a matter of shaping the timing, pacing, and trajectory phrasing into a rhythm that modulates emphasis and places the tension of the open question in the appropriate place.

The Godfather (Francis Ford Coppola, 1972)

I return now to *The Godfather*, which was also discussed in Chapter 8, to look in more detail at the Baptism sequence and the parallel action between Michael Corleone (Al Pacino), a young man on the cusp of becoming the Godfather of the New York underworld, and a series of murders his henchmen are executing around the city.

In this famous sequence Michael is in church taking on the role of being a spiritually responsible godfather to his sister's newborn baby. But this baptism is a metaphor; the baby is not the only one being baptized, Michael is too. The baby's baptism is ceremonial, sonorous, and richly decorated in lace and ritual, but the new Godfather's baptism is in blood.

This parallel action sequence has been very carefully planned, and its efficacy relies a great deal on the composition of the shots and the

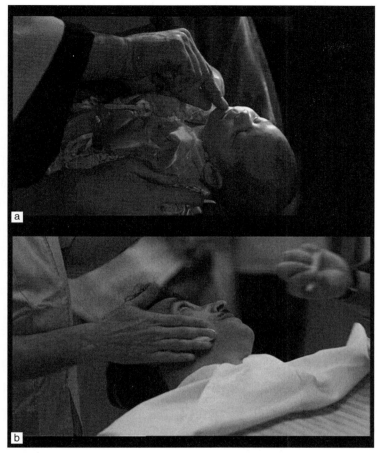

FIGURE 10.3
The comparison of the similarities of these two figures having their chins anointed in the baptism/murder sequence of The Godfather *(Francis Ford Coppola, 1972) highlights the irony of their differences.*

action to draw the metaphor between the two baptisms. The editors, William Reynolds and Peter Zinner, cut from the priest's action of preparing the baby for baptism to a hitman preparing his gun, from the priest anointing the baby's chin with a holy ointment to a barber anointing a hitman's chin with shaving cream. These are physical indicators of the metaphor, images and movements from which the audience can draw a metaphoric connection between the two sides of the action. The emotional connection between the two sides of the parallel action comes from two things: the organ music and sounds of the service, which are artfully cut across from the grand church to the sordid sites of violence, and the precise timing of image cuts to cue clearly to the audience that Michael Corleone knows what is going on and condones it.

The music imbues the whole sequence with the association of the holy, the sanctified, and the just, which of course is ironic because only half of the action is sanctified by God; the other half is a series of brutal, sudden, and alarming murders. The sound of the baby crying is heard only over shots of hitmen getting ready to kill. In shots inside the church the baby is sleepy and peaceful. The sound of the dialog is drawn over shots in disparate locations. When the priest asks Michael if he accepts God, Michael replies affirmatively, in sync (meaning we see him in the church saying the words we are hearing). But the priest presses the point, in accordance with the ritual, asking Michael if he believes in Jesus and if he believes in the Holy Spirit. When Michael replies to these questions, we hear his affirmation, but we see something different: images of his thugs going about their work. Later, when Michael is asked repeatedly if he renounces the devil and his work, the questions are heard over images of someone being gunned down; their terror and spurting blood are then juxtaposed immediately with a close-up of Michael, looking down and inward, affirming that he does renounce the devil.

A very important part of making this ironic and metaphoric cutting work is the editors' timing of cuts on Al Pacino's performance. It is the precise timing that allows us to surmise that Michael is fully aware of the violent action taking place, knows it is taking place at his behest, and both regrets and sanctions it.

The first close-up of Michael in the sequence is a slightly high-angle shot looking at Michael from the roughly the perspective of the priest, who is standing a step above Michael on the altar. At the beginning of this shot Michael is looking down and appears to be listening to the priest, gazing at the baby (Fig. 10.4a). He then he looks up toward the priest (Fig. 10.4b), then his eyes shift to the middle distance and glaze over slightly, as he looks into his own thoughts (Fig. 10.4c). Once

FIGURE 10.4

Just before the killings start in the baptism/murder sequence of The Godfather *(Francis Ford Coppola, 1972), there is a shot of Michael (Al Pacino) that tells us, just through the shifts of his eyes, that his mind is in two places at once: here with the holy ritual in the church and away with the unholy ritual taking place at his behest.*

his inward gaze is established, there is another shot of the baby, but Michael is not looking at him, Michael's gaze is on the images in his mind's eye: the preparations for the killings. Had the editors left the shot 46 frames, or 1½ seconds earlier, they would have left us with the impression that Michael's thoughts were with the baptism. Instead, the timing leaves us with the impression that his thoughts are far away.

From there forward, as both the music and the mayhem escalate throughout the sequence, the editors use a repeating pattern of cutting back to Michael as he is looking inward and then holding on the shot as he responds to the priest. The response is performed calmly, even beatifically, and allows us to align with his thoughts, to believe, with him, that he can be both good and bad at the same time. It is the timing of the cut to Michael as he looks inward that tells us he knows what is going on, the holding on the shot as he responds that aligns us with him emotionally, and then the cutting back to the violence that creates the irony: we are emotionally aligned with the perpetrator of inhuman acts, who is reflective, sorrowful, and imbued with the righteousness of the Church. And this is the irony of the entire film. The good people in the film, the ones we understand, like, and feel with in the cycles of tension and release, are the monsters. The film form, including performances, shooting, cutting, sound, music, and devices, moves our understanding, caring, and allegiance toward the protagonist at the same time it reveals his stately, mindful, even responsible descent into base thuggery.

PRACTICAL EXERCISE

Parallel Action Part 5

Three very useful principles are demonstrated in *The Godfather's* parallel action:

1. Metaphoric connections between the two sides of the action are made by choreographing the juxtaposition of actions and images to imply relationships;

2. Overlapping sound and music reshape our understanding of the relationship between the two sides of the action completely; and

3. Timing of cuts throws the energy from one shot to the next and, when used in combination with performance, shapes our empathetic responses.

As you write the next sequence of shots, try to make use of these three principles to shape your story. Even if the images are not being placed to mirror each other directly the way they are in *The Godfather*, it is important to think about how they build a sequence of ideas when juxtaposed. Cutting a shot of the desert from one side of the action with a shot of a swimming pool on the other side will contrast the two sides. Cutting bird wings flapping with tissues fluttering will compare them. This is, of course also a stylistic question. As discussed in Chapter 9, if you make collisions of screen direction, energy, line, or movement, the two sides of the parallel action will read in a relationship to each other that is different than if you make smooth linkages.

The overlapping of sound or music will draw the emotional color from one side of the action to the other, which can be used ironically. But overlapping sound in parallel action can also be used to create an emotional resonance or stronger alliance with one side of the action. It may even create a sense of premonition, as in the possibility that the audience will surmise that one side of the action has a presence in the mind's eye of the characters on the other side. Is there one side of your scenario you would take the sound from at this point and draw it over the other?

The timing of your cuts will, as discussed in Chapter 7, throw the energy or intention of one shot to the next shot, making the energy or action of the second shot feel as though it is responding to the first shot. This sense of timing is how the editors of *The Godfather* align us with Michael in the Baptism sequence. It would be useful to you now to make sure you know who you want the audience to be aligned with in your sequence (it could be more than one figure) and to think about how timing of the cuts will strengthen that alignment.

As you write the final convergence of the two sides of your parallel action, you may want to think about style, metaphor, and sound connecting the two sides and the timing of cuts shaping audience responses as the impact of convergence occurs.

Having come to the final convergence for your sequence, you now have the opportunity to do the most fun part of filmmaking: editing! As this is a written, not a shot, sequence, you will have to imagine the flow rather than experience it, but this still provides an opportunity for you to sing the rhythms in your head as you read through your scenario. Listen to the song for a modulated build of tension and be aware of release points as you, for example, introduce complications in the forward trajectory of characters in pursuit of their goals or dwell on some of the emotional moments that do not drive action forward but do create feeling for what is at stake. The releases are as important as the builds of tension in creating a compelling rhythm. You might go back to your scenario at this point and exclude some information from the earlier parts of the sequence to have it to reveal later, and you might think about cutting points throughout and how you use them to align the audience with the characters.

This parallel action exercise is a writing exercise as well as an editing exercise, designed to bring the two phases of filmmaking into a deeper understanding of each other. Certainly editors who work on it gain a new sympathy for the challenges of writing. At the same time, writers who work on it understand much more acutely what is meant by the expression "editors write the last draft of the script." By imagining all of the principles of parallel action as they will come into play in the edit suite, writers and directors can see the huge impact of rhythm and cinematic devices on storytelling.

Snatch (Guy Ritchie, 2000)

The parallel action sequence in *Snatch*, the most recent and most self-conscious film of the five discussed, is, like *The Great Train Robbery*, not really parallel action. In fact, Guy Ritchie takes filmmaking back almost 100 years and makes a slyly winking sequence that brings the viewer in on three "parallel" sides of a story by taking us backward and forward in time, just as Edwin Porter did in 1903.

FIGURE 10.5

Dennis Farina and Vinnie Jones get ready to go on more than just a car ride in Snatch *(Guy Ritchie, 2000). [Photo credit: Columbia/SKA Films; The Kobal Collection; Sebastian Pearson]*

In *Snatch*, as three sets of interests converge on their common objective, they collide, literally, in a violently fatal car crash that is absurd and clever. We see the crash three times, as though we can see all points of view, not in parallel, but sequentially.

The absurdity of this sequence arises from the dialog and the situation, and the cleverness arises from the sequential way in which information is revealed. Just as Hitchcock makes use of our expectations to subvert them in *Strangers on a Train*, Ritchie knows we know what to expect from parallel action. And he plays with our expectations, thwarting them by manipulating the conventions of the device. As the three cars approach a common destination, the editor (Jon Harris) subverts classical parallel action so that it is not just showing what is happening in one spot and meanwhile what is happening in another spot. Instead, one set of characters goes forward to a certain point in time and space, and then the edit jumps back to an earlier time and shows another set of characters on their journey to converge, not just in space, but in time. This manipulation of linear time makes the viewer feel like God. As well as showing information the characters would not know about things going on, meanwhile, in another place, it reveals information that the characters could not know about their own actions or trajectories.

This playing with the device shifts our allegiance; it takes us outside of the story so that we do not feel with any of the characters, exactly; it is as though we feel allegiance with the filmmaker instead. We stand in his shoes, playing with time and space. We feel clever, omniscient, just as the director might feel because he, of course, like God, knows more about the story than any of his characters could.

This case study does not have an exercise to go with it, because the principle behind it, that explicit manipulation of a convention will draw attention away from the story and toward the film as a film, is a principle likely to be used only in very specialized scenarios. However, this case study does provide an opportunity to consider another implication for the audience that relates to French film theorist Christian Metz's idea that cinematic space and time allow the audience a kind of godlike quality, an omniscience of always being in the right place at the right time. Parallel action allows spectators to be where the action is. It places the viewer in the important place at the important time, even if the two actions are taking place worlds apart. In this way, parallel action creates one of the unique and enjoyable sensations of the movies. Unlike life, in the movies we can always be where the action is. If this unique sensation is not, to quote singer/ songwriter Paul Simon, "why God made the movies," it is certainly one reason the device of parallel action arose so early in the development of film form and remains so robust. This function of placing the spectator in the right place at the right time gives rise to a final and very useful question an editor can ask herself when putting together a parallel action sequence: Where is the action? Because that, of course, whether it is physical, emotional, or event action, is where the audience wants to be.

SLOW MOTION

Slow motion is a simple technical device and can be quite useful in the shaping of rhythm and affect.

Technically speaking, slow motion of live action can be created one of two ways: if shooting on film, it is a matter of running the film through the camera at a faster rate. That way, more frames are shot per second, and when the film is projected at normal speed (24 frames per second), the action looks slower and smoother because there are more frames of it. An action that took 1 second to perform but which was covered with 48 frames of film now takes 2 seconds to project and looks much smoother because the action's flow is captured in twice as much detail.

The other way to create slow motion is in the edit suite. When you use the motion effect functions in a digital nonlinear editing program to create slow motion, what the program is doing is duplicating frames so that the action takes longer to occur. If you specify that the shot should run at 50% of its original speed, the program will duplicate each frame and make the shot last longer by playing each frame twice. This does not create exactly the same smooth effect as in-camera slow motion, but really this becomes noticeable only when you go to more extremes of slow motion, such as running the shots at one-quarter or one-eighth their normal speed. Then the fact that frames are being repeated becomes more visible, and there is a stuttering effect created as one frame is held for the length of time it would normally take eight frames to pass. In filmmaking processes before the advent of video cameras or digital edit suites, slow motion created in postproduction was called step printing and was done with an optical printer by repeating frames, just as it is done in the digital nonlinear edit suites. This repeating of frames creates a effect different from running the film faster through the camera, but it is still an aesthetic effect that can be put to good use for many purposes.

But what are these purposes? Why make something slow motion? The major function of slow motion is to prolong for the purpose of heightening whatever effect the gesture or action covered is meant to have; i.e., to make it more poetic, romantic, glorious, horrifying, or otherwise heighten the emotionality or importance of a moment.

Why would seeing something for a longer time make us more emotional about it? There are, I believe, at least two answers to this question. The first is a simple matter of temporal emphasis. If an emotion or action is in progress and it is portrayed in slow motion, then it will automatically have more emphasis by duration than it would normally have. The other reason slow motion heightens affect is emphasis by stress. As discussed in Chapter 3, the emphasis by stress is the accent or emphasis created by the energy or quality of movement, not by its duration.

Slow motion changes the energy or quality of a normal movement and thus gives it a greater emphasis. It increases the magnitude of an occurrence in our perception and changes the quality of our kinesthetic empathy, I believe, because it creates an image of a greater effort of bodies in motion. Bodies (and these could be human bodies, bodies of water, bodies of objects) expend greater energy to do an action when they appear not just to push against obstacles on their journeys but also to be pushing the resistance of time. This "resistance of time" can, in some cases, also create the opposite quality of movement; not greater strain but a floating, buoyant quality can be created by that temporal resistance. In this case, time becomes a sort of cushion of air holding a body up as it moves in slow motion. As viewers, our kinesthetic response to the effort involved is heightened as the bodies appear to strain against time or float within it, unable or unwilling to break free and move with normal gravity and tempo. The great Soviet documentary filmmaker Dziga Vertov[7] is quoted as saying that "slow motion is time in close-up." The idea of time being close-up suggests that slow motion does for time what the close-up does for space, which is make us more intimate with it, more cognizant of it, and more sensually affected by it.

The following case studies look at a few examples of slow motion in films to extract some principles about how and why it is used, what the particular effects of our heightened kinesthetic empathy may be, and also to consider when slow motion might be cliché or overused.

SLOW MOTION CASE STUDIES

Chariots of Fire (Hugh Hudson, 1981)

Chariots of Fire is the Best Picture Academy Award-winning tale of the religious and ethical conflicts experienced by members of the British track team in the 1924 Olympics in Germany. The races that take place in the film are very important ways of showing the story. They show us the characters in competition with each other, with other teams, and with themselves, drawing a physical metaphor between running a race and the competitions and cooperations of life. Variations on speed of motion are often used in depicting these races to underline, enhance, or create emotional impact, the tensions of the conflict, and most importantly, the kinesthetic empathy required for us, the viewers, to have a felt experience of the runners' stories.

In the climactic gold medal-winning race there is the use of a couple of different speeds of slow motion in the sequence, all done "in-camera." There is a range of slow motions in the athletes' bodies, but the crowd is in normal time. This signals that the athletes are having a special kinesthetic experience. Some athletes are slower and more glorious or expending more effort than others, as they prepare for the race, line up on their marks, get set into their starting postures, and go. But the race itself, the first time we see it, is mostly in long shot and normal time

FIGURE 10.6

Ben Cross as Harold Abrahams pushes against time to reach the finish line in Chariots of Fire (Hugh Hudson, 1981). [Photo credit: 20th Century Fox/Allied Stars/Enigma; The Kobal Collection]

and, given that these are Olympic athletes running a mere 100 meters, very quick. Under 6 seconds, including the win.

Given that this is a climactic moment of the film and many of the emotional and plot lines are riding on its outcomes, running it in under 6 seconds is a very interesting choice and one which, I believe, was probably made in the edit suite. As soon as the race ends, in fact as it is won, the editor, Terry Rawlings, returns to slow motion. The winner, our hero, Harold Abrahams (played by Ben Cross), breaks the tape in a surge of effort against time that seems as though his chest is literally pushing the weight of time in front of him as he pushes across the finish line (Fig. 10.6). His friends and teammates in the crowd run down to congratulate him in slow motion, and then the editor makes another interesting choice: he replays the race, this time in slow motion. One could surmise that this is the memory of the race as it was felt by the characters, but the shots are not really set up to encourage us to infer that. There is no shot of Abrahams's head or face or gaze that would imply we are shifting into his memory. So to me, this replay of the race feels as though it is for my benefit as an audience, so that I can feel the effort, this time in slow motion, feel the physical and psychological exertion as Abrahams strains against time and circumstances toward victory. In short, the race is replayed so that I can have the experience of kinesthetic empathy that can be created by slow motion. When I watch the race the first time, the tension of the question of who will win is foremost in my experience. Slow motion here might have the effect of making me impatient rather than making me empathetic. Also, the extreme quickness of the race is, to my mind, a more accurate representation of what it might feel like to the athletes. After all the build up, the training, the tensions, the politics of getting to this point, that race would feel very quick indeed. The second time allows me the kinesthetic experience of being in the race as a value in itself, a heightened, more glorious, more effort-filled experience than anything in my real life.

The Navigator (Vincent Ward, 1988)

Another very useful aspect of slow motion has to do with prolonging the occurrence of an event for storytelling purposes. Slow motion prolongs the sensation of an action occurring rather than having occurred. To clarify this point, I refer to screenwriting teacher Robert McKee's book *Story: Structure, Substance, Style and the Principles of Screenwriting.* McKee discusses the idea that emotion is something an audience experiences while something is going on.[8] We experience feeling as something is occurring, not once it is over and we already know the result. This of course is similar to the tension of the open question I have been referring to throughout the book, and it is also a way of describing the kinesthetic empathy that occurs while the question is open. Not only do we feel tension about what will happen, but we feel with the characters as they go through an event. Once an event is resolved, their emotions and ours dissipate.

McKee says there are only two emotions: pleasure and pain. They each have a lot of variations—joy, love, happiness, rapture, fun, ecstasy, etc., or misery, stress, grief, humiliation, remorse, etc.—but they all come back to pleasure and pain. "As audiences we experience emotion when the telling takes us through a transition of values. As soon as the plateau is reached, however, emotion quickly dissipates. An emotion is a relatively short-term, energetic experience. Now the audience is thinking, great, he got what he wanted, what happens next?"[9]

So if we experience the emotion during the journey, but as soon as we get there, we stop feeling the energy of the emotion, then slow motion, quite simply, prolongs the journey, so that we either can pay more attention to it or feel it for longer.

At the end of Vincent Ward's moving and inventive film *The Navigator*, the protagonists have reached a very hard fought objective, which is to raise a cross on the steeple of a church. Because it is a mythical parable being told in two time frames, present-day New Zealand and medieval plague-ridden Europe, the storyteller, a young boy, knows that there will be a great triumph but also a terrible tragedy once the goal is reached. He doesn't know what the tragedy is, and neither do we, until the cross has been raised and the boy starts to fall from the spire. There are a series of jump cuts that repeat and prolong the action of the boy falling away from the spire, and then there is a slow motion shot, not of the boy, but of his glove, drifting gracefully across the sky, never quite reaching the ground.

The slow motion is necessary to prolong the occurrence of the event, to give us time to realize who is falling and what the story implications of that fall are. It is also very necessary emotionally. A quick fall would change the emotional quality of the event from a lyrical sacrifice to a bad accident. But what I think is really interesting is that the slow motion shot of the fall is not a shot of the boy, but of the glove. I think that the editor, John Scott, and director, Vincent Ward, knew that putting in a slow motion shot of the boy falling would be too much. It might be maudlin or sentimental, it would almost certainly be a cliché, and it could never be lyrical, because it's just too awful. Using the glove as a metonym allows us to see the beauty of the fall, to feel suspension of the moment as the glove is suspended by time, and to experience the grace of its movement as the grace of letting go.

Thelma and Louise (Ridley Scott, 1991)

This final case study on slow motion is from the end of *Thelma and Louise*, the 1991 Academy Award nominee for editing by Thom Noble. *Thelma and Louise* was a controversial film when it was released. The controversy was over the feminist credentials, or lack thereof, of the story, and one aspect of the controversy centered on the end: When the two women drive off the edge of a cliff rather than surrender to the law, is it defiant liberation or just suicidal wreckage and waste?

The use of slow motion, music, and a slow fade to white in the last shot are aspects of form that fuel the controversy. As the two women drive off the cliff's edge, the car soars in a glorious, triumphant, arc in the air, in a gracious slow-motion suspension of time. The car doesn't fall. Ever. Rather, the editor stops time and motion with a freeze-frame, and then the slow fade to white, timed with the rising cadence of the music, leaves us with the impression that the protagonists are flying, not falling. The very upbeat tune continues into a credit sequence montage of all of the happiest moments of the film. All of these techniques are used to convince us of one thing: a happy ending. And they succeed, largely owing to the physiological responses we can be depended on to have when we see smiling faces and graceful flows and hear happy music that synchronizes us to its infectious beat. It is only on a cognitive level that this film's ending is sad. Only if you think about the wreckage and dead bodies that, of course, you never see, do you think about the waste and horror the events imply. How different would this movie have felt if the car had flown at regular speed? What if it had actually crashed?

FIGURE 10.7
Geena Davis and Susan Sarandon as the title characters in Thelma and Louise *(Ridley Scott, 1991). When they make the decision to go forward rather than surrender, is their decision noble, lyrical, and redemptive or ignominious and wasteful? The filmmaker relies on slow motion and a few other editing devices to show his perspective. [Photo credit: MGM/Pathe; The Kobal Collection]*

This film uses slow motion at the end of the story to sustain the emotional energy generated by the action. Placed at the end, the slow motion sustains our emotional energy as we leave the cinema and, even more importantly, sustains the emotion we feel about the action in progress rather than having the feeling that freedom and flight have come to an end.

FAST MOTION

Technically speaking, fast motion is the opposite of slow motion. It can be created either by running the film more slowly through the camera or by dropping out frames in the edit suite using the motion effects function. Unlike slow motion, there is no perceptual difference in using one of these techniques or the other. Running the film through the camera more slowly means that the action is covered in fewer frames, which is the same effect as dropping frames out in editing so that action goes by more quickly.

Affectively speaking, the function of fast motion may also be the opposite of slow motion. If the function of slow motion has been to make something more poetic, romantic, glorious, horrifying, or otherwise heighten the emotionality of a moment, then is the function of fast motion to make you feel less?

In many cases, we laugh at fast motion or experience it as a light moment. By being too speeded up to be real, fast motion is kinesthetically comic; it creates absurdity by ellipses.

According to Robert McKee, comedy is predicated on the audience feeling that no one gets hurt. So, if fast motion makes us feel less, perhaps it does so by leaving the impression that the characters feel less. Our kinesthetic empathy is activated by the recognition of an on-screen figure's kinesthetic experience, so if those figures don't feel an event, we don't either.

This kinesthetic effect could be said to be drawn from the technical means of production of fast motion. It is almost as though, by dropping out frames, you eliminate the points of contact at which the body would normally feel pain. The actual crash of the body into the ground is missed or passes to quickly to hurt. Instead of straining against time or feeling it as a force of support or cushioning, bodies on screen slip through time with very little contact, too little to have an impact.

TWO QUICK FAST MOTION CASE STUDIES

- *Romeo and Juliet* (Baz Lurhmann, 1996)
- *Two for the Road* (Stanley Donen, 1967)

In Baz Luhrmann's 1996 version of Shakespeare's *Romeo and Juliet*, editing rhythms and style do a great deal to update the story to contemporary

Southern California. In the scene in which Juliet's mother asks Juliet if she would like to marry Paris, the editor, the audacious and daring Jill Bilcock, conveys a great deal about the mother's character and her relationship with her daughter by use of fast motion. The scene is cut with absolute respect for the rules of classical continuity cutting. There are no jump cuts or even jarring cuts from long to close-up shots. Shot sizes and composition progress from wide to medium to close in an orderly and reliable way.

As Juliet, Claire Danes's performance is unaffected and sincere. Meanwhile, however, her mother (played by Diane Venora) is getting ready for a costume party, which she intends to go to as a Las Vegas-style Cleopatra in a gold wig and sequins. She is chain smoking, barking at servants, and stressing equally about her daughter's future prospects and her own appearance. Bilcock supports and conveys the mother's manic energy and scatterbrained approach to life by speeding up her action, so that by contrast with Juliet she appears silly, slightly insane, and, even more importantly, utterly lacking in feeling. The point of the scene is that Juliet's mother is oblivious to Juliet's emotions, and this is conveyed through use of fast motion. She dashes, spins, and slips through the scene feeling nothing, being impacted on by no one, and letting nothing touch her.

In *Two for the Road* Albert Finney and Audrey Hepburn play lovers on a road trip to explore Europe and their love. The couple inadvertently meet up with some old friends of Finney's character and get dragged along on a tourist trip to see a chateau somewhere in France. The whole sequence of visiting the chateau, taking photos, getting ice creams, and attending to other needs takes place in under 2 minutes, all in fast motion. The players look, exclaim, pose, snap, eat, smile, and carry on just as tourists ought to but at such a rate that none of the experiences has any meaning whatsoever, and this, of course, is the point. This tourists' view of an antique culture is a kind of desecration of time, the friends' grotesque parody of family living is a warning to the young lovers, the whole event is a travesty of a felt experience, but a funny one because although they miss the actual meaning of anything they are doing, they don't feel bad. At this rate of fast motion, they don't feel anything.

MIXED MOTIONS AND SPEED RAMPING

One exception to fast motion being funny is that it can be confusing or about confusion. Fast motion can be used to create a head space in which things are moving so quickly that a crisis is precipitated. But this use of fast motion is quite often mixed with slow motion and various speeds in between, the effect being one of disorientation in time and therefore a loss of one's sense of place in the world. A useful reference for this is the ending of Arthur Penn's 1967 film *Bonnie and Clyde*. When Bonnie and Clyde are suddenly and very gorily gunned down, Penn and the editor Dede Allen use a rapid-fire mix of slow and faster shot speeds to convey the confusion, panic, and depths of feeling of the characters.

More recently, mixed motion speeds are used in action films to convey a kind of superhuman control and power in fight scenes wherein the hero might slip into a slow motion preparation, creating tension and a heightened sense of his gravitas and the power of the obstacle he faces, a feeling that he not only has to push against his enemy, but push against time itself. Then he will spin into a faster-than-the-speed-of-light kick, signaling his incredible dexterity and mastery of the elements of time, space, and gravity. Then he'll land in a perfectly controlled normal speed, regrounding us in real time and space and preparing us for the next onslaught.

Another variation on the use of slow and fast motion is a relatively new device called speed ramping. Again, this can be done in some high-tech cameras in which variable speed settings can be employed or in the edit suite, where motion effects can be controlled and modified in a range of ways. The device involves starting at one speed—for example, one-eighth normal speed—and then ramping up to, for example, eight times faster than normal speed, in one shot.

If the function of slow motion has been to make poetic, romantic, glorious, horrifying, or otherwise heighten the emotionality of a moment, and the function of fast motion is the opposite, to minimize the emotional significance, to make us feel less, then what is the function of speed ramping, which, in one very cool and exciting shot does both? The device is probably too recent to theorize effectively. The fact that it appears in stylish recent films and lots of music videos now does not mean that it will always be associated with being stylish or cool. In fact, its prevalent use in music clips, and the wave of British "gangsta" films that were very popular in between 1998 and 2003, or so, makes it already look dated by association with a style that is no longer stylish. So the question is open as to whether it will become a cinematic device with conventional associations and reliable emotional resonances. The most I'm willing to say about it at the moment is that sometimes it is used as a subjective expression of the character's state of mind, but more often it seems to be an aesthetic effect in which shifting from the emotional qualities of slow motion to distancing qualities of fast motion creates a foregrounded sensual experience of time.

SUMMARY

There are many more devices available to editors and filmmakers to vary their storytelling and rhythms, and very likely some still to be invented. The two discussed herein, motion effects and parallel action, were chosen because they have an easy accessibility to editors. It is possible for an editor to create parallel action in a story that is plodding along or to create motion effects to change the texture and feel of time—characters' time and movie time. Both of these will complicate the unfolding of a story and, if used well, enhance expression as well as providing interest or variation.

Parallel action is particularly interesting as well, not just because it is one of the oldest devices, but because, in a sense, any cutting that uses a shot–reverse shot is parallel action. If there are two people in a conversation and the editor cuts between them, she is very often showing us not just what the action and reaction are—in other words, just what is happening sequentially—but is subtly manipulating time to show us what is going on meanwhile. If she cuts from a man drumming his fingers impatiently to a woman staring out the window she could be saying "he is impatient; meanwhile, she is lost in her thoughts." If there are two characters, there are two stories, and the questions for the editor will be the same in handling any two stories running parallel to each other: questions of emphasis, of where is action and where is emotion, and which one needs to be emphasized more to give this story the right balance. This question will be taken up further when we look at two examples of common scenes in the next chapter.

ENDNOTES

1. Turim, M., *Flashbacks in Film: Memory & History*, p.5.

2. In his book *The Eye Is Quicker*, Richard D. Pepperman writes extensively about story showing and how editors do it.

3. See Eisenstein, S., "Dickens, Griffith and the film today," in *Film Form*, p. 205.

4. See Fairservice, D., *Film Editing: History, Theory and Practice*, for more information on the evolution and development of practices and devices in editing.

5. Ibid., pp. 42–48.

6. This example of great editing technique first came to my attention when I was reading *The Technique of Film and Video Editing: Theory and Practice*, by Ken Dancyger. So rich are the innovations that Hitchcock brought to the film form that Chapter 6 of that book is completely devoted to experiments in editing by this master filmmaker.

7. Vertov is quoted in the DVD commentary by film scholar and Soviet film expert Yuri Tsivian on Vertov's masterpiece *Man with a Movie Camera*.

8. For more information on McKee's ideas about emotional transitions, see pp. 33 and 34 in *Story: Structure, Substance, Style and the Principles of Screenwriting*, Emotional transitions and some of McKee's other principles of scene design will also be looked at in more detail in the chapter on Common Scenes.

9. Ibid.

CHAPTER 11

Common Scenes

This chapter will look at two types of common scenes: two-handers (scenes with two characters talking in them) and chases. The two-handers are trickier to cut, but the chases are what win the editing awards because they are flashier, more visible editing. The analysis of each of these types of scenes draws on the theories and vocabularies proposed in this book, as well as theories proposed by others, and applies both to the practice of editing common scenes. In the case of two-handers, I will use the definition of a scene proposed by Robert McKee in *Story*[1] to provide a framework for extracting cutting principles. When discussing chases, I will make use of the work done by Ken Dancyger in *The Technique of Film and Video Editing*[2] in defining the elements of an action sequence. His explanation of the kinds of shots found in these sequences helps define some of the options an editor has when working with her material.

TWO-HANDERS

To look paradigmatically at two-handers, that is, look at what any of them may have in common, wherever they sit in the syntax or structure of a production, a definition of scene has to be established first. The definition I'm going to use comes from Robert McKee's book on screenwriting, *Story: Substance, Structure, Style and the Principles of Screenwriting*. I'm using this definition rather than the standard definition that a production manager would use because McKee looks at a scene as an emotional or story event, whereas a production manager would look at it as a technical or practical event.

For a production manager a scene is the action that takes places in a given location at a given time, and when the time of day or location changes, the scene, for production purposes, is given a new number. This scene numbering does not need to take into account flow of emotions, image, or story events in the final edit because scene numbering is concerned only with getting the production shot, not with storytelling.

The following definition of a scene by Robert McKee looks at a scene the way an editor needs to look at it: in terms of its opening and closure as an emotional or story event. McKee says:

> A scene is an *action through conflict* in more or less continuous time and space that *turns* the *value-charged condition* of a character's life on *at least one value* with a degree of perceptible significance.[3]

I have put the italics into that definition of a scene to highlight the important parts for an editor, which I will provide some more detail about in a moment. McKee discusses each of these italicized phrases in his book, and I will draw on his breakdown of terms to explain what the above quote means at a practical level. But I will also reinterpret these terms slightly to make them a bit more directly applicable to what an editor, as opposed to a screen writer, is doing.

Action Through Conflict

Action through conflict is something that is happening (action) that is not what one or more of the characters wants. In conventional drama, characters are pursuing goals, and conflict arises when they confront an obstacle to achieving their goals or getting what they want. Very often that obstacle is another person, a person with different or competing goals.

So a two-hander is action through conflict when two characters, who are each other's obstacles, meet and try to move, change, negotiate, get around, or defeat each other to achieve their goals. It is important to remember that the conflict may not be an overt conflict. It is not necessarily a fist fight or even an argument. The characters may just be talking about tea and cake, but the screenwriter and the editor both need to understand the underlying desires the characters are operating from to create drama. As discussed in Chapter 7, one character may ask for cake, but his underlying emotion is his desire for love. The other character may give him cake, but the underlying emotion she is operating on is her desire to escape. The conflict is not the subject of the scene, but it is the substance, and it is therefore what the editor is shaping. The editor shapes the emotional rhythm of a two-hander to convey the emotional conflict.

McKee says that a scene takes place in "more or less continuous time and space" because for him a scene is the rise and resolution of a particular conflict or event of emotional substance, not a change of location or of time of day.

Turns

When McKee says a scene involves a "turn," he simply means a change to another direction. So in a two-hander, a character may come in expecting to achieve his material or emotional goals and have his expectations thwarted or turned in another direction, so that by the end of the scene he doesn't expect to get what he wants anymore; rather, he has a new problem to deal with: not getting what he wants. Turning a scene is the heart of the editor's craft contribution to shaping a two-hander, but to turn a scene the editor has to understand what the action through conflict of the scene is, and also, as per the explanation below, what the "value-charged conditions" of the characters are.

Value-Charged Condition

McKee says, "Story values are the universal qualities of human experience which may shift from positive to negative or negative to positive, from one moment to the next. For example alive/dead (positive/negative) is a story value, as are love/hate, truth/lie.... All such binary qualities of experience that can reverse their charge at any moment, are story values."[4] So if a value is a universal quality of human condition that can shift from positive to negative, then where it starts is its value charge: its positiveness or negativeness at the beginning of the scene. The value charge is either the positive or the negative state that a character is in with regard to her desires and her life.

In a dramatic two-hander scene a character will perform an action that will be in conflict with another character's goals, and, for at least one of them, the value charge will change from positive to negative or negative to positive depending on who wants what and who gets what he or she wants.

On At Least One Value

Characters are not simple; they don't just want one thing, they may want love and security or love and adventure or revenge and money. So their conflicts are not necessarily simple either. McKee describes three levels of conflict that a character may be experiencing at any given time, or that may be running through the story: internal, interpersonal, and social or environmental. Internal conflict is obviously something going on in a character's own emotions or conscience, whereas interpersonal conflict is a collision of two or more characters' desires. Social or environmental conflict refers to the material or external world and how it may block or facilitate a character getting what he wants. When McKee says a scene turns on "at least one value," he means that a character may accomplish one thing he expected to but be thwarted in another. So in our example of one character asking for cake but wanting love, well, he gets cake, so that is one emotional state that doesn't change its value charge. However, in this case he is optimistic about his chances of getting love, too, and doesn't get that. So on another level, the interpersonal one, the value charge does change from positive to negative.

This notion of three levels of value charge is well worth the editor exploring further as she works on a scene. The question to ask herself is: What is the value charge of each character coming into the scene, internally, interpersonally, and socially or environmentally? (A given scene or production may not have all three operating at once, but the most fascinating, cinematic, and engaging characters often will have all three at work at some point.)

The editor also has to determine, in collaboration with the director, which of these values is the real substance of the scene, because that is the value she will use to shape the flow of the performances. The substance and rhythm of a two-hander, as we shall see from the case studies that follow, are shaped by the editor's choices about which character's performance to emphasize and when. These choices direct the spectator's attention to aspects of performance and character that provoke our own hopes and fears about what will happen.

The editor can also make vitally important choices about where and when to *turn* the scene; that is, what shot or character to be on, and what moment of his performance to show, to shape the emphasis and empathy we experience as the emotions in the scene turn. Turning a scene is not just a one-way street from script to final cut. The editor can create or realize a turn through choices of editing patterns and shots. A scene may be written with a particular point at which it turns, but this may not be convincing or energetic enough in the performances or shots or story. In the end we find that a scene can play as written, but the editor can rewrite by shaping the scene's flow. A scene can turn, or the editor can turn it.

The case studies that follow rely on the reader having read Chapter 7 of this book, or at least bringing his own foreknowledge of the terms used in that chapter, such as beats, actions, and intentions, to his reading of these case studies, because these terms are used to elucidate the strategies the editors are using in the given scenes to shape their emotional flow.

PRACTICAL EXERCISE

Goals and Actions

To understand how this idea of characters pursuing goals works, it is helpful to have an experience yourself of what you are doing to achieve your goals at any given moment. This practical exercise could be done in a number of circumstances to create an experience of analyzing your own and others' actions, goals, and value charges and when those value charges turn from positive to negative or vice versa. In this case we'll use a classroom, but we could just as easily use a party, dinner with the family, or a date. In any scenario with more than one person it is possible to look at the psychology of the two people involved and identify what, at some level anyway, each of them wants and how he or she is pursuing it.

This is not, however, an exercise in understanding drama, just an exercise in understanding how characters pursue goals. If it were an exercise in understanding drama, we would have to pick a scenario in which the two people's goals are in conflict with each other. Your classroom, party, dinner table, or date may be harmonious in that no one's goals conflict with anyone else's. In this case your scene would probably not end up in a movie. When people say "drama is life with the boring bits cut out," what they mean is that scenes in which nobody is struggling against obstacles to achieve their goals are undramatic.

That said, the following exercise is useful for understanding what is meant by pursuing goals and identifying how actions are taken in pursuit of goals.

If you're in a classroom, try asking the students what they want, as in: Why are you in class today, what did you come here for? It is likely that they will come up with a fairly small range of answers that might include knowledge, skills, and to see their friends, but will almost definitely include the answer

"to pass the class or to get a good grade." Once a goal such as "gain knowledge" or "get a good grade" has been established, then you can ask them: What will you do to get what you want? The answers will vary, from showing up to staying awake, paying attention and asking questions, making comments that make them look smarter than the other students or even putting other students down so that they look better, bringing an apple for the teacher or doing the readings or helping shift the tables into position, and so on.

At this point students discover that they can easily identify in themselves a range of behaviors they might undertake to get what they want. In fact, just as with the Stanislavski tradition of acting technique, their behavior is dictated by two things: wanting something (desire or goal) and what seems to be working as they move toward that goal.

If they try cracking jokes to get a good mark, they will keep doing this behavior if it gets a smile from the teacher and stop doing it if it gets a frown. So their goals and behavior create a cause-and-effect chain in life. The effect their behavior causes will determine whether they continue using that behavior to get what they want or change actions and try something else to achieve their goals. Or they may change their goals. If they switch to cracking jokes to make their friends laugh and to irritate the teacher, then the behavior they choose will have changed based on the change in their goals, and a new cause-and-effect chain will have been set in motion.

Armed with this immediate, embodied knowledge of how they themselves perform actions to achieve goals, students can begin to see what actions the characters are doing to achieve their goals and then to identify where a scene turns when the actions they take to achieve their goals do or do not work.

TWO-HANDER CASE STUDIES

Gone with the Wind (Victor Fleming, 1939)

Gone with the Wind is an epic romance about Scarlet O'Hara (Vivien Leigh) and the changes she and the "Old South" undergo during the

FIGURE 11.1

Clark Gable as Rhett and Vivien Leigh as Scarlet in Gone with the Wind *(Victor Fleming, 1939). Scarlet is trying to stop Rhett from leaving her, and her emotional dynamic is shown physically through the blocking: Rhett takes the lead and walks out of shots so that after each cut, Scarlet has to run into the new shot, chasing Rhett as he moves ahead of her. In the background of this still, a portrait of her and other details of their surroundings are clearly visible, as they are in most of the shots of this scene, but these details are not visible in the climactic close-ups at which the scene turns. Why? [Photo credit: Selznick/MGM; The Kobal Collection].*

American Civil War. Scarlet experiences inner conflict as she has to shift from being what she was raised to be, a Southern belle helplessly dependent on slaves and protective men, to being who she really is: a successful, independent, and shrewd businesswoman. Her interpersonal conflicts are many; in fact, just about everyone in the story presents her with conflict as they either try to repress her independent spirit and initiative or rely on her to solve all of their problems. In her love relationships the inner and the interpersonal conflicts intertwine for Scarlet as they overlap with her own understanding of who she is or ought to be. Socially and environmentally, conflict is everywhere: the story is set during war, but only when the war changes Scarlet's life does Scarlet come into conflict with it.

The last scene of *Gone with the Wind* is the scene in which we hear Clark Gable, as Scarlet's husband Rhett, say the famous line, "Frankly my dear, I don't give a damn," and then leave her. Up until this scene, Scarlet has been known, even by Rhett, to be in love with another man, Ashley. In the scene just before this final one, Ashley's wife dies. For reasons that are not quite clear, probably owing to conventions of the epic romance, which at the time would have dictated that successful independent women should be punished by being failures in love relationships, as soon as Ashley's wife dies, Scarlet realizes she isn't really in love with Ashley at all; rather, she loves her husband, Rhett. She races home to tell him that she loves him, filled with the uplifting optimistic expectation that he will rejoice in her declaration and they will live happily ever after, only to have her expectations thwarted.

The scene is beautifully shot, with the director Victor Fleming taking tremendous care with the framing and shot sizes to convey the power shifts and changing expectations between the two characters cinematically. Consequently, the editor has few choices to make throughout the bulk of the scene about where to cut or what to cut to. The scene is played in a series of shots that start on a framing of Rhett, then Scarlet moves into the frame to talk to him, then Rhett leaves the frame. Then the editor, Hal C. Kern, cuts to the next shot, framing Rhett and forcing Scarlet to run into the shot, to pursue Rhett, to ask, plead, and finally beg him not to leave her. Throughout this scene Scarlet is being refused and denied what she wants, but she keeps hoping. She keeps believing she will get what she wants, she keeps changing her action as she pursues her goal, until a specific moment when the realization dawns on her that she has lost. This one moment is the turn of the scene, and I would argue that, in this case, the editor created it.

If you watch the scene, you can't help but notice how beautifully the mise-en-scène is articulated in most of the shots. It is shot with a fairly wide but not distorting lens, so that the backgrounds and the foregrounds are sharp. It is important that the backgrounds are sharp because the set contributes to the meaning of the scene as the characters move through it. It frames them and creates opportunities for the balance of power to be visible in the shot's composition and movement. The whole scene is shot this way until it turns. The moment when Scarlet realizes her desires have been thwarted, the cinematographer suddenly changes from a wide lens to a long lens, the backgrounds go completely soft and blurry, and, at the same time, the shot pattern changes from medium-wide two-shots (shots in which both characters are in frame) to a much tighter two-shot and then a tight close-up on Scarlet. Now it would be possible to surmise that the director planned this change in the shot pattern *in order* to turn the scene at this moment. But I would hypothesize that in fact what happened was that the editor realized the scene did not have a satisfactory turn, and he ordered a "pickup" of the moment at which the emotional expectations actually change.

A pickup is a shot the editor asks for after main shooting has been completed. If, as he would have been in the Hollywood studio in 1939, the editor is assembling the rushes or dailies during the production period, he can recognize if there is an important moment missing in the coverage before the cast and crew disperse and the shoot is finished. In *Gone with the Wind*, I hypothesize that the editor realized the scene didn't have a change in shot pattern that would help him to turn it, and he notified the director. The director then got shots according to the editor's specifications, but, as the crew had probably moved on from the location of the original scene, he picked them up with a long lens, which blurs the background, rather than a wide lens, which would have revealed the fact that they were not on the original set. By blurring the background the director was able to make the pickup shots match the original coverage closely enough to get away with it.

So my hypothesis that in the climactic scene of the most expensive motion picture ever made up until then, *Gone with the Wind,* the editor actually engineered the turning of the scene is based on three things:

1. The lens changes;

2. The background, which had been so articulated and significant before, suddenly becomes blurred; and

3. Most importantly, the pattern of shots changes from the carefully choreographed pattern of two-shots to a single in which the character doesn't move.

The last reason is the most important because, even if I am wrong and the scene was shot all at once and didn't use pickups, the change of the pattern of shots is the key to understanding the editor's control over the turn of a scene. Changing the pattern of shots is the editor's cinematic tool for underlining and crystallizing emotional change or change of the value charge from positive to negative. In a two-hander the change in pattern could be from two-shots to a single, as it is here, or from singles to a two-shot. It could be from many cuts to no cuts or from no cuts to one cut or from long shots to close or close to long. The point is not how the pattern changes but that it does. In *Gone with the Wind* the change in pattern of shots is the key to understanding that Scarlet's value charge has changed from positive to negative. It is subtle in this case because the value charge would seem to be changing throughout the scene. But I would argue that the turn is the actual moment at which the realization dawns, when the character who has been hopeful gives up hope, stops maneuvering or negotiating, or even pleading and begging, and accepts the new state of things, allowing the audience and the drama to move on to what happens next.

Postcards from the Edge (Mike Nichols, 1990)

Postcards from the Edge is a film Robert McKee uses to talk about screen-writing technique in his seminars and lectures. After attending one of these seminars I watched the film again and realized it also has some interesting things to reveal about constructing the "last draft of the script," the edit.

Postcards from the Edge is obviously a much more recently made film than *Gone with the Wind*, and the shooting and production style are therefore quite different. It is likely that, rather than setting up each shot so that it could be cut only in a certain way, the director, Mike Nichols, would have covered most scenes from two or more angles and thus given the editor, Sam O'Steen, many more options for shaping the scene in the edit suite. In this case O'Steen didn't have to ask for pickups to shape the emotional dynamics by shaping the shot patterns; he had the material available for him to manipulate into patterns that underline the scene's emotions and changes.

One reason the change in pattern of shots is so important in turning the scene is that it is a visual cue, not a dialog cue, to the change. In other words, it can occur on and emphasize the subtext rather than simply supporting the text. Changing the pattern of shots is something the editor can do to reveal, punctuate, support, or even, in some cases, create the subtext. She can construct the rhythm of the scene by using the beats or changes of actions that the actors play in the most engaging and believable emotional cause-and-effect chain the material allows—whether that is the chain that was written or not. If she creates this cause-and-effect chain with a pattern of shots and then changes the pattern when the scene turns, then she is creating a visible, physical expression of the emotional dynamic of the scene.

Unlike *Gone with the Wind*, the scene I'm going to analyze from *Postcards from the Edge* is just a scene, not a sequence or act climax. It's a smallish turn, and the cutting is minimal, but there are some key cuts that make the most of the performances, and the places where there is no cutting are also significant in telling us how the values are shifting for the protagonist. The rhythm of this scene is very much contained in the performances, which are very finely rehearsed. The physical rhythm is fairly minimal, there are no cutaways to add texture, color, or movement; the emphasis is on the actors, their performances, and their spatial relationships. These performances and spatial relationships are carefully set up and shot to be about the static nature of the balance of power between the two characters.

Postcards from the Edge is a coming-of-age story, which is interesting considering the protagonist, Suzanne (Meryl Streep), is 35, which is much older than most people are when they come of age. Suzanne has had a recreational drug overdose and is in a rehab center when her mother (Shirley MacLaine), a once-famous movie star, comes to visit.

PRACTICAL EXERCISE

Analyzing a Scene

The following five questions are the ones I used to make my analysis of *Postcards from the Edge*. I have found, over the years, that they are pretty robust and can be applied to most two-handers you would like to try them against.

1   Define the conflict

What do the characters want and what forces of antagonism are blocking them? You may find it useful to ask this question on a number of levels, as in: What do the characters want in their lives, what do they want in the whole movie, what do they want in the sequence, the scene, and from moment to moment?

2   Note the value at the beginning

Once you know what your protagonist wants, decide what her value charge is at the beginning of the scene; is she positive or negative in her expectations? Does she think she'll get what she wants or not? Another facet of this is to note her current emotional state: Is she in a positive state—e.g., happily in love—or a negative state; e.g., pining with unrequited love?

3   Break the scene into beats

What are the characters doing to get what they want? When those actions don't work, what do they try next? Can you see the beat, or the place at which they shift their action from one thing to another?

4   Note the closing value and compare it to the opening value

You can now map the emotional trajectory of the whole scene from its starting charge, through the changes the characters undergo as they play their actions and come into conflict with each other, to their final emotional charge in the scene.

5   Survey the beats and locate the turning point

At what point in the sequence of beats does the value charge actually change? Once you have found the beats, you can identify the key beat on which the values change, and, at this point, you may discover that there is a change in shot pattern or at least a cut on this moment.

Define the Conflict—What Does the Character Want?

At the beginning of this sequence of *Postcards from the Edge*, Suzanne just wants to get through this visit from her mother without a fuss. She wants a peaceful, cheerful visit with no tears, traumas, accusations, or confrontations. In the bigger picture of the whole film, Suzanne has a slightly different goal. Her desire is to grow up, to be successfully in charge of her own life and not susceptible to her mother's manipulations. The force of antagonism blocking her is her mother, who is too self-absorbed to see Suzanne as anything but her child, certainly not as her own person. This is useful knowledge for analyzing this scene because once there are tears and confrontations, they stem from this bigger subtextual issue, not from the immediate subjects being discussed.

Note Value At Beginning

The scene starts when Suzanne's mother arrives at the rehab center. Suzanne is optimistic about her chances of getting through the visit without a fuss. She brushes off the fact that her mother is late and waits pretty patiently while her mother is adored by fans. In a sense, you could say that Suzanne is strategizing. She is being patient and lighthearted because if she can get through this visit without Mom affecting her too much, maybe she can start to achieve her larger objective, which is to get through life without Mom on her back.

Break the Scene Into Beats

Once Suzanne and her mother reach Suzanne's bedroom and begin to talk, Suzanne goes through a number of beats to try to keep the peace, all of which are ignored by her mother as she railroads through her monolog, taking charge of Suzanne's life and career.

It is worth noting here that, although it is Suzanne's story, this part of the scene is covered in one shot that features Mom at the center of the screen, talking animatedly. Suzanne, stretched out on her bed at the bottom of the screen, is barely visible. I would be very confident in suggesting that the whole scene was probably covered from the reverse position, over Mom's shoulder, and that Sam O'Steen, the editor, chose to use the shot in which Mom is featured to enhance the magnitude of the forces of antagonism arrayed against Suzanne; that is, to make Mom a bigger force.

Also, and perhaps more importantly, he features Mom to keep our sympathies aligned with Suzanne. Suzanne tries a number of actions to stem the flow of Mom's tide of plans and accusations, and most of these are to put Mom down, to belittle her, to mock her. These don't work, of course, but if we were to see them center screen they would be much stronger and the result would probably be that we liked Suzanne less. As the scene is cut, Suzanne's interjections are clever, but she is David against Mom's Goliath. She is low in the frame and a victim. If she were large and centered, she would seem to be more of an ungrateful brat than a sympathetic target for Mom's inane rant.

Note the Closing Value and Compare It to the Opening Value

At the end of the scene, when Mom leaves Suzanne's bedroom, the value charge for Suzanne has changed from positive to negative with regard to her immediate and her long-term expectations and desires. Mom has managed to cry and blame Suzanne, Suzanne has had to confront and accuse Mom, the confrontation has not been effective, Mom has ignored the implications of Suzanne's accusations and left, still planning and taking charge of Suzanne's life.

Survey the Beats and Locate the Turning Point

There is a specific point at which Suzanne's desire for a peaceful, tear-free visit is thwarted, and that, of course, is when Mom starts to cry. As noted earlier, there is only one shot from when Suzanne and Mom start talking together on the beds in the room, and that shot is held for quite a long time, through quite a few small beat changes for Suzanne as Mom takes charge of the action. When Mom suddenly starts to cry, O'Steen makes his first cut. He changes the pattern of shots, draws our attention to Suzanne, and effectively turns her value charge from an optimistic expectation that she'll slide through to a negative expectation that she won't make it.

This is a very interesting choice of a moment to turn the focus to Suzanne. When I screen it for students and ask them what Suzanne is doing in the shot O'Steen has cut to, they often say "nothing" on first viewing. However, if you go back and play the cut again, you find that, in fact, Suzanne is incredibly busy in the shot. Not only is she holding her breath and freezing her movements, which are active physical actions, she is hurtling through an array of emotional actions. She is biting her tongue, holding back accusations, repressing angry outbursts, and giving up hope, all in the space of about 3 seconds. You could say that her optimism for achieving her scene goal disappears before our eyes, but you would have to add that this is because O'Steen has chosen to show us that moment, to turn the scene there, and not at any number of other points at which she could have appeared to give up hope.

O'Steen then cuts back to the original shot in which Mom is center frame again, holds this for a moment, and then, as Suzanne sits up to confront Mom, changes the pattern of shots again. O'Steen goes from holding on one shot for a long time to a much quicker back and forth, for four shots. The change of pattern signals that not only has Suzanne's immediate scene value charge changed from positive to negative, but her hopes of achieving her larger goal, of getting Mom to recognize her as her own person, are also receding.

Then Mom gets up to leave and O'Steen returns to his original shot and holds it to the end of the scene. As the ending of the scene plays out, Suzanne and Mom have their most explicit argument yet, over who will do Suzanne's laundry. But there are no cuts here. This argument is loud and overt, but it is not the substance of the scene. The scene has already turned, Suzanne has lost, and now the consequences of her loss are just being played out. O'Steen chooses to hold on the one shot for the entire argument and Mom's departure because he is in fact saying "no change." Mom held power when she came in; she got what she wanted, which was to dominate Suzanne; she is leaving, impervious to the pain she has caused; and we are in the exact same place as we were when we started. The shot and the balance of power remain unchanged, only Suzanne's value charge has changed from positive to negative.

I have argued up to now that the editor can take charge of how and when a scene turns by changing the pattern of shots and choosing what to show and when. The next three very quick case studies are all, to some extent, cutting oddities, interesting variations on the idea that changing the cutting pattern can turn the scene. They are highly visible cutting responses to underlying themes in a scene or story, and so they draw some attention to themselves; but on close examination, it is possible to see how each supports or creates the actual emotional intentions of the scene.

Notorious (Alfred Hitchcock, 1946)

In *Notorious*, Ingrid Bergman plays a degenerate and degraded woman, Alicia, who is called upon by the U.S. Government to do a spy job that can redeem her in her own eyes, and those of the world. Cary Grant plays the agent, Devlin, who recruits her and, not surprisingly, the two fall in love. One of the key two-hander scenes between them takes place in Alicia's apartment, before she knows what her exact mission is and after Devlin has recruited her. In this scene, the two embrace and banter and kiss each other continuously until Devlin gets a phone call asking him to come to the office. Although there is lots of conversation between Alicia and Devlin over this time, there are no cuts. It is all one shot, and I would argue that this is because nothing really changes. In fact, this is sort of half a scene interrupted by a completely different series of scenes. When Devlin returns to the apartment an hour later, the scene takes up where it left off, but then there are lots of changes. Value charges change for both of them, and there are plenty of cuts reflecting the textual and subtextual conflicts they are now engaged in.

Kiss or Kill (Bill Bennett, 1998)

Kiss or Kill is an Australian film with a very distinctive style, pace, and subject matter. The underlying themes of the film are that you never really know where you stand with other people, that at any moment a person could kiss or kill. In the story, fugitives played by Francis O'Connor and Matt Day are on the run. At one point they pull into a gas station, get some gas and snacks, and then leave. This is a 1-minute scene in which nothing really happens as far as changes of values go, but there are lots of cuts. The editor, Henry Dangar, ASE, has established a style for editing the film that involves rapid jump cutting throughout. On the editing style chart in Chapter 9, this film would be an extreme example of decoupage and collision. Every shot collides with the next, creating an uneasy feeling that the ground is shifting beneath you; you never really know where you stand, which, of course is a cinematic expression of the film's themes.

The dozens of edits are a way of saying that things are always in flux. By constantly shifting our point of view slightly, the edits and shots imply that these characters, if looked at a bit differently, would change. Or, in fact, they are changing. So, Dangar establishes and sustains an editing style that conveys a meaning different from what quick cutting often conveys. Instead of conveying lots of changes, the dozens of cuts say the opposite, that change is a constant.

Howard's End (James Ivory, 1992)

In contrast to the highly visible stylization of *Kiss or Kill*, *Howard's End* is a stately and classical costume drama. However, there is one scene that jumps out for its editing choices and its radical shift away from the cutting style that has been used up to that point. This is the scene in which Meg Schlegel, played by Emma Thompson, confronts her new husband, Henry J. Wilcox, played by Anthony Hopkins, over an affair he had years ago.

FIGURE 11.2
Anthony Hopkins as Henry and Emma Thompson as Meg, apparently healing a rift in their relationship in Howard's End *(James Ivory, 1992). [Photo credit: Merchant Ivory; The Kobal Collection]*

In the scene, Meg forgives Henry and reassures him that it will never be thought about again. The value charge appears to change in the scene, from negative to positive, in favor of their loving relationship staying the course. Then there is a fade to black and a fade up to the same scene in which the characters seem to be having a variation of the same conversation, and the exact same value change, from negative to positive in favor of the stability of their relationship, occurs again. Then fade to black again, then fade up and the same conversation, virtually, and the same value change occurs a third time. In each iteration there are changes and variations, of course. We are not seeing the same lines or blocking or shots, but substantively, we are seeing the same action, and this has a very curious effect on the value change in the scene.

On first viewing I surmised that the husband just needed a lot of reassurance and the scene keeps repeating because it takes a long time for him to believe his wife forgives him. But on reviewing the sequence it is possible to see that this is not the case at all. It may be what is occurring textually, but subtextually the opposite is happening. It is not a matter of Meg forgiving her husband, but of him stubbornly resisting her forgiveness until it becomes obvious that his real goal is to get her to see that she is the one who needs to be forgiven. He is not to blame for having been unfaithful, she is to blame for having witnessed his indiscretion. By repeating the apparent change from negative to positive three times, the editor actually undercuts the shift of the value charge and turns it into its opposite. The scene is not about the wife forgiving her husband, it is about the husband succeeding in getting his wife to take the blame. Instead of moving from negative to positive, the result of the repetition is to show them stuck. We learn that although the damage will be covered up and masked, their relationship will never recover.

SUMMARY—TWO-HANDERS

At the end of the discussion on parallel action (Chapter 10, "Devices"), I noted that cutting two-handers has something in common with parallel action as a device, in that if there are two characters, there are two sides to the story going on. Although we may be seeing the relationship of these two sides of the story sequentially—that is, in a cause-and-effect chain rather than in parallel—the questions of editing parallel action can still be useful.

When working on a two-hander it is very useful, for example, to identify where action is and where emotion is. In the scene from *Howard's End*, action appears to be with the wife and emotion with the husband. She appears to have to do the forgiving; his feelings and their relationship appear to be at stake. However, the opposite is revealed to be true; he is action and she is emotion, and the future of their relationship depends not on her driving the scene and forgiving him, but on her letting him drive the scene and taking the blame.

In the scene from *Postcards from the Edge*, Mom is action and Suzanne is emotion all the way through. As discussed above, their relationship does not change, and that, of course, is the problem.

In the scene from *Gone with the Wind*, Scarlet starts out as action, rushing in to declare her love and make everything all right again. But when Rhett starts to leave her, he takes charge of the scene. He becomes action and she becomes emotion. So, just as with parallel action, the question for the editor becomes: Which side are we on, when, and for how long?

CHASES

The chase is often referred to as pure cinema because it is a scenario in which the conflict is always made manifest in visible and audible action. Chases do not, therefore, have the same problems as the two-handers; in many ways, the problems are the opposite. The scene objective is always the same in a chase, for one entity to catch the other, so the editor does not need to interrogate the behavior to find out what the subtext is, or who wants what. However, the editor does have to shape the behavior to create the impression of a strong cause-and-effect chain and modulate the cycles of tension and release. Just as in a two-hander, she does these things by choosing whose side to be on, when, and for how long. This section will look at the elements an editor could take into consideration as she makes these decisions.

Some very useful principles about chases have been articulated by Ken Dancyger in *The Technique of Film and Video Editing*.[5] In the section on action from page 223 to 225, Dancyger writes about four key issues for constructing an effective action sequence: identification, excitation, conflict, and intensification. Each of these four also applies to a chase, and I will use Dancyger's definitions of them to begin constructing a "recipe" for effective chase cutting.

Identification

There is much theory available on the question of identification and even the validity of it as a concept. One of the current theoretical questions is: Do spectators "identify" with a character, as in transferring their own sense of who they are onto the character? Or, as spectators, could what we are doing be more accurately described as aligning with the character, as in hoping for the same things he hopes for and fearing with his fears, and thus, in a sense, developing an allegiance with him? Or is the action more accurately referred to as empathizing? I have tended, in this book, to promote the idea that we empathize, and that we empathize physically or kinesthetically as well as or as a part of our emotional empathy.

For our purposes in discussing chases it is not really necessary to solve this theoretical question and choose between identifying, aligning, and empathizing. It is sufficient to say that the spectator must care. As viewers we have to know enough about who the character is, and feel close enough to him, or closely aligned enough with his goals, to understand why he does what he does, to hope he achieves his desires, and to fear he won't. Then this "identification" has to be maintained throughout the chase. We can't get too far away from the character we care about or we will cease to care.

So, to create what Dancyger calls identification, he suggests we need close-ups and point-of-view shots. Close-ups bring us into greater intimacy with the characters by bringing us into closer proximity, and they reveal more minute details of their feelings and expressions than do long shots. Point-of-view shots literally give us the same view of the situation that the characters have, thus making it easier for us to understand what they feel, because we see what they see.

Excitation

Excitation, in Dancyger's view, is accomplished through movement: movement within shots and movement of shots (pans, zooms, tracks, dollies, cranes, etc.). Excitation is also accomplished, he says, through increasing the pace, or rate of change of movement. The earlier chapters of this book offer an expansive explanation of how this works for the spectator and for the editor in the discussions of movement activating our mirror neurons and our kinesthetic empathy. It comes down to saying that movement is what we can shape in order to shape rhythm, and the purpose of rhythm is to create the cycles of tension and release that keep us engaged in the story. So in a chase, excitation is accomplished by shaping movement into the cycles of tension and release that get our heart rates going and our pulses pumping.

An aspect of cutting that is particular to the creation of excitation is this question: Do we cut before or after the peak of the content curve? "Content curve" means how long it takes to recognize the content of a shot, to understand it, and to be ready to move on. Cutting before the peak of a content curve—that is, just as the spectator is beginning to understand what is in a shot but hasn't fully grasped it—creates a kind of uneasiness and edginess. The viewer knows something is going on but is not sure what. This can contribute to excitation, though, of course, too much of this uncertainty can also diminish excitation and create irritation. If we really don't know what's going on for long enough, we lose the thread of the action and stop being excited about it or even caring about it, in part because, when we lose the thread of the action, we also loosen our understanding of what's at stake.

Conflict

According to Dancyger, conflict is developed by crosscutting. By going back and forth between the two sides of the action, we stay in touch with how close each character is to his goal. The cutting back and forth between chaser and person being chased also keeps the stakes in the foreground of our thoughts and increases the activity of our minds as we consciously or unconsciously conjecture about what will happen. Each time, we are reminded of how close each side is to achieving its

PRACTICAL EXERCISE

Content Curve

You can get a small group of people together to help you test out what the content curves of various images are and how cutting before or after the peak of the content curve changes perception.

Gather a few images together. Try to make them quite different from each other so that your viewers can't get used to looking in just one way. For example, you might use a print of an Italian renaissance painting of a battlefield, a black-and-white print of a photograph, and a child's drawing.

Gather your group around a table and then show them one of the images for half a second. Start with it face down on the table, lift it so they can see, and then put it down again and ask them what they saw.

Depending on how complex the image is, they may be able to report seeing figures or colors or even relationships or moods. Or they may have just seen figures and colors and surmised relationships and moods. If you play around with the images and timings for a while, you will begin to get a sense of how much complexity and detail can be absorbed in how much time. From there you can ask yourself how long you would need to hold on a given image for an audience to understand it completely and how much time you

could consider shaving off of that duration so that they grasp figures and colors and maybe surmise relationships and moods, but still experience some excitation of not quite knowing what is going on.

One thing to note is that the second time you show an image, even if you show it for a very short time, your viewers will grasp much more of the content. This is because they are accumulating information from successive viewings, of course. They are using what they learned the first time they saw it to augment what they grasp the second time. Obviously this is useful for editors to play around with because they may well return to a shot a few times, and they can use this process of the viewer accumulating knowledge to create suspense and a reveal.

Be warned though; people can get quite irritated in this experiment if they feel they are being tested on how quickly they grasp the content of an image but they aren't being given sufficient time to grasp it. This irritation is a valuable part of the learning for the person doing the experiment, because it helps them to understand when the audience's excitation might turn to irritation. But make sure your colleagues know it is just a game and they are not being judged, because you don't want that irritation directed at you.

goal and what is at stake; and the open question of "what will happen?" and the tension of that question are renewed.

There is another idea about conflict that is also very useful in the context of cutting a chase, which is Eisenstein's notion of conflict: the conflict created when cutting together shots of unequal size or lighting values or movement or direction or line, shape, or mass. This sense of conflict more rightfully belongs in the category of excitation, though, because what is happening is that by cutting between shots that don't link smoothly, that collide in some aspect of their composition, you are creating more movement between shots. The viewer's mind has to move more quickly to recognize each new shot, and the jagged quality of movement is also more foregrounded.

Intensification

To quote Dancyger directly, "Intensification is achieved through varying length of shots."[6] This has not just to do with shortening shots but really has to do with modulating the rhythm, the points of emphasis by duration and energy, to make surprising and engaging movement phrases or patterns of accent. In different cases this could mean holding on one shot for a long time until the question of "what will happen next?" intensifies and then rushing into a flurry of short sharp shots. Or intensification could be achieved by setting up a pattern of very even cuts and then jumping into an erratic pattern of lengths. And so on. There are many, many possible variations, but overall the intensification created by varying the length of shots has more to do with the patterns of movement created, sustained, and judiciously broken than with the actual length of shots themselves.

By breaking the elements of a chase down into the categories of identification, excitation, conflict, and intensification, Dancyger has, I believe, provided us with a very useful basis for understanding how an effective chase is made. If we were to think of these four elements as ingredients, just as flour, eggs, butter, and flavoring are the basic ingredients of a cake, then we would have the first half of a recipe for cutting a chase.

The question then becomes: What kind of a chase are we making? To draw the analogy a bit further, if we were making an intense chocolate cake, we would use more chocolate and butter and less flour. If we were making a light cake, we'd put in more flour and less butter, but possibly the same amount of chocolate. Similarly, the questions for an editor are: What are the proportions of the ingredients and how will different mixes make different effects?

The following case studies look at the balance of ingredients in different chases. But this recipe is also easy to apply to analysis of scenes that you are curious about or that you are cutting. The ingredients are identification, excitation, conflict, and intensification. What are the proportions and timings of these that are going to make the most effective chase in the context of the story and style you have established?

CHASE CASE STUDIES

The Girl and Her Trust (D. W. Griffith, 1912)

The chase in *The Girl and Her Trust* is between robbers trying to steal the safe from a train station and a train racing to foil them. As the thieves try to make their escape, the "girl" of the title, played by Dorothy Bernard, an energetic and enterprising lass if ever there was one, jumps on board the robber's handcart and impedes their progress.

The chase lasts for 2 minutes and although there are only 23 cuts, all of the four elements of a chase—identification, excitation, conflict, and intensification—are visible in some measure.

Conflict is by far the most prevalent element in this chase, as 12 of the shots are cut together to move from one side of the action to the other. There is also a very substantial amount of excitation; that is, movement within shots and of the camera, which is sometimes mounted on a vehicle moving in parallel with the train and handcart to track their progress. However, this excitation does not look very exciting to a contemporary viewer because to our eye there is relatively little movement going on. Griffith has cleverly utilized still objects in the foreground to emphasize the speed and trajectory of the train as it passes, but to our eye he never cuts before the peak of the content curve, the shots are very similar in composition, so we have no trouble recognizing and assimilating the information within them, and they are all in long shot so their movement is not felt, kinesthetically, with the same intensity a close-up would provide.

There are only two shots in the whole sequence that would qualify as shots that promote identification or alignment with the character and her goals. These are high-angle shots looking down at the girl and the robbers on the handcart. The girl looks up toward the camera, allowing us to see her face and care about her emotions, but these shots don't show up until the middle of the chase, so their effect is somewhat minimized. Because we don't align with the girl intimately from the beginning, it is harder to engage later. Interestingly, the last shot of the girl, after she's saved the day, reveals her to be witty and vivacious; in other words, well worth aligning with. But our identification up to then has been more abstract, more with an archetype than a character.

Intensification, as in establishment of a pattern of shots and then varying it to create a particular "ride" through the action, is probably the least visible of all the elements in this particular chase. Cuts do come faster toward the end, but the framing of the shots does not add to the intensity of movement or emotion, so the speed of cuts, by itself, does not have as strong an effect of intensification as it might.

Although there are many aspects of *The Girl and Her Trust* that are somewhat outside of our contemporary experience of what a cinematic chase might look or feel like, this doesn't mean it wasn't a good chase at the time. In fact, it demonstrates that in some sense we have changed very little in our construction of chase sequences. To a greater or lesser extent all of the elements are there. What is interesting is what the proportions of ingredients in the recipe tell us about what was important to the filmmaker and his contemporary audiences. The reliance on long shots of the train barreling down the tracks does not so much indicate naiveté about creating identification as it signals a fascination with the machine. This great, powerful locomotive was cast in the role of the force for good, and if we see it that way and recognize the novelty and powerful cultural mythological engagement with trains, we can see that the filmmaker chose shots of the train because that was what mattered to him and to his audience. The shots of the train create an understanding of the meaning and dynamics of this particular story and chase. As we shall see in each of the chases that follow, there is an ongoing fascination with new technology, and although the movement gets faster and the close-ups get closer, filmmakers are still using machines to create excitation and still shaping a balance of their ingredients to deliver the meaning of their particular chase.

The French Connection (William Freidkin, 1971)

The chase between the cop (Gene Hackman) and the drug dealer (Marcel Bozzuffi) at the end of *The French Connection* won a well-deserved Academy Award for its editor, Jerry Greenberg. The editor's artistry is particularly apparent in this chase from the way Greenberg balances the chase's ingredients to make us feel the story.

FIGURE 11.3

Gene Hackman as the cop and Marcel Bozzuffi as the drug dealer in The French Connection *(William Freidkin, 1971). This shot shows the almost lyrical final moment of a chase that has been characterized by extraordinary effort. [Photo credit: 20th Century Fox; The Kobal Collection]*

Like most contemporary chases, this one is composed of fragments of action cut to look like they're happening at a frenetic pace next to each other. Which, of course, they weren't. Chases are very arduous to shoot, involving dozens of setups; that is, moving the camera, the crew, and the actors to a new place, lighting it, and then just grabbing a short sharp burst of action on camera before the lumbering process of moving the crew begins again. To make an effective chase, the editor has to take all of these little fragments and compose them into a convincing cause-and-effect chain, a chain of shots by which we can believe that the action in the first shot causes the action in the second shot. The cause-and-effect chain has to be more than convincing, though. It has to be compelling. And this is where the balancing of identification, excitation, conflict, and intensification, to tell the particular story of your chase, comes into play.

The chase in *The French Connection* is unusual because at one point the person being chased, the drug dealer, jumps onto a subway train and thinks that he has eluded his chaser. But he doesn't relax, and neither does the tension of the chase. Instead, the editor uses parallel action between the drug dealer and the cop to make us feel that the two characters know where each other is and are feeling the immediate pressure of each other's presence, when in fact the opposite is true. But the intercutting or use of the element of conflict in the edit keeps both sides of the action so present in our minds that we forget this and feel that the characters are under extreme pressure.

Excitation is a big element in *The French Connection* chase. Even though it was made in 1971, it still feels as though the rate of movement within and between shots is dazzlingly high. In particular, Gene Hackman's performance as the cop is filled with very dynamic and revealing movement. His body language speaks of intense focus, the ravages of the long chase, and the fury that fuels the effort he has to make to reach his goal. Excitation emanates from all of the shots associated with him, too—his car windshield, tires, the subway tracks overhead, and the architecture and inhabitants of the city around him all whip past with fast-moving, high-contrast shadows, lines, colors, or directions.

The spinning of tires and slamming of feet on the pedals have now become old chestnuts of shots to enhance excitation in a chase (in fact, they were used as far back as 1916 in D.W. Griffith's *Intolerance*), but they do their job here and keep our heart rates up. Part of the success of these elements is the soundtrack for this scene. Unlike most chases, this one does not use music. Instead, it relies on sound to articulate the rhythms and pulse of the sequence. Therefore, the sounds of things moving are fully exploited and enhanced in the sound design, and this contributes to our sense of the immediacy of the excitation.

Another very important device that comes into play in *The French Connection* is what I call jeopardy-enhancing elements. These are the innocent bystanders who are endangered by the chase: the baby carriage narrowly missed, the passengers on the subway car. All of these add to our sense of the danger and tension of the scene and allow for some variation in the patterning of shots. The conflict is more intense when Greenberg does not just cut back and forth between protagonist and antagonist but develops some stronger sense of identification or knowledge of who they are, in each of their stories, by use of jeopardy-enhancing elements. We have emotional responses to each of the characters when we see their response to these. The cop is alarmed and almost hysterical when he narrowly misses a baby carriage. The dealer is calm and callous when the subway train driver dies of a heart attack. In both cases, close-ups and point-of-view shots are used and we understand more about each of them.

Intensification is beautifully realized at the end of this frenetic and high-anxiety chase when the two opposing sides finally meet on the subway entrance stairs. At first it seems that the dealer will just surrender. But then he starts to make a run for it, and after all the fast and furious cutting, the shot in which he is killed is elegiac, almost lyrical, and held for a long time as the cop, exhausted and spent, slumps down onto the stairs after the very hard won capture of his prey.

Identification, excitation, conflict, and intensification are very equally balanced in this chase, unlike *The Girl and Her Trust*, in which there is plenty of conflict but almost no identification. The difference created by using a different balance of these ingredients is that the chase becomes a different story. Both have the same plot in the sense that someone is being chased by someone else. And the chases end in the same way, with capture. But they are very different stories. *The Girl and Her Trust* is the story of unexpected elements, a girl and a train, foiling the villain's plans. It is a story of archetypes colliding and simple good triumphing. The chase in *The French Connection* is much more a story of humans against machines, rather than working harmoniously with machines. The characters have some complexity to them, which is made apparent through the elements of identification and intensification. The characters strategize and persist against overwhelming odds, and in the end their emotions, their frailty, and the magnitude of their effort tell a story of humanity locked in a struggle with overwhelming forces and succeeding, but just barely, and at a cost.

Terminator 2 (James Cameron, 1991)

There is a chase early on in *Terminator 2* between the new model Terminator, T-1000 (played by Robert Patrick); the 12-year-old boy, John (Edward Furlong), who he has been sent to kill; and the old model Terminator (Arnold Schwarzenegger), who has been repurposed for this sequel and given the mission of saving the boy.

This chase is once again a battle of vehicles and, just as in the other two chases, in which the cop's car becomes a beat-up version of him and the train is a stand-in for the hero, the vehicles become part of the identity of the characters themselves. The boy, John, is riding a motor scooter. On it he has some power—it is not as feeble as a bicycle would be—but he is small, exposed, and vulnerable nonetheless. T-1000 commandeers a massive shiny black truck. Its façade is the size of a small house and in it T-1000 is elevated way above John. Midway through the chase, Schwarzenegger rides in on a huge motorbike, its bass roar replacing the scooter's anxious whine in a patriarchal sweep as Schwarzenegger pulls John off his bike and deposits him in his lap. John's scooter gets crushed under the wheels of the truck that is pursuing them, but this is not just a jeopardy-enhancing element. It tells us how much danger John is in by crushing an aspect of him with barely a bump to the truck's suspension system. This may be a vehicle getting crushed, but it is definitely a use of identification to heighten our emotional responses.

In fact, this chase relies primarily on identification and conflict to achieve its affect. There is very little intensification. The cuts come evenly throughout the whole, about a second apart. The music and sound effects add to this blanket feeling of even pace by being evenly intense and carrying the same pulse throughout. The only exceptions are when Schwarzenegger leaps into the fray and time is momentarily suspended, and the end, when the pace slows down considerably, once the heroes think they have vanquished the villain.

There is also surprisingly little excitation in this sequence. Although, of course, everything is in motion, the rate of movement stays roughly the same. The actors are not using body language to express subtext or any layers of feeling, in part because the boy's feelings are very simple and the other two of them are machines without feelings. So performer movement is minimal, vehicle movement is even, and there are almost no cutaways to objects hurtling or other things moving. The main exception to this is shots of the truck hitting the cement sides of the laneway it is hurtling down. When the truck is driving straight forward its mass fills the frame and very little movement is actually visible. When a part of it slams into cement we can see the contrast between wall and wheel and the resulting shower of sparks.

Almost every shot is either of the protagonists (the boy and Schwarzenegger) or of the antagonist, meaning that the majority of shots are in conflict or a crosscut relationship to one another. A great deal of tension arises from us knowing just how close T-1000 is to overrunning the boy. But it is identification that sells this chase and tells its story.

Of the 170 or so shots, depending on where you locate the start and end of the chase, almost forty of them, or almost one in four, are shots of the boy (or his bike being crushed) that are close enough for us to see his expression and emotion. Another fifty are, or could be, his point of view. The rest of the shots belong to either Schwarzenegger or the environment or are shots that could not be the kid's point of view, but they still serve the purpose of raising the levels of anxiety for the kid by showing the imposing force of his pursuer. The primary expressive and anxiety-creating element in this chase is the boy. A great deal of the power of this chase rests in the tug on the emotions that a boy being pursued by a giant truck would create. Therefore, none of the other available elements for engaging our sensations or emotions, such as intensification or excitation, come anywhere near the prevalence of close-ups and shots of the boy's point of view. The editor is relying on the boy as emotion, or what's at stake, and the truck as action, or what's driving the scene, to tell the story.

The story this chase tells is once again man against machine, but this time the machines are men, too, so the result of the chase is not really a victory for the boy or for the power or intelligence of life; rather, it is one machine managing to, temporarily, elude another. Although the story of John's vulnerability and Schwarzenegger's strength comes through, it comes through with little of the musicality or rise and fall of excitement that a stronger mix of excitation and intensification could have given it. So, in the end, the chase reads as somewhat mechanical, but, given it's really about the battle of the two Terminators, perhaps that is how it was intended to feel.

At around 170 shots in 4 minutes, *Terminator 2* has about forty cuts per minute as opposed to the eleven or twelve per minute in *The Girl and Her Trust*, but both, in different proportions, have all of the elements of a chase, even though *The Girl and Her Trust* relies of conflict and excitation, and *Terminator 2* consists almost entirely of identification and conflict. *The French Connection* balances the four elements roughly equally and is, in my view, the most consistently satisfying of the three.

SUMMARY—CHASES

The point of analyzing these chases is to understand that each of these different recipes or balances of different elements tells a different story. The questions that are useful for an editor then are, not surprisingly: What is my story? What is the balance of elements I need to tell it? Is your story more about the people or the problem, the energy or the effort, the intensity or the confusion? Does it rely on us feeling empathy with character, being excited by movement, being anxious about the pressure of the conflict, or riding the rise and fall of intensity? Or some judicious combination thereof? Understanding your chase as its own particular story will let you use the four ingredients of the chase—identification, excitation, conflict, and intensification—not just as a recipe but as a way of creating a physical and emotional experience of story. You can shape what you see and hear, using a combination of these four types of images and sounds, into the psychokinetic ride you want your spectator to take.

ENDNOTES

1. McKee, R., *Story: Substance, Structure, Style and the Principles of Screenwriting.*
2. Dancyger, K., *The Technique of Film and Video Editing, Theory and Practice.*
3. McKee, R., *Story: Substance, Structure, Style and the Principles of Screenwriting*, p. 35.
4. Ibid., p. 34.
5. Dancyger, K., *The Technique of Film and Video Editing, Theory and Practice*, pp. 223–225.
6. Ibid., p. 224.

CHAPTER 12

Conclusion

In the introduction to this book, my approach was described as "problem-driven research,"[1] the problem being to find a way to describe modes of thinking about rhythm and the processes and purposes of shaping rhythms, so that rhythmic creativity in film editing can be understood and extended.

Because editors always say that shaping rhythm is intuitive, I began by inquiring into what editors mean when they say that. I found that what an editor is doing when creating rhythm is creating something that "feels right," but that that sense of feeling right—that rhythmic intuition—is an explainable psychosomatic phenomenon and not a veiled and indefinable one. Making an edit feel right is the editor's contribution to a film, her special skill, her signature, but it is not just a gift or talent. Knowing when something feels right is an awareness of the rhythms of the world and the rhythms of the body—an awareness that can be trained and developed.

Feeling rhythm is "a body thing."[2] The intuition that informs the process of cutting rhythms is based on knowledge of rhythm in the world that is acquired physically: through kinesthetic empathy and mirror neurons, as discussed in Chapter 1. Rhythmic thinking is also informed by the body's own rhythms. In the process of cutting a film, knowledge of rhythms of the world and rhythms of the body support, extend, and enhance the creativity, judgment, expertise, and sensitivity that editors use to cut rhythms. Knowing what some sources of intuitive knowledge are, and how that knowledge is assimilated, opens to the editor the possibility of actively developing and articulating her rhythmic intuition.

One body of articulated knowledge that offers editors ways of extending their intuition about rhythm is the art of choreography. The ways in which dance makers create affect have some things in common with the ways editors create rhythm, because choreographing and editing are both manipulations of movement. Consideration of the choreographic possibilities for shaping movement and energy over time is one way of understanding and possibly expanding the craft of cutting rhythms.

Choreographers make dance phrases, and editors make cine-phrases, but both are shaped by the tools of timing, pacing, and trajectory phrasing. In editing, timing works on choosing precise frames, durations of shots, and placement of shots in the film. Pacing manipulates the frequency of cuts and the concentration of movement or change between shots in scenes, sequences, and the overall film. Trajectory phrasing is a term I arrived at by bringing together research in dance and in editing. It is the phrasing of movement energy and direction. It governs the choices about smooth linkage or abrupt collision of shots, the selection of movement energies to be juxtaposed by cuts, and the stress accents that punctuate the movement of energy.

Timing, pacing, and trajectory phrasing are generally all at work in any given sequence, not just as tools that an editor is employing, but also as attributes that rhythms have and faculties that editors possess. As faculties, they are part of the editor's somatic intelligence and function without being verbally articulated. However, a clear definition of each of their functions may help editors in their conversations with colleagues and collaborators. These definitions may provide editors with more specific ways of articulating their intentions or more precise ways of interrogating their own work.

The intuitive, choreographic shaping of movement and energy over time, through timing, pacing, and trajectory phrasing, creates the rise and fall of tension and release in a film. That is the purpose of rhythm in film: to shape understanding and emotions through cycles of tension and release. Rhythm signals the story's meaning and the character's intentions at an immediate, physically recognizable level. By creating the waves of tension and release, the editor creates the film's "beat or 'pulse.'"[3] By riding the waves of tension and release, the spectator's body rhythm is drawn into a kind of synchronization with the film's rhythm. This physiological syncing function of rhythm in film makes movies a form of meditation for the unquiet mind, not one that is likely to result in enlightenment, but one that nonetheless gives the mind's fluctuations a unity of focus for the duration of the rhythmically articulate film.

An editor may shape rhythms according to the film's dominant priorities: the physical movement, the emotions, or the events. The distinction being drawn between types of rhythm is actually a distinction between types of movement to which an editor chooses to sensitize herself when making cutting decisions. In most films, all three types of rhythm are always present, but they can be prioritized at different moments, and there are some principles about cutting each that can be articulated.

If the film prioritizes physical movement, then the editor is dealing primarily with physical rhythms. Her choices pertain to linkage or collision, to the rise and fall of energy, to the rate and concentration of movement, the pulses and cycles of tension and release of the visible and audible movement in shots and between them. Choreographic ideas about shaping movement phrases and refining the movement's flow and cadence can be useful to an editor working on physical scenes such as dance scenes, chase scenes, or fight scenes.

If the movements of emotions are the focus of the film (or a sequence within a film), then the editor's work is focused on the rise and fall of emotion, not the phrasing of the physical. But, the shaping of emotional rhythm actually involves shaping of the physical images and sounds, for the ways in which emotion moves through them. Knowledge of techniques that actors use to create the movement of emotions in the movement of their bodies and voices can help train the editor's eye to "see feeling." The editor can see cycles of preparation–action–rest, actions and beats that course through the physically visible performance, and use the movement of these cycles to throw the emotional energy from one shot to another. In this way, the editor can shape the performance and the emphasis on a given emotional moment by using the time, energy, and movement of one performance in a cause-and-effect relationship with another.

Shaping event rhythm relies, in the first instance, on knowledge of the audience the film is addressing and their likely physical rhythms, rates of assimilation of information, and expectations of change. The editor uses this knowledge, and her own feeling for sustaining the tension of dramatic questions, to organize the plot events into a rhythmically coherent and compelling structure. To shape event rhythm effectively, the editor has to continually refresh and retune her awareness of her own kinesthetic responses to the movement of the events in a film. Editors sculpt the tension and release in scripted events by working with the timing, pacing, and trajectory phrasing of ideas and information across the flow of the whole, not just the individual scenes or parts.

In most films, editing involves working with all three kinds of rhythm. The physical, emotional, and event rhythms come together to create the rhythm of the film. This rhythm and its components are not necessarily experienced cognitively. Rhythm in a finished film is a *"felt phenomenon,"*[4] just as it was in the cutting room during the creative process of shaping it. As award-winning editor Merle Worth says in *First Cut: Conversations with Film Editors:*

> It is not cognitive in the conventional way that we understand the word. You are looking from inside the bloodstream of what's going on. Initially you are working exclusively in the realm of intuition.[5]

The objective of this book is to respect intuition at the same time it provides specific information about the materials, processes, and purposes of rhythm in film editing. My own mix of practical and theoretical work has demonstrated that intuition can work effectively with the knowledge of what intuition is, how it is informed and developed, and what the processes, tools, and purposes of rhythm in film editing are. This knowledge supports the somatic impulses and gives the editor options to consider, consciously or subconsciously, when making something feel right.

Explicit knowledge about rhythm is not prescriptive, but it is useful when an editor is stuck and doesn't know how to make something feel right. At that point it gives her questions to ask herself about what may be wrong. Readers who have come this far in this book will be aware that I have not at any point described a "good" rhythm or a "bad" rhythm. In the last three chapters I talked about specific instances of cutting and the tools, conventions, and operations that may often be at work in shaping their rhythms. But the application of these principles is always particular to the material available and the premise it is trying to convey. Rhythms can be manipulated to give shades of meaning, subtext, and impact to material that may be quite surprising to both director and editor, even within the conventions and operations described herein. The methods I propose are methods of asking questions of the material that will yield the rhythms its story requires.

This articulated knowledge of what rhythm is, how it is shaped, and what it is for has a place in conversations between editors and directors, where it can be used, diplomatically, to establish common vocabularies and ways of working. It also has a place for directors and writers long before they even get to the edit. A director and writer who have a developed consciousness about rhythm and the ways it conveys their meanings will be able to work much more effectively with collaborators in performance, images, sound, and music to come up with the material the edit will shape into the production's finished form. The ideas about rhythm in this book may also be useful to screen studies scholars who are interested in the effects editors have on shaping a film, and the effects of rhythm on the spectator's experience of film.

Through practical application of these ideas to films I've cut, especially *Thursday's Fictions*, I have found that the knowledge I have researched and articulated herein is useful in the creative process. It has expanded my own intuitive resources by making me aware of the confluence of rhythms in the rushes, the rhythms of the world, and the rhythms of my body working together on shaping the rhythms of the film. The ideas in *Cutting Rhythms* are about moving fluidly between the conscious process of evaluating work and the intuitive process of feeling it. These ideas are written to support and legitimize body knowledge or somatic intelligence as a credible and educated resource and, at the same time, to make the body knowledge accessible, even within a complex or verbally driven collaborative process. My own experience of practical and theoretical research has been, for me, a successful exercise in archeology of my own intuition and "thinking body."[6] My hope is that my findings will also be useful to other editors, to filmmakers, and to screen studies scholars who are interested in an integrated somatic, kinesthetic, and cognitive approach to the study and creation of rhythms in film.

ENDNOTES

1. Bordwell, D., and Carroll, N., *Post-Theory: Reconstructing Film Studies*, p. xvii.
2. Rowe, K., "Dany Cooper interview," *Inside Film Magazine*, p. 43.
3. Bordwell, D., and Thompson, K., *Film Art: An Introduction*, p. 197.
4. Preminger, A., and Brogan, T. V. F., editors, "Rhythm," in *The Princeton Encyclopedia of Poetry and Poetics*, p. 1068.
5. Worth, M., as quoted in Oldham, G., *First Cut: Conversations with Film Editors*, p. 320.
6. *Todd, M. E., The Thinking Body: A Study of the Balancing Forces of Dynamic Man.*

Bibliography

Allen, R.J., *Out of the Labyrinth of the Mind: Manifesting a Spiritual Art beyond Dualism*, D.C.A. thesis, University of Technology, Sydney, 2004.

Allen, R., and Smith, M., editors, *Film Theory and Philosophy*, Oxford University Press, Oxford, 1999.

Allman, W.F., *Apprentices of Wonder: Inside the Neural Network Revolution*, Bantam Books, New York/London/Toronto/Sydney/Auckland, 1989.

Arnheim, R., *Film as Art*, University of California Press, Berkeley, Los Angeles/London, 1957.

Aronson, L., *Scriptwriting Updated: New and Conventional Ways of Writing for the Screen*, AFTRS Publishing/Allen & Unwin, Sydney, 2000.

Bartenieff, I., with Lewis, D., *Body Movement: Coping with the Environment*, Gordon & Breach New York/London/Paris, 1980.

Barthes, R., "Musica Practica," in *Image–Music–Text*, essays selected and translated by Heath, S., Fontana–Collins, London, 1979.

Bazin, A., *What Is Cinema?* essays selected and translated by Gray, H., foreword by Renoir, J., new forward by Andrew, D., University of California Press, Berkeley, 2004.

Benedetti, J., *Stanislavski: An Introduction*, Methuen Drama, London, 1990.

Bergen, R., *Sergei Eisenstein: A Life in Conflict*, Overlook Press, Woodstock/New York, 1999.

Berger, J., *Ways of Seeing*, British Broadcasting Corp./Penguin, London, 1972.

Bergson, H., *Introduction to Metaphysics*, translated by Anderson, M.A., Philosophical Library, New York, 1961.

Bergson, H., *Matter and Memory*, translated by Paul, N.M., and Palmer, W.S., Zone Books, New York, 1991.

Birdwhistell, R.L., *Kinesics and Context: Essays on Body Motion Communication*, University of Pennsylvania Press, Philadelphia, 1970.

Bogue, R., *Deleuze on Cinema*, Routledge, New York/London, 2003.

Bordwell, D., *The Cinema of Eisenstein*, Routledge, New York, 2005.

Bordwell, D., "Intensified continuity: Visual style in contemporary American film—Critical essay," *Film Quarterly*, Spring 2002, Volume 55, Number 3, pp. 16–28.

Bordwell, D., *Narration in the Fiction Film*, University of Wisconsin Press, Madison, 1985.

Bordwell, D., *On the History of Film Style*, Harvard University Press, Cambridge, MA/London, 1997.

Bordwell, D., and Carroll, N., *Post-Theory: Reconstructing Film Studies*, University of Wisconsin Press, Madison/London, 1996.

Bordwell, D., Staiger, J., and Thompson, K., *The Classical Hollywood Cinema*, Routledge, London, 1985.

Bordwell, D., and Thompson, K., *Film Art: An Introduction*, 5th edition, McGraw–Hill, New York, 1997.

Bottomore, S., "Shots in the dark: The real origins of film editing," in *Early Cinema: Space, Frame, Narrative*, edited by Elsaesser, T., with Barker, A., BFI Publishing, London, 1994.

Bottomore, S., "The panicking audience? Early cinema and the 'train effect'," *Historical Journal of Film, Radio, and Television*, June 1999, Volume 19, Issue 2, p. 177.

Brannigan, E., *A Cinema of Movement: Dance and the Moving Image*, Ph.D. thesis, School of Theatre, Film and Dance, University of New South Wales, Sydney, 2004.

Brogan, T.V.F., "Rhythm," in *The Princeton Encyclopedia of Poetry and Poetics*, edited by Preminger, A., and Brogan, T.V.F., Princeton University Press, Princeton, NJ, 1993.

Carroll, N., *Theorizing the Moving Image*, Cambridge University Press, Cambridge, UK/New York/Melbourne, 1996.

Claxton, G., "The anatomy of intuition," in *The Intuitive Practitioner*, Atkinson, T., and Claxton, G., editors, Open University Press, Buckinghamshire/Philadelphia, 2000.

Cook, D., *A History of Narrative Film*, Norton, London/New York, 1996.

Dancyger, K., *The Technique of Film and Video Editing: Theory and Practice*, 2nd edition, Focal Press, Boston/Oxford/Johannesburg/Melbourne/New Delhi/Singapore, 1997.

Dancyger, K., and Rush, J., *Alternative Scriptwriting*, Focal Press, Boston/Oxford/Johannesburg/Melbourne/New Delhi/Singapore, 1995.

Decety, J., Grezes, J., Costes, N., Perani, D., et al., "Brain activity during observation of actions: Influence of action content and subject's strategy," *Brain*, October 1997, Volume 120, Issue 10, pp. 1763–1777.

Deleuze, G., *Cinema 1: The Movement Image*, translated by Tomlinson, H., and Habberjam, B., University of Minnesota Press, Minneapolis, 2003.

Deleuze, G., *Cinema 2: The Time Image*, translated by Tomlinson, H., and Galeta, R., University of Minnesota Press, Minneapolis, 2003.

Deren, M., "The visual arts today," in *Film Theory and Criticism*, Mast, G., and Cohen, M., editors, Oxford University Press, New York/Oxford, 1985.

Durr, W., Gerstenberg, W., and Harvey, J., "Rhythm," in *The New Grove Dictionary of Music and Musicians*, Sadie, S., editor, Macmillan, London/Washington, DC/Hong Kong, 1980.

Dymtryk, E., *On Film Editing*, Focal Press, London, 1984.

Eikhenbaum, B., "Problems of cine stylistics" (1927), translated by Sherwood, R., edited by Taylor, R., in *The Poetics of Cinema*, Special Issue, *Russian Poetics in Translation*, RPT Publications, Oxford, 1982, pp. 5–18.

Eisenstein, S., *Film Form: Essays in Film Theory*, edited and translated by Leyda, J., Harcourt Brace, San Diego/New York/London, 1977.

Fairservice, D., *Film Editing: History, Theory and Practice*, Manchester University Press, Manchester/New York, 2001.

Feuerstein, G., *The Yoga-Sutras of Patañjali: A New Translation and Commentary*, Inner-Traditions International, Rochester, VT, 1989.

Feury, P., *New Developments in Film Theory*, Macmillan, Hampshire/London, 2000.

Fisher, L., "Film editing," in *A Companion to Film Theory*, Miller, T., and Stam, R., editors, Blackwell, Malden, MA/Oxford/Carlton, VIC, 2004.

Fraleigh, S.H., *Dance and the Lived Body: A Descriptive Aesthetics*, University of Pittsburgh Press, Pittsburgh, 1996.

Gannon, S., and Life, D., *Jivamukti Yoga*, Ballantine Books, New York, 2002.

Giannetti, L., *Understanding Movies*, 4th edition, Prentice–Hall, Upper Saddle River, NJ, 1987.

Gibson, R., "Acting and breathing," in *Falling for You: Essays on Cinema and Performance*, Stern, L., and Kouvaros, G., editors, Power Publications, Sydney, 1999.

Goddard, J.-L., "Montage mon beau souci," in *Godard on Godard: Critical Writings*, Narboni, J., and Milne, T., editors, Secker & Warburg, London, 1972.

Greenfield, A., "Filmdance: Space, time and energy," *Filmdance Catalogue*, Elaine Summers Experimental Intermediate Foundation, New York, 1983.

Grodal, T.K., *Moving Pictures: A New Theory of Film Genres, Feelings and Cognition*, Clarendon Press, Oxford, 1997.

Henderson, B., "The long take," in *Movies and Methods: An Anthology*, Nichols, B., editor, University of California Press, Berkeley, 1976.

Hooper, G., "Science and the fear of 20th century art," *Real Time + On Screen*, Number 60, April–May 2004; online at http://www.rt.airstrip.com.au/article/60/7376. Accessed April 2004.

Humphrey, D., *The Art of Making Dances*, Grove Press, New York, 1959.

Kennedy, B.M., *Deleuze and Cinema: The Aesthetics of Sensation*, Edinburgh University Press, Edinburgh, 2004.

Kimergard, L.B., "Editing in the depth of the surface: A few basic principles of graphic editing," *P.O.V.*, Number 6, "The Art of Film Editing," online at http://imv.au.dk/publikationer/pov/Issue_06/section_1/artc6A.html.

Kirsner, K., Speelman, C., Maybery, M., O'Brien-Malone, A., Anderson, M., and MacLeod, C., editors, *Implicit and Explicit Mental Processes*, Erlbaum, Mahwah, NJ/London, 1998.

Kivy, P., "Music in the movies: A philosophical inquiry," in *Film Theory and Philosophy*, Allen, R., and Smith, M., editors, Clarendon Press, Oxford, 1997.

Konigsberg, I., *The Complete Film Dictionary*, New American Library, New York/Scarborough, ON, 1989.

Kuleshov, L.V., *Kuleshov on Film*, selected, translated, and edited, with an introduction by Levaco, R., University of California Press, Berkeley, 1974.

Le Fanu, M., "On editing," *P.O.V.*, Number 6, "The Art of Film Editing," online at http://imv.au.dk/publikationer/pov/Issue_06/section_1/artc1A.html.

Leyda, J., *Kino: A History of the Russian and Soviet Film*, 3rd edition, Princeton University Press, Princeton, NJ, 1983.

Malloch, S.N., "Mothers and infants in communicative musicality," *Musicae Scientiae*, Special Issue, *Rhythm, Musical Narrative and Origins of Human Communication*, 1999–2000, pp. 13–28.

Malloch, S.N., and Trevathen, C., "The dance of wellbeing: Defining the musical therapeutic effect," *Nordic Journal of Music Therapy*, 2000, Volume 9, Number 2, pp. 3–17.

McGrath, D., *Screencraft: Editing & Post Production*, Rotovision, Crans-Pres-Celigny, Switzerland, 2002.

McKechnie, S., Grove, R., and Stevens, K., *Conceiving Connections: Further Choreographic Research*, Australian Research Council, Canberra, online at www.ausdance.org/au/connections.

McKechnie, S., Grove, R., and Stevens, K., *Unspoken Knowledges: New Choreographic Research*, Australian Research Council, Canberra, online at www.ausdance.org/au/unspoken.

McKee, R., *Story: Substance, Structure, Style and the Principles of Screenwriting*, Methuen, London, 1999.

McLean, A.L., "Feeling and the filmed body," *Film Quarterly*, Spring 2002, Volume 55, Number 3, pp. 2–15.

Meyerhold, V., *Meyerhold on Theatre*, translated and edited with a critical commentary by Braun, E., Methuen Drama, London, 1998.

Michotte, A., *The Perception of Causality*, Basic Books, New York, 1963.

Mitoma, J., Zimmer, E., and Steiber, D.A., editors, *Envisioning Dance on Film and Video*, Routledge, New York/London, 2002.

Mitry, J., *The Aesthetics and Psychology of Cinema*, translated by King, C., Athalone Press, London, 1998.

Modell, A.H., *Imagination and the Meaningful Brain*, MIT Press, Cambridge, MA/London, 2003.

Motion Picture Editors Guild Newsletter, online at www.editorsguild.com/newsletter/SpecialJun97/directors.html.

Mundal, S., "Notes of an editing teacher," *P.O.V.*, Number 6, "The Art of Film Editing," http://imv.au.dk/publikationer/pov/Issue_06/section_1/artc4A.html.

Murch, W., *In the Blink of an Eye*, AFTRS Publishing, Sydney, 1992.

Murch, W., *In the Blink of an Eye, Second Edition*, Silman–James Press, Los Angeles, 2001.

Neill, A., "Empathy and (film) fiction", in *Post-Theory*, Bordwell, D., and Carroll, N., editors, University of Wisconsin Press, Madison, 1996.

Newlove, J., and Dalby, J., *Laban for All*, Routledge, New York/Nick Hern Books, London, 2004.

Noddings, N., and Shore, P.J., *Awakening the Inner Eye: Intuition in Education*, Teachers College Press, Columbia University, New York/London, 1984.

O'Steen, S., *Cut to the Chase: Forty-five Years of Editing America's Favorite Movies*, as told to O'Steen, B., Michael Wiese Productions, Studio City, CA, 2002.

Oldham, G., *First Cut: Conversations with Film Editors*, University of California Press, Berkeley/Los Angeles/Oxford, 1992.

Ondaatje, M., *The Conversations: Walter Murch and the Art of Editing Film*, Bloomsbury Publishing, London, 2002.

Orpen, V., *Film Editing: The Art of the Expressive*, Wallflower, London/New York, 2003.

Panikkar, K.N., "Rhythm and its applications," in *Creative Arts in Modern India (Essays in Comparative Criticism)*, Parimoo, R., and Sharma, I., editors, Books & Books, New Delhi, 1995.

Panofsky, E., "Style and medium in the motion pictures," reprinted from "Bulletin from the Department of Art and Archeology," in *Film Theory and Criticism: Introductory Readings*, 3rd edition, Mast, G., and Cohen, M., editors, Oxford University Press, Oxford/New York, 1985.

Pearlman, K., and Allen, R.J., *New Life on the 2nd Floor*, Tasdance, Launceston, 1996.

Pearlman, K., and Allen, R.J., editors, *Performing the Unnameable: An Anthology of Australian Performance Texts*, Currency Press and *RealTime*, Sydney, 1999.

Pepperman, R.D., *The Eye Is Quicker: Film Editing: Making a Good Film Better*, Michael Weise Productions, Studio City, CA, 2004.

Peters, J.M., *Pictorial Communication*, translated by Coombes, M., Philip, Cape Town, 1977.

Pitches, J., *Vsevolod Meyerhold*, Routledge, London/New York, 2003.

Preminger, A., and Brogan, T.V.F., editors, *The New Princeton Encyclopedia of Poetry and Poetics*, Princeton University Press, Princeton, NJ, 1993.

Pudovkin, V., "Film technique," reprinted in *Film Theory and Criticism*, 3rd edition, Mast, G., and Cohen, M., editors, Oxford University Press, Oxford/New York, 1985.

Pudovkin, V.I., *On Film Technique and Film Acting* (revised memorial edition—1st edition 1929), Vision Press, London, 1974.

Ramachandran, V.S., "Mirror neuron and imitation learning as the driving force behind 'the great leap forward' in human evolution," online at www.edge.org/3rd_culture/ramachandran/ramachandran_p2.html, 11/09/2004.

Reisz, K., and Millar, G., *The Technique of Film Editing*, Focal Press, London/Boston, 1984.

Restak, R., *Brainscapes: An Introduction to What Neuroscience Has Learned about the Structure, Function and Abilities of the Brain*, Hyperion, New York, 1995.

Restak, R., *The New Brain: How the Modern Age Is Rewiring Your Mind*, Rodale, Emmaus, PA, 2003.

Rosenblum, R., *When the Shooting Stops, the Cutting Begins: A Film Editor's Story*, Penguin, New York, 1979.

Rowe, K., "Dany Cooper interview," *Inside Film Magazine*, November 2004, 71, pp. 43–44.

Salt, B., *Film Style and Technology: History and Analysis*, Starwood, London, 1983.

Sayles, J., *Thinking in Pictures: The Making of the Movie 'Matewan'*, Houghton Mifflin, Boston, 1987.

Schmidt, M.R., and Stivers, C., "You know more than you can say: In memory of Donald A," *Schon (1930–1997)*. *Public Administration Review*, May 2000, Volume 60, Number 3, pp. 265–274.

Schmidt, P., "Introduction," in *Meyerhold at Work*, Schmidt, P., editor, Applause, New York/London, 1996.

Scholes, P.A., *The Oxford Companion to Music*, 10th edition, edited by Ward, J.O., Oxford University Press, Oxford, 2000.

Schon, D., *The Reflective Practitioner: How Professionals Think in Action*, Basic Books, London, 1991.

Sheets, M., "Phenomenology: An approach to dance," in *The Dance Experience*, Nadel, M.H., and Miller, C.N., editors, Universe Books, New York, 1978.

Smith, M., *Engaging Characters: Fiction, Emotion and the Cinema*, Clarendon Press, Oxford, 1995.

Smith, M., "Imagining from the inside," in *Film Theory and Philosophy*, Allen, R., and Smith, M., editors, Clarendon Press, Oxford, 1997.

Sobchak, V., *The Address of the Eye: A Phenomenology of Film Experience*, Princeton University Press, Princeton, NJ, 1992.

Sokolowski, R., *Introduction to Phenomenology*, Cambridge University Press, Cambridge, UK/New York/Melbourne/Madrid, 2000.

Sollberger, A., *Biological Rhythm Research*, Elsevier, Amsterdam/New York/London, 1965.

Stam, R., *Film Theory: An Introduction*, Blackwell, Malden, MA/Oxford/Carlton, VIC, 2000.

Stein, J., and Urdang, L., editors, *The Random House Dictionary of the English Language*, unabridged version, Random House, New York, 1966.

Stern, L., and Kouvaros, G., editors, *Falling for You: Essays on Cinema and Performance*, Power Publications, Sydney, 1999.

Stevens, K., McKechnie, S., Malloch, S., and Petocz, A., "Choreographic cognition: Composing time and space," in *Proceedings of the 6th International Conference on Music Perception & Cognition*, edited by Woods, C., Luck, G., Brochard, R., Seddon, F., Sloboda, J.A., and O'Neill, S., Keele University, Keele, UK, August 2000.

Tarkovsky, A., *Sculpting in Time*, translated by Blair-Hunter, K., University of Texas Press, Austin, 1986.

Tobias, J., "Cinema, scored: Toward a comparative methodology for music in media," *Film Quarterly*, 2004, Volume 57, Number 2, pp. 26–36.

Todd, M.E., *The Thinking Body: A Study of the Balancing Forces of Dynamic Man*, Dance Horizons, Hightstown, NJ, 1973.

Turim, M., *Flashbacks in Film: Memory & History*, Routledge, New York/London, 1989.

Van Leeuwen, T., "Rhythmic structure of the film text," in *Discourse and Communication: New Approaches to the Analysis of Mass Media Discourse and Communication*, van Dijk, T.A., editor, de Gruyter, Berlin/New York, 1985.

Van Leeuwen, T., *Introducing Social Semiotics*, Routledge, New York, 2005.

Vertov, D., *Kino-Eye: the Writings of Dziga Vertov*, edited by Michelson, A., translated by O'Brien, K., University of California Press, Berkeley/Los Angeles/London, 1984.

Wartenburg, T.E., and Curran, A., *The Philosophy of Film: Introductory Text and Readings*, Blackwell, Malden, MA/Cambridge, UK/Carlton, VIC, 2005.

Weidman, V., "Film editing—A hidden art?" *P.O.V.*, Number 6, *The Art of Film Editing*, online at http://imv.au.dk/publikationer/pov/Issue_06/section_1artc2A.html.

Weiss, E., and Belton, J., editors, *Film Sound: Theory and Practice*, Columbia University Press, New York, 1985, online at www.moviemaker.com/hop/vol3/02/editing2.html.

Index

Page numbers followed by "f" denote figures